KNOWLEDGE DOESN'T EXIST AND OTHER THOUGHTS ON CRITICAL THINKING

Critical thinking (CT) is essential in education, the workplace and everyday life, yet many struggle to understand or apply it effectively. This book breaks down the 'what, how and when' of CT in a clear, accessible way, making it practical for readers from all walks of life. Drawing on almost twenty years of researching CT, Dr Christopher Dwyer presents accessible, evidence-based lessons and strategies for using CT in real-world situations, helping readers navigate the overwhelming flood of information we face daily. Written in an informal, engaging tone, this book makes CT approachable for anyone looking to improve their decision-making skills.

DR CHRISTOPHER DWYER is a senior psychology researcher and lecturer at the Technological University of the Shannon, in the Department of Technology Education. He has authored over forty peer-reviewed research papers; an ongoing blog for *Psychology Today*, *Thoughts on Thinking*; as well as this book's predecessor, *Critical Thinking: Historical Perspectives & Practical Guidelines*, published by Cambridge University Press in 2017.

KNOWLEDGE DOESN'T EXIST AND OTHER THOUGHTS ON CRITICAL THINKING

CHRISTOPHER P. DWYER

Technological University of the Shannon

Shaftesbury Road, Cambridge CB2 8EA, United Kingdom

One Liberty Plaza, 20th Floor, New York, NY 10006, USA

477 Williamstown Road, Port Melbourne, VIC 3207, Australia

314–321, 3rd Floor, Plot 3, Splendor Forum, Jasola District Centre, New Delhi – 110025, India

103 Penang Road, #05-06/07, Visioncrest Commercial, Singapore 238467

Cambridge University Press is part of Cambridge University Press & Assessment, a department of the University of Cambridge.

We share the University's mission to contribute to society through the pursuit of education, learning and research at the highest international levels of excellence.

www.cambridge.org
Information on this title: www.cambridge.org/9781009602730

DOI: 10.1017/9781009602754

© Christopher P. Dwyer 2025

This publication is in copyright. Subject to statutory exception and to the provisions of relevant collective licensing agreements, no reproduction of any part may take place without the written permission of Cambridge University Press & Assessment.

When citing this work, please include a reference to the DOI 10.1017/9781009602754

First published 2025

Cover credit: Tim Knepp/PIXNIO. CC0 1.0

A catalogue record for this publication is available from the British Library

Library of Congress Cataloging-in-Publication Data
NAMES: Dwyer, Christopher P., author.
TITLE: Knowledge doesn't exist and other thoughts on critical thinking / Christopher P. Dwyer, Technological University of Shannon.
DESCRIPTION: Cambridge, United Kingdom; New York, NY, USA : Cambridge University Press, 2025. | Includes bibliographical references and index. | Summary: "This book offers an accessible, evidence-based guide to critical thinking for everyday use. With a conversational tone, it breaks down the "what, how, and when" of applying critical thinking to navigate today's overwhelming flow of information, making it valuable for readers from all backgrounds" – Provided by publisher.
IDENTIFIERS: LCCN 2024061748 (print) | LCCN 2024061749 (ebook) | ISBN 9781009602730 (hardback) | ISBN 9781009602723 (paperback) | ISBN 9781009602754 (epub)
SUBJECTS: LCSH: Critical thinking.
CLASSIFICATION: LCC BF441.D896 2025 (print) | LCC BF441 (ebook) | DDC 160–dc23/eng/20250106
LC record available at https://lccn.loc.gov/2024061748
LC ebook record available at https://lccn.loc.gov/2024061749

ISBN 978-1-009-60273-0 Hardback
ISBN 978-1-009-60272-3 Paperback

Cambridge University Press & Assessment has no responsibility for the persistence or accuracy of URLs for external or third-party internet websites referred to in this publication and does not guarantee that any content on such websites is, or will remain, accurate or appropriate.

For EU product safety concerns, contact us at Calle José Abascal, 56, 1°, 28003 Madrid, Spain, or e-mail eugpsr@cambridge.org

For Mara

Contents

List of Figures	*page*	x
List of Tables		xi
Foreword		xii
Robert J. Sternberg		

	An Introduction	1
1	What Exactly Is 'Critical Thinking'?	5
	Skills	10
	Dispositions	13
	Reflective Judgment	16
	Cognitive Continuum Theory and Dual-Processing	20
2	When and Why Do We Think Critically?	23
	Applying Critical Thinking to Things You Care About	24
	Burden and Value	26
	Care versus Passion	28
	Does Time of Day Matter?	29
	Concluding Thoughts	31
3	Knowledge Doesn't Exist: The Nature of Certainty and Problems with 'Theory' and 'Proof'	32
	Is It *Really* 'Just a Theory'?	34
	'Proof': The Dirtiest Word in CT	36
	The Psychology of Certainty	37
	Knowledge as 'Theory', Not 'Truth'	39
	Implications	41
	Potential Criticisms	43
4	Understanding the Flaws of Experience and Memory	46
	Experience versus Expertise	47
	The Personalised Nature of Experience …	50
	… And How It Affects Memory	55

vii

viii   *Contents*

	Misremembering Mandela	58
	Concluding Thoughts	61

5   Evaluating Information Sources and Credibility   63

Personal Experience/Anecdotal Evidence	67
Common Sense/Common Belief	68
Research	71
Expert Opinion	73
Statistics	77
Concluding Thoughts	79

6   Changing Minds   80

Being Practical	83
Being Right Is Not Enough	87
How Can We Change the Minds of Those Who Haven't Thought Critically?	87
How Can We Change the Minds of Those Who Believe They Have Thought Critically, yet Are Still Wrong?	91
Changing 'Hearts and Minds'	92
Rationalisation: Who Are You Trying to Convince, Me or Yourself?	96
Changing One's Own Mind	98
Concluding Thoughts	100

7   Eureka Moments, Problem-Solving and Creativity   101

Eureka Moments	102
The Creative Element of Eureka Moments	104
The Problem with Thinking Outside the Box	106
Concluding Thoughts	110

8   Critical Thinking Training   112

In Preparation of Content and Materials	113
Instructional Typology	113
Assessment Design	115
Active Learning and Knowing Your Cohort	118
As the Course Unfolds	119
Questions	119
Acknowledging Student Preconceptions	121
Approaches to Content Presentation and Style	122
Underlying Themes and Concluding Thoughts	125

9   Implications of Social Psychology on Critical Thinking and Practical Lessons Learned in Recent Years   127

'Noisy Information': Are We, as a Society, Getting Worse at CT?	129

Contents

ix

Contextual Applications in Real-World Scenarios	131
Conspiracy Beliefs	132
Value-Signalling	136
Politics	139
Fake News and Misinformation	143
Concluding Thoughts	149

10	How Can We *Really* Think Critically? Engaging and Expressing Critical Thinking in Our Everyday Lives	151
	CT as Expression	151
	Clarify the Definitions of Important Terms	151
	Address the Importance of the Topic	152
	Do Your Research – Properly	153
	CT and Writing	154
	Know the Nature of an Argument	155
	Develop an Organised Structure	156
	How to Start Writing an Argument	156
	'Quality, Not Quantity'	158
	Write as if Your Granny Was Reading	159
	Recognising That Some People Don't Want Your Expression	160
	A Tale of Two 'CT's	161
	Mindware: 'Fighting Fire with Fire'	162
	CT in Reality	166
	Final Thoughts	168

References	171
Index	183

Figures

1.1	Interdependencies among CT processes	*page* 19
10.1	Example template for an argument	157

Tables

1.1	Examples of dispositions towards CT	*page* 14
4.1	Common cognitive biases	52
6.1	Common persuasion strategies	84
7.1	Problem-solving checklist	102
10.1	Real-world applications of CT	152

Foreword

I started studying critical thinking, and first edited a book on it, four decades ago. At the time, I was one of many psychologists and editors who believed critical thinking was a construct whose time had come. We all knew at the time the importance of critical thinking: our goal was for this importance to be recognized in action – in teaching and testing in schools and in society in general. At the time, the prospects looked bright: education was in a busy period of reform and societies were looking for ways to improve upon their educational offerings, especially to diverse students who in the past had been underserved. The prospects looked especially bright because James Flynn, a philosopher at the University of Otago, had discovered what came to be called the Flynn effect – the increase of IQs around the world by thirty points during the twentieth century. If people were indeed so much smarter, it seemed, they all should be in a good position to enhance their critical thinking and to function at more advanced cognitive levels than had been true in the past.

That, of course, was all then. It was before the current age, when the combination of social media and now generative AI threaten the prospects of any serious critical thinking at all. Social media have lowered attention spans, successfully stifled critical thinking, or even the perceived need for it, and brought into prominence the notion that feelings matter a whole lot, almost certainly more than carefully curated thoughts.

Meanwhile, Kellyanne Conway, an American in the first presidential administration of Donald Trump, introduced the notion of 'alternative facts', which appear to be fictions that one accepts as facts because it is convenient to do so. Meanwhile, aspiring autocrats and other populist politicians learned how to use social media and other modern means of communication to persuade people that whatever grievances they have, they are real, and they are someone else's fault.

One would hope that schools would have successfully countered the effects of social media and too much time on screens through their

Foreword xiii

assiduous teaching of critical thinking, and perhaps that would have happened were it not for the COVID pandemic that broke out in 2020. Suddenly, for many students, screens became all they had. They were omnipresent. Since the pandemic, many schools have largely switched to screen-based education. Many students are scarcely learning to think critically. Their loss may be in part due to an increasingly unused ability that is getting rusty, yet also in part due to an attitude that critical thinking was once important, but, in the current age of memes, it is passé.

Dr Christopher P. Dwyer's book on critical thinking thus has special relevance in our current age. Whereas once I might have hoped that by the mid-2020s, critical thinking would be so common that we hardly need another book on it, the opposite has proved to be true. Critical thinking is becoming increasingly less common, and we have a greater need for a book such as this one than perhaps we have ever had before. We all are fortunate, therefore, that Dwyer has written this book at a time when the world is so challenged to teach its younger people to think critically. The book covers the important topics in the field and is a needed, valuable and highly readable contribution not only to the field of critical thinking but to our armamentarium of texts that can teach students to think critically before the world descends further into chaos, and it becomes too late.

Robert J. Sternberg

An Introduction

Following the publication of my first book, *Critical Thinking: Conceptual Perspectives & Practical Guidelines* (Cambridge University Press, 2017), I was invited by *Psychology Today* to write an ongoing blog regarding all things critical thinking, with opportunities to extend beyond that as appropriate. I took up the offer and started 'Thoughts on Thinking'. Let me be clear by saying that I never thought I would write a blog. I recall even making fun of some bloggers before having been presented the opportunity. Does that make me a hypocrite? Maybe.

Another way of looking at it is as being consistent with one of the core fundaments of critical thinking (CT) – exhibiting the willingness and ability to change one's mind. That's what I did. I changed my mind, because a specific purpose for the blog became clear to me – I had the opportunity to reach a larger, wider audience than ever before with respect to informing people about CT, its importance and how we can improve it. Indeed, that has always been the goal of my research. Does the format of how I share my message really matter? As an educator, I saw this blog as a tool for education.

Don't get me wrong; I'm not so self-important as to think that I could change the world with a blog. Honestly, for as cliché as it might sound, I genuinely felt that if the blog could meaningfully impact just a handful of people beyond the reach of my book, then it'd be worth it. Besides, it's not like I'd have to regularly produce pages upon pages; blog posts are relatively short – you need to get your point across quick and strong. If anything, it might help my writing.

So, I started the blog and one of the first things I noticed confirmed this notion: people won't read it if your entries are too long – TL; DR (too long; didn't read), as they say online. If I wanted to have meaningful impact on anyone – especially those not from an academic tradition – I'd need to maintain their attention. I had to be as succinct and concise as possible, while still maintaining clarity. However, academics often have

2   An Introduction

this implicit desire to be as accurate as possible with their wording so as to not be misconstrued. If you're familiar with academic papers, they're generally a good bit longer than a typical blog post, regardless of how 'succinct and concise' they can be. That was one pitfall of communicating with the public through the blog – I couldn't be as thorough and, subsequently, as accurate as I would like to have been with my language. Thus, pretty early on, I found myself writing the blog in an almost serialised way – constantly referring back to previous posts where complex concepts were 'fleshed out', so as to save me from reiterating the same things over and over.

On the other hand, one thing that ended up being quite a strength of the blog format was the informal nature of the communication. I found myself telling stories and getting my point across to readers through examples and analogies. As research suggests, examples and personalised anecdotes are very powerful means of communicating messages, even though they're not the most credible way of arguing for one's perspective (see Chapter 5 for more on that). Nevertheless, I figured 'fight fire with fire'; and so, I looked at the narrative structure and colloquial nature of blog writing as a potentially more entertaining means of achieving my goal of conveying educational material to readers and, also, a welcome break from the stylistically limited nature of typical academic writing.

I've taken pride in the fact that I've received positive feedback on the blog over the past eight years that it has been on the go. The most useful pieces of feedback have pertained to indicating topics of interest, different avenues to explore, new research to read and, of course, disagreement in perspective (be it from academic or non-academic readers), which inevitably leads to re-evaluation of my own thinking – a true example of CT. Simply, it has been a learning process for me just as much as I hope it has been for readers.

Over the course of writing the blog, my mind has changed on topics, new ideas have arisen and my excitement for the field of CT research has further grown. The fun I've had writing the blog and engaging readers, along with the feeling that I am, in many ways, achieving the aforementioned purpose and goal of my blog, has led me to write this book – while taking into consideration both the strengths and weaknesses of the blog medium.

The goal of my first book was to engage academics, students and anyone who wanted to learn about CT and get better at it. While I do imagine (and hope) that many readers of this book will be academics and students interested in CT, its target audience – much like my blog – is truly anyone,

An Introduction 3

regardless of academic background, who wants to learn about CT and get better at it. This book is for everyone. Thus, I'm going to take a page out of my blog-writing experience in my approach to *Knowledge Doesn't Exist*; I'm going to adopt a conversational approach – following the more informal tone and narrative structure of my blog – in discussing the various topics and concepts within this book. But, given that it is a *book*, I'm allowed more room to play with in terms of being accurate in my wording and meaning – and ensuring you, the reader, are provided a sufficient amount of information to take in and consider for yourself in your own CT. Sure, one goal of this book is to similarly tell you about what CT is and how it can be improved, just as it was in its predecessor (in light of more recent research and further consideration since my first book's publication). However, another important goal is to address the complexities surrounding what CT *really* means, in a conversational way, with respect to applying it in our modern world.

Specifically, this book starts with a thorough discussion of what CT actually is in Chapter 1, before moving on to the 'why' and 'when' of its application in Chapter 2, where the conversational tone really 'kicks in'. Chapter 3 introduces the nature of the information we think about and how that affects what we might conceptualise as 'knowledge', thus addressing the book's titular perspective. Chapter 4 discusses how we might store, retrieve and apply whatever it is we refer to as 'knowledge', before addressing the issue of such information's credibility – and how to evaluate that – in Chapter 5. Assuming we have appropriately evaluated such information, Chapter 6 presents a discussion of how one might go about changing the minds of others (and even our own) who hold misinformed views as true. Chapter 7 begins the move of our focus to a more applied look at CT, specifically through a discussion of the nature of problem-solving. Chapter 8 presents ways one might enhance their CT, particularly through training methods. Chapter 9 discusses how other people and the world around us can affect our application of CT, with respect to various examples of real-world events from recent years. Finally, Chapter 10 concludes the book and discusses the various ways one might express CT in real-world scenarios; the possibility of separating the ideal from the practical (in terms of how we might *really* go about application); as well as the implications of our considerations throughout the book, and where such associated efforts to enhance CT might focus on in the future.

The information we 'think about' in real-world settings, how we do it and the very nature of both information and thinking are fundamentally important issues for consideration. When we think critically, the process

An Introduction

must be applied to some information. In a very basic way, we can consider that information to be *knowledge*, regardless of whether it's true, false or even somewhere in between – a half-truth if you will. But, what is knowledge *really*? Isn't it just the information that someone stores in their head? If that's the case, then knowledge isn't necessarily 'true'; rather, it's just the way in which someone understands something. If we look at it in a collective sense, knowledge might refer to all the existing information out there, over the course of history. Regardless, once we start collating it, we start seeing discrepancies and contradictions.

Did humans evolve over millions of years to become what we are today, or were we intelligently designed by some omnipotent force to serve some purpose in the world? These rather 'foundational' perspectives represent two different 'knowledges' that often seem to be in direct contrast. So, which one is right? Or can they co-exist? For the purpose of this example, it doesn't matter because without a definitive answer (and means to check it), can we really say that one is 'knowledge'?

Isn't knowledge supposed to be correct? Sure, you might argue that this is an issue of semantics regarding how one defines knowledge – or even 'right' for that matter; but in a colloquial sense, we must question whether or not knowledge actually exists or if everything is just a series of stand-alone or integrated concepts that are considered with varying degrees of likelihood. Thus, if you care enough about an idea or concept, you will think critically about it – regardless of label – because without it, how can you *know*? Perhaps such consideration has never been so important as now, in light of the exponential increase in the amount of information created over the past twenty-five years and the 'age of misinformation' that many have argued we find ourselves living in (e.g. with respect to 'fake news', gaps between political views in the general population, various social movements and the COVID-19 pandemic). Indeed, never in human history has there been such an abundance of health information and misinformation from sources so wide-ranging in levels of trustworthiness (Abel & McQueen, 2020), noted in the recent literature as an 'infodemic' (Rubinelli et al., 2021) – and this was based on research data from before the COVID-19 pandemic!

So, when it comes down to it, this book is about CT – as a process. But it's also about the *nature* of thinking, as well as the nature of the information we think about. Happy reading and critical thinking.

CHAPTER I

What Exactly Is 'Critical Thinking'?

Despite often being considered a 'buzzword' in the realm of educational outcomes, the term critical thinking is typically thought to have been introduced in the early 1940s by Edward Glaser. However, its concept can be said to transcend such terminological tradition, given its use and value in Greek antiquity. Nevertheless, it has been argued that there remains confusion regarding what critical thinking actually is, which might help explain its 'reinvention' or 'rediscovery' every so often – like a 'buzzword' in the zeitgeist.

Critical thinking (CT) is a 'metacognitive process consisting of specific skills and dispositions, that, when applied through purposeful, self-regulatory, reflective judgment, increase the chances of producing a logical solution to a problem or a valid conclusion to an argument' (Dwyer, 2017; Dwyer et al., 2014). No wonder confusion exists over CT's definition. It's long and full of abstract concepts. Most definitions of CT are this way, even the good ones (see, for discussion, Dwyer et al., 2014; Ennis, 1998; Halpern, 2014). To be fair, 'well, they did it that way, so I should too' is not a good rationale for individuals hoping to provide a description of CT to engage such length and abstraction in defining the term; but, in this context, it does reveal a trend. CT definitions – and many definitions in general – are long for the purposes of ensuring accuracy and to avoid being vague (even if they might come across as vague or ambiguous to novices in the field). No one likes reading a *short* definition of some term and then still being baffled by what it means. On the other hand, sometimes *too long* a definition has a similar effect. So, a lengthy definition of CT for the sake of accuracy perhaps isn't a very good excuse – especially for the non-academic population who should, arguably, be at the fore in terms of a target audience.

So, I admit that my own definition, as presented earlier, may not be the most accessible one either. As a result, when I teach CT, I often break to summarise what it is as simply as possible – accruing, over the years,

6   What Exactly Is 'Critical Thinking'?

various simplified descriptions. On one occasion, I was asked as part of an exercise to explain/describe CT within the confines of 140 characters (as per some social media). Here are a few of my attempts:

1. 'Playing devil's advocate'[1]
2. 'Taking your time and using caution with thinking'
3. 'Leaving emotion at the door'
4. 'The application of specific skills, dispositions and reflective judgment to draw a conclusion or solve a problem'
5. 'Skill involving the identification of the structure of an argument, the role propositions play within, as well as their sources'
6. 'Skill in assessing an argument's strengths and weaknesses regarding credibility, relevance, logical strength, balance and biases'
7. 'Skill in gathering evidence and drawing a reasonable conclusion'
8. 'An inclination, tendency or willingness to perform the necessary cognitive skills'
9. 'Understanding the nature and limits of *knowing*, and how this can influence the defence of reasoning and potential falsification'

Though the first four explanations are accurate, they remain problematic: the first three explain CT to some extent but don't truly encapsulate the 'full story'; and the fourth explanation, though comprehensive of CT's 'full story', remains vague with respect to some abstractions. What skills? What disposition? What's reflective judgment?

So, I tried further in the next five offerings, as it seemed that the first four were insufficient without further explanation. Without being able to rely on the fourth entry as an 'umbrella' for the following five, these attempts did nothing to advance progress either. None could both address the 'full story' and ensure enough clarity for any real meaning to be derived by those unfamiliar with educational research – or perhaps even those *in* the field of educational research!

Though I received some positive feedback from this exercise, I ultimately viewed it as a failure (making the positive feedback worry me a bit – we'll get to that). But, despite such failure, something positive

---

[1] Refers to arguing against your own point as a means of ensuring multiple perspectives are accounted for within decision-making. Essentially, it makes you ask yourself 'what if I'm wrong?' and forces you to develop an alternative conclusion/solution, working well to combat confirmation bias (see Chapter 6). I explain it here because, though I assume many readers are familiar with the phrase, on one occasion following my recommendation of 'playing devil's advocate', I was questioned by a student (who had not previously heard the phrase) regarding how I could recommend messing around with the occult. Yikes. This is just one of many examples of why we need CT.

emerged in my thinking – a great lesson was learned. It may be the case that efforts made to simplify the concept of CT actually lend themselves to increasing the confusion, uncertainty and/or debate. The reality of why good CT definitions are as long as they are is because CT is quite a complex concept. Indeed, conducting CT is not easy either; otherwise, everyone would be doing it and we'd live in a world with far fewer poor decisions. It is, perhaps, the case that long explanations are necessary to ensure not only accuracy but clarity as well (albeit with some level of needing to break it down to its component parts). With that, the issue of defining CT has never been easy.

In a 2007 study, the University of Western Australia found that while 92 per cent of academic staff believed it important to provide students with opportunities to engage critical evaluation of their personal beliefs and perspectives with a view towards changing them, 54 per cent of students felt that they were not actually provided such opportunities by their educators. A potential explanation can be found in the response of one university lecturer interviewed as part of research by Lloyd and Bahr (2010) exploring qualitative descriptions of CT provided by academics: 'we expect students to do it [think critically], but now you are questioning me on my understanding of it, I wonder if I actually understand it myself'. Further reinforcing this notion, Lloyd and Bahr found that only 37 per cent of academics involved in instructing or assessing CT in university courses at least acknowledged the dispositional and self-regulatory aspects of CT; and only 47 per cent described CT in terms of involving processes or skills! Assuming there is a 'trickle effect' (i.e. from educators to students, to the wider population), if those teaching CT are in the dark about it, how can we expect others to know its meaning?

For many years, I believed one of the biggest issues faced in the area of CT was that of debate regarding definition – that too many definitions exist and state disparate things. However, it's also the case that many, if not most, of the more highly cited definitions agree that CT is a purposefully engaged process of cognitive and metacognitive strategies, consisting of both skills and dispositions (e.g. Dwyer, 2017; Ennis, 1996; Halpern, 2014; Ku & Ho, 2010a; Perkins & Ritchhart, 2004). Indeed, forty-six experts in the field of CT gathered in 1988 to discuss conceptualisation and definition, as part of the Delphi Report. They identified analysis, evaluation and inference as the core skills necessary for CT (i.e. through 95 per cent consensus agreement), alongside a number of positive dispositions towards thinking (Facione, 1990a). Despite this, it is often concluded that debate lingers on. Perhaps this is a result of historical

8   What Exactly Is 'Critical Thinking'?

convention (i.e. with respect to describing such a complex concept) or not seeing the level of CT development we might hope to see in light of a standard description of CT (see Chapter 8 for further discussion).

Sure, it could be the case that 'debate lingers on' (particularly with respect to the more intricate details) to some extent, but perhaps the real issue is that researchers in the field of CT fail to see beyond the boundary of expertise. Just because we 'get' what CT is, in the broad sense, doesn't mean everyone else does. So, maybe it's not a matter of whether the experts are on the same or even a similar page regarding what CT is (with respect to the intricacies); rather, perhaps the problem is what's conveyed to others – be they teachers, students or the public (alongside their willingness or ability to engage it).

Both for good and bad, *critical thinking* has become a buzzword. We all know it's important, useful and we want both others to do it and to do it ourselves; but, maybe it's the case that, consistent with the qualitative excerpt earlier, many educators don't really know what 'critical thinking' is and/or simply haven't researched it themselves (see also Eigenauer, 2017). *So, what can we do?*

There's the very idealistic academic's answer, of course, which would suggest that initiatives need to be developed to reinforce a better understanding of CT and its instruction as part of teaching programmes. Though I agree with this sentiment wholeheartedly, I'm also not naïve. Such initiatives cost money, and more often than not, it seems, education is underfunded (especially if a specific topic seeking funding is not on trend in the 'zeitgeist'). Moreover, not everyone has the opportunity to engage such education. Couple that with the fact that there is no guarantee that such an initiative would work.

Playing devil's advocate (consistent with the earlier recommendations), I can imagine being on a teacher-training course and not really giving my all to topics in which I have little interest. It's not about being a 'bad student' in this context, but rather having only so much time to complete *all* coursework and maintain other concurrent responsibilities. Sure, some individuals will; but, many won't – and again, we must not assume everyone's interest in the field. I, along with many colleagues in the past, have 'got stuck' with teaching topics in which we have no interest. Why should CT be any different for anyone else?[2]

---

[2] At the start of a new semester, I was introduced to a new lecturing colleague (from a different department in one of the institutions where I've worked) and noticed they were carrying a book on CT. I won't mention the author of said book for reasons of courtesy, but it's not a book I would rate

What Exactly Is 'Critical Thinking'?

Of course, I don't mean this as an indictment against educational systems or individual teachers not interested in teaching CT. Rather, it's simply an observation that may have a seed of truth; in which case, the implications are important. It needs to be made clear that if one is not getting training in CT to the requisite standard – or if they want supplementary material – they should be independently engaging literature on CT. This goes for educators, students and people interested in CT alike. In fact, that's part of the impetus for this book and this chapter specifically: to provide readers with the full story of what CT is, thoroughly exploring its complexities, but in a manner that clarifies the abstractions.

A better understanding of CT facilitates many positives, especially for those who engage it – CT allows people to gain a better understanding of complex information (Dwyer et al., 2012; Halpern, 2014); it facilitates good decision-making and problem-solving in social and interpersonal contexts (Gambrill, 2006; Ku, 2009); it decreases the effects of cognitive biases and heuristic thinking (Facione & Facione, 2001; McGuinness, 2013); and it yields a higher likelihood of better grades, becoming more informed and more active citizens, and being employable (Barton & McCully, 2007; Holmes & Clizbe, 1997; National Academy of Sciences, 2005). Arguably, these notions have been given a 'louder shout' over the past fifteen–twenty-five years in light of advancing technology and growing political, economic, social and health-related concerns (Dwyer, 2023). Thus, we shouldn't rely or wait on others to develop our CT through training, particularly when opportunities to engage good CT training aren't always feasible. So, let's work it out for ourselves and go back to the drawing board to break the definition down. CT is:

> A metacognitive process consisting of a number of sub-skills and dispositions, that, when applied through purposeful, self-regulatory, reflective judgment, increase the chances of producing a logical solution to a problem or a valid conclusion to an argument. (Dwyer, 2017; Dwyer et al., 2014)

---

as particularly 'good'. I jokingly asked why they didn't go with the book by Chris Dwyer, and so as to not look so 'full of myself' upon introduction, despite it being a joke (one can't assume their humour will land for everyone), I mentioned other books by researchers I highly rate (e.g. Halpern and Ennis). The reply I got was concerning for someone in my field. This lecturer – who would be delivering a full semester module on CT – had not heard of those other researchers and had only been 'landed' with the module in recent days. The book they were holding was one they 'just found' in the library. Given that CT was not a field that particularly interested them (hence being 'landed' with the module), coupled with the lack of time to adequately prepare for the module, all I could think about was how much of a missed opportunity this class might well turn out to be for the students.

10 What Exactly Is 'Critical Thinking'?

In the definition, there are three key concepts that require attention: (1) skills, (2) dispositions and (3) reflective judgment.[3] The remainder of this chapter will address each in turn.

Skills

Consistent with the Delphi Report (Facione, 1990a), analysis, evaluation and inference are the core skills necessary for CT. This is not to say other cognitive skills are not important – they are, and fundamentally so, namely memory and comprehension (e.g. see Anderson & Krathwohl, 2001; Bloom et al., 1956; Dwyer et al., 2014). For example, if you can't remember specific information and understand it at an appropriate level, how can you think critically about it (see, for example, Halpern, 2014; Maybery et al., 1986)? However, beyond a foundational ability to store and retrieve information learned and encoded as knowledge, the CT process begins with analysis.

Analysis is used to identify and examine the structure of an argument,[4] the propositions within an argument and the role they play within this network of reasoning (e.g. the main conclusion, the reasons of support, objections to propositions and inferential relationships among them), as well as the sources of the propositions. Through such analysis, an argument's hierarchical structure begins to appear. This structure can be extracted (e.g. from dialogue and text) for subsequent evaluation.

Evaluation refers to the assessment of propositions and claims (identified through the previous *analysis*) with respect to their credibility, relevance, balance, bias as well as the logical strength among propositions. Such assessment facilitates justified judgment regarding the overall strength or weakness of an argument. If an argument (or its propositions) is not

---

[3] Though the term 'metacognition' (i.e. thinking surrounding one's own cognitive processes, their regulation and their outcomes; see, for example, Flavell, 1979; Ku & Ho, 2010b) is important, it's role as 'thinking about thinking' is self-evident in discussion of the three key concepts addressed, particularly in reference to reflective judgment.

[4] An argument, as conceptualised throughout this book, refers to any verbal-based representation (e.g. through written or spoken word) of two or more propositions that interact in a manner to justify (or refute) some standpoint, typically signposted through words such as 'because', 'but', 'however', 'yet', 'therefore' and 'thus'. The 'heatedness' of debate plays no role in its classification as an 'argument'. We engage arguments all the time, across a variety of different forms; for example, a TV commercial provides a one-sided argument for why you should purchase some breakfast cereal, an editorial in the newspaper pushes an argument for a policy change, a two-sided argument at work determines which pitch is best to present to your potential client, or a two-sided argument with your spouse could be about how best to potty-train your toddler.

credible, relevant, logical and/or unbiased, consider excluding it or discussing its weaknesses as an objection.

Specifically, evaluating *credibility* involves progressing beyond merely identifying the source of propositions in an argument (as in analysis) to actually examining the 'trustworthiness' of those identified sources (e.g. personal experience/anecdotal evidence, common sense/beliefs, expert opinion and scientific evidence). This is particularly important because some sources are stronger, or more credible, than others (see Chapter 5 for a more detailed discussion of credibility). Evaluation also implies deep consideration of the *relevance* of propositions within an argument – accomplished through assessing the contextual pertinence – that is, the applicability of one proposition to another and to the central claim. With respect to *balance* and *bias*, it's important to consider an argument's 'slant'. If an argument seems imbalanced in favour of one line of thinking, then it's quite possible that the argument has omitted key, opposing points that should also be considered.[5] Imbalance may also imply some level of bias in an argument – another factor that should also be assessed. However, just because an argument is balanced does not mean that it isn't biased. For example (and there are many), it may very well be the case that the 'opposing views' presented have been 'cherry-picked' because they are easily disputed (akin to building a 'strawman', that is, a purposefully misrepresented proposition), thus making supporting reasons appear stronger than they may actually be. In any argument, one should construct an understanding of the author's or speaker's motivations and consider how these might influence the structure and contents of the argument.

Finally, evaluating the *logical strength* of an argument is accomplished through monitoring both the inferential relationships among propositions and the claims made in light of these. Assessment of logical strength – through the skills of evaluation – can be aided by the subsequent application of inference (i.e. the final core CT skill), as a means of double-checking the logical strength. For example, this can be checked by asking whether or not a particular proposition can actually be inferred based on the propositions that precede it.

Similar to other educational concepts such as synthesis (e.g. see Bloom et al., 1956; Dwyer, 2011, 2017), the final core CT skill, *inference*, involves

---

[5] Of course, this issue of omission only applies to propositions of a credible nature. If an argument excludes reference to certain perspectives you might have anticipated seeing, it may not be an issue of imbalance or bias; rather, it may be that the perspectives based on beliefs and opinions do not warrant discussion in such an argument. If the latter, you may consider evaluating your own perspective with regards to the credibility of such beliefs and opinions.

the 'gathering' of credible, relevant and logical evidence based on the previous analysis and evaluation, for the purpose of drawing a reasonable conclusion (Dwyer et al., 2014; Facione, 1990a). Though inference implies synthesis, with respect to putting together 'parts' of information to form a new whole (Dwyer, 2011), it is a unique form of synthesis in that it involves the formulation of a set of conclusions derived from a series of arguments or a body of evidence. Such inference may imply accepting a conclusion pointed to by an author in light of the evidence they present, or 'conjecturing an alternative', equally logical, conclusion or argument based on the available evidence (Facione, 1990a). The ability to infer a conclusion in this manner can be completed through formal or informal logic strategies (or both; see Dwyer, 2017) in order to derive intermediate conclusions and a central claim.

Another important aspect of inference involves the querying of available evidence, for example, by recognising the need for additional information, gathering it and judging the plausibility of utilising such information to draw a conclusion. In this context, inference can be seen to overlap with evaluation, to a certain extent, in that both skills are used to judge the relevance and acceptability of a claim or argument. Furthermore, after inferring a conclusion, the resulting argument should be *re-evaluated* to ensure that it is reasonable to draw the conclusion that was derived – again, akin to double-checking. Notably, this cautious approach – especially in light of uncertainty – is a tenet of CT and, in particular, its reflective judgment component (as detailed later).

Overall, the application of the three CT skills is a process. One must analyse, evaluate and then infer; and this can be repeated to ensure that a reasonable conclusion has been drawn. In an effort to simplify the description of this process, I've used the analogy in class over the past few years of *picking apples for the purpose of baking*. We begin by picking apples from a tree. Consider the tree as its own analogy for an argument, which is hierarchically structured, as in a tree diagram. By picking apples, we are analysing – identifying propositions and the role they play. Once we pick an apple, we evaluate it – making sure it isn't rotten (i.e. lacks credibility, is biased) and is suitable for baking (i.e. relevant and logically strong). Finally, we infer – we gather the apples in a basket, bring them home and group them together based on some rationale for construction – perhaps four for a pie, three for a crumble and another four for a tart. By the end of the process, we have baked some apple-based goods, or developed a conclusion, solution or decision through CT *skills*.

I stress the phrase CT *skills* here because there is more to CT than just the application of skills – a critical thinker must also have the disposition to think critically and engage reflective judgment. For example, though one might be aware of which CT skills to use in a given context and may have the capacity to perform well when using these skills, they may not be disposed to use them. On the other hand, one might be willing to apply CT skills and engage reflective judgment, but without the appropriate ability to use these skills, it is not likely that CT will be applied (Valenzuela et al., 2011).

Dispositions

Though the skill aspect of CT is well researched, there is significantly less research focused on the *dispositional* aspect, despite the aforementioned common conceptualisation of CT as composed of both skills and dispositions. Disposition towards CT refers to an inclination, tendency or willingness to perform a given thinking skill (Dwyer, 2017; Facione et al., 1997; Ku, 2009; Norris, 1992; Siegel, 1999; Valenzuela et al., 2011). Different types of CT dispositions (CTDs; see Table 1.1 for examples) are essential for understanding how we think and how we can make our thinking better, in both academic settings and everyday situations (Siegel, 1999).

Notably, it's difficult to read these descriptions of CTDs and not, on some level, interpret them as some sort of personality frameset; but, this is not the case. CTDs are not personality traits. Consider the traditional behaviourist approach to personality. Such an approach would argue that personality doesn't really exist (apart from the fact that people just like to label and categorise things (and people) to create nice, neat little packages; see Chapter 3) and that the various personality traits are simply a series of 'response tendencies'. For example, where personality theory might label me an 'extrovert', it doesn't necessarily account for all the times I'm introverted and doesn't necessarily account for the reason why I'm 'extroverted'. Moreover, the behaviourist approach might suggest that my *response tendency* towards extroverted behaviour exists because it has been reinforced over time, as a result of positive outcomes yielded from such extroverted behaviour. Why this is an important aside is because CTDs – though different from personality traits – can be usefully conceptualised in a similar manner: as response tendencies. Indeed, this is a core part of how they are defined: as tendencies, inclinations and willingness.

14 What Exactly Is 'Critical Thinking'?

Table 1.1 *Examples of dispositions towards CT (adapted from Dwyer et al., 2016; Quinn et al., 2020)*

Disposition	Description
Reflection	An inclination to reflect on one's behaviour, attitudes, opinions, as well as the motivations behind these; to distinguish what is known and what is not, as well as limited knowledge or uncertainty; to approach decision-making with a sense that some problems are necessarily ill-structured, some situations permit more than one plausible conclusion or solution and judgments must often be made based on analysis and evaluation, as well as feasibility, standards, contexts and evidence that preclude certainty.
Open-mindedness	An inclination to be cognitively flexible and avoid rigidity in thinking; to tolerate divergent or conflicting views and treat all viewpoints alike, prior to subsequent analysis and evaluation; to detach from one's own beliefs and consider, seriously, points of view other to one's own without bias or self-interest; to be open to feedback by accepting positive feedback and to not reject criticism or constructive feedback without thoughtful consideration; to amend existing knowledge in light of new ideas and experiences; and to explore such new, alternative or 'unusual' ideas.
Organisation	An inclination to be orderly, systematic and diligent with information, resources and time when determining and maintaining focus on the task, conclusion, problem or question, while simultaneously considering the total situation and being able to present the resulting information in a fashion likewise, for purposes of achieving some desired end.
Perseverance	To be resilient and to be motivated to persist at working through complex tasks and the associated frustration and difficulty inherent in such tasks, without giving up; motivation to get the job done correctly; a desire to progress.
Intrinsic goal orientation	Inclined to be positive, competitive and enthusiastic towards a goal task, topic of focus and, if not the topic itself, enthusiasm for the process of learning new things; to search for answers as a result of internal motivation, rather than an external, extrinsic reward system.
Attentiveness	Willingness to focus and concentrate; to be aware of surroundings, context, consequences and potential obstacles; to have the 'full picture'.
Truth-seeking	To have a desire for knowledge; to seek and offer both reasons and objections in an effort to inform and to be well informed; to have a willingness to challenge popular beliefs and social norms by asking questions (of oneself and others); to be honest and objective about pursuing the truth even if the findings do not support one's self-interest or preconceived beliefs or opinions; and to change your mind about an idea as a result of the desire for truth.
Scepticism	Inclination to challenge ideas; to withhold judgment before engaging all the evidence or when the evidence and reasons are insufficient; to take a position and be able to change position when the evidence and reasons are sufficient; and to look at findings from various perspectives.
Inquisitiveness	An inclination to be curious; to have a desire to fully understand something, discover the answer to a problem and accept that the full answer may not yet be known; to make sure to understand a task and its associated requirements, available options and limits.

Dispositions 15

One problem with CTDs is that they're difficult to measure. Unlike CT skills, which you can assess through objective skill- or application-based assessment, CTDs are not skill-based and, instead, are commonly measured via self-report. There may be CTDs that an individual values, in theory, but don't actually match the manner in which they behave (e.g. akin to cognitive dissonance). For example, I may genuinely value open-mindedness and believe that I am an open-minded person (and report that on such a scale), but whether or not I act in a manner that reflects this sentiment might be a different story. Though CTDs aren't behaviours per se (i.e. rather, they are tendencies towards behaviours), they should be applied as such, and, subsequently, observable (e.g. through interpretation of their associated behaviour – not giving up on a task might reflect perseverance and not jumping to conclusions might represent reflection). Nevertheless, it remains that 'willed tendencies towards behaviours' arguably boil down to an individual's values and worldviews, which again are not the most easily measured without encroaching into the realm of self-report. This is not to slam the idea of self-report as a means of measuring CTDs; indeed, it's more or less the best approach we currently have available (e.g. observation of behaviour and response tendencies isn't the most feasible means of assessing CTDs, especially with large samples). With that, I've been heavily involved in the development of a CTD self-report scale (see Quinn et al., 2020). However, we must also recognise that it is far from a perfect format of CTD measure, and it is recommended that novel means of assessment are researched.

Consistent with Table 1.1, there are a variety of different CTDs. Of course, some people will score higher on some CTDs than others. Ideally, a critical thinker will want to score high in all of them; but, depending on the topic at hand and what's contextually required, some CTDs will be more important than others. The point is, CTDs can interact and there can be overlap among them (e.g. inquisitiveness, truth-seeking and perseverance).

As a result, important distinctions are worth noting. For example, in many ways, open-mindedness and scepticism may appear as at odds with one another. To better understand their relationship, consider again their definitions from Table 1.1. Though it might be interpreted that the two reside on opposite poles of a spectrum, they are largely distinct concepts – an individual can be both sceptical and open-minded at the same time. Open-mindedness doesn't mean you have to *accept* divergent ideas, but rather just consider them. It's about being open to changing your mind in light of new evidence; detaching from your beliefs and focusing on

16   What Exactly Is 'Critical Thinking'?

unbiased thinking void of self-interest; and being open to constructive criticism and new ideas. People who are sceptical do all of this as well – they challenge ideas and they withhold judgment until sufficient evidence is provided; they are open to all possibilities until sufficient evidence is presented one way or another. Remember, scepticism is not the same as cynicism. So, despite what we might initially think about scepticism and open-mindedness on the surface, they go hand in hand once we *reflect* on them in light of comprehensive description. Notably, this example again illustrates the importance of understanding definitions and the way we engage them and arguments more generally. This notion will continue to play an important role throughout this book.

Reflective Judgment

Remember, CT is a metacognitive process (i.e., thinking about thinking), and the ability to do this (Flavell, 1976, 1979; Ku & Ho, 2010b) and apply CT skills to a particular problem implies a reflective sensibility and the capacity for *reflective judgment* (King & Kitchener, 1994).

Perhaps the simplest description of reflective judgment (RJ) is that of 'taking a step back' in your thinking and not jumping to a conclusion. Perhaps equally as simple is *self-regulation* of one's own thinking.[6]

I once had a very thought-provoking conversation with a colleague – one to which I frequently refer – about some people who get so 'good' at applying certain aspects of CT that progressing through the process is no longer effortful – it becomes like second nature; it becomes automatic.

---

[6] Self-regulation is a key feature of metacognition (see, for example, Boekaerts & Simons, 1993; Brown, 1987; Ku & Ho, 2010b); and as CT is a metacognitive process, self-regulation plays a vital role in it, as addressed in the context of RJ earlier. To provide more specific context, self-regulation can be conceptualised as the ability to control emotions, attention and behaviour, including self-monitoring and response inhibition (Gestsdottir & Lerner, 2008), which in many ways is a concept akin to executive functioning (see Miyake et al., 2000). Consistent with self-regulation's role of working in unison with CT skills, dispositions and RJ, self-regulated thinkers are metacognitively, motivationally and behaviourally active participants in their own thinking and learning (Zimmerman, 1989). Notably, a topic of study that is aligned with self-regulation and has gained traction in pop culture over recent years is *emotional intelligence* – regulation through appraising, monitoring and managing our feelings and associated thoughts (Casey, 2018; see also Goleman, 1995; Salovey & Mayer, 1990). I highlight emotional intelligence here as a form of self-regulation because it brings to light an important theme that will be engaged throughout this book – the negative effect that emotion can have on CT and why we should 'leave it at the door' when entering critical thought, as much as we can. Of course, it's not possible to entirely eliminate emotion or its associated biases from thinking, hence the usefulness of emotional intelligence for CT. By being aware of emotion's impact and engaging our emotional intelligence, through processing our feelings about a topic (e.g. through appraising and regulating them), we can work to account for such influence in how we draw conclusions and make decisions.

Automaticity (i.e. the ability to complete a task without paying attention to it) of cognitive processes is achieved through frequent engagement (Anderson, 1981; Bargh, 1997; Strack & Deutsch, 2004), given that through extensive use, procedural schemas[7] will be constructed for such processes. The problem with this is that when thinking becomes automatic, it's implied that little or no attention is paid to the task – which is the antithesis of CT. Thus, RJ must be engaged in an effort to combat automatic thinking. In fact, RJ should be engaged in all scenarios where CT is required, regardless of how skilled, fast or efficient one is in applying it. That is, one must take a step back and think about the argument or problem a little bit longer (a behaviour that significantly increases decision accuracy; e.g. Teichert et al., 2014). At the very least, it will aid identification of possible bias by the thinker, if not bring to light mistakes or gaps in logic.

Some existing definitions of CT include this notion to some extent; for example: *reasonable, reflective thinking focused on deciding what to believe or do* (Ennis, 1987), or *reflective thinking in which a person evaluates relevant evidence and works to draw a sound or good conclusion* (Bensley, 1998). They imply avoidance of jumping to a conclusion or relying solely on intuitive judgment. Similarly, a useful way of considering RJ is as 'System 2 thinking' (see, for example, Kahneman, 2011; Stanovich, 1999) – the rational, reflective side of thinking associated with conscious awareness, as opposed to the automaticity associated with System 1 thinking.

However, there is more to RJ, more that's necessary for CT, than just that. A longer, better-elaborated and, perhaps, more accurate, description implies an *epistemological understanding*. That is, RJ can be conceptualised as an individual's understanding of the nature, limits and certainty of *knowing* and how this can affect how they defend their judgments and reasoning in context, as well as an individual's acknowledgment that their views might be falsified by additional evidence obtained at a later time (King & Kitchener, 1994).

The ability to acknowledge levels of certainty and uncertainty when engaging in CT is of utmost importance. Often, the information a person is presented with (along with that person's previous knowledge of associated information) provides only a limited source from which to draw a conclusion – they don't have *all* the information. Thus, who is to say that

---

[7] Schemas refer to mental frameworks or cognitive representations regarding how individuals interpret the world around them. See Chapter 4 for a more detailed discussion.

18   What Exactly Is 'Critical Thinking'?

the cross-section of information that they're working with is actually facilitating an accurate account of the situation? Perhaps the information they're working with is biased towards one perspective and doesn't allow for them to evaluate multiple sides of the story.

Problems that cannot be solved with absolute certainty are known as *ill-structured problems* (King et al., 1990; Wood, 1993). Though it can be argued that there is no certainty at all in the arena of knowledge or problem-solving (see Chapter 3), specific thinking activities are necessary when people realise the questionability around certainty, at the very least, in *some* cases (Dewey, 1933; King & Kitchener, 2004; Wood, 1993). RJ is one such activity that should be engaged when an ill-structured problem is encountered, where the uncertainty associated with the problem indicates that multiple paths of reasoning and action are possible (e.g. 'what is the best way of decreasing global warming?').

Ill-structured problems like this often lead thinkers to reasonably consider multiple, alternative solutions (e.g. 'make everyone drive electric cars' or 'cut down on cattle farming in order to lower methane emissions'). Consider the recommendation earlier about 'playing devil's advocate'. Good thinking doesn't mean you develop one solution and forge on with that. You consider it from numerous perspectives and generate responses in light of these. Of course, some solutions are better than others; and this can be based on the organisation, complexity and careful consideration of the propositions within an argument. For example, in comparison with the earlier unsupported singular claims, a more complex and better-considered response might propose that 'although research is still ongoing in this area, mathematical models based on existing research findings suggest that by making small decreases in emissions in all walks of life, whether it be travel, farming, industry or energy production, emissions around the globe will decrease substantially'. Thus, it isn't only the conclusion that is reached – regardless of it being wrong or right – it's how you got there that counts. I recognise how corny that may sound – 'it's the journey that counts, not the destination' – but, in this context, it's true. Let's say that your response is 'right'. That's all well and good, but if you can't walk people through how you came to that conclusion – the analysis, the evaluation and the inference – then people will doubt you, and rightly so. In RJ and CT, just as important as the conclusion/solution/inference is the manner in which one *arrives* at it. Notably, this description of RJ, as involving inferential processes, further reinforces the interdependence between it and CT.

Reflective Judgment

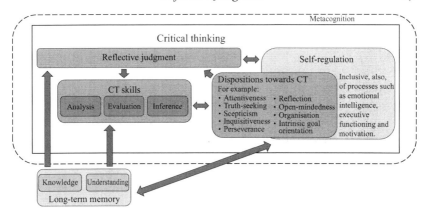

Figure 1.1 Interdependencies among CT processes
(adapted from Dwyer, 2017; Dwyer et al., 2014, 2015, 2016)

Furthemore, RJ is considered a component of CT because it allows one to acknowledge that epistemic assumptions (i.e. assumptions about one's knowledge) are vital to recognising and judging a situation in which CT may be required (King & Kitchener, 1994), and it may influence how well an individual applies each CT skill (King et al., 1990) – perhaps, even how well they 'engage' their CTDs (Dwyer et al., 2015). Indeed, research investigating the link between these concepts indicates a correlational relationship between RJ and both CT skills and dispositions, with a suggestion that the two develop in an interdependent, cyclical manner (Brabeck, 1981; Dawson, 2008; King & Kitchener, 1994; King et al., 1990). Furthermore, RJ development is not a simple function of age or time, but more so a function of the amount and nature of engagement an individual has with problems that require CT (Brabeck, 1981; Dawson, 2008; Dwyer et al., 2015; Fischer & Bidell, 2006). Research also suggests that RJ performance may be moderated by CT dispositions (Dwyer et al., 2015), in that RJ requires willingness to both understand the epistemological nature of things and engage it. With that, RJ stands out as distinct from CTDs and skills in that it represents a combination of self-regulation and engagement with both extant and ongoing understanding of the nature of knowledge and its relationship with information engaged in context. In this context, Figure 1.1 shows the interdependencies among CT processes, including RJ.

20   What Exactly Is 'Critical Thinking'?

Cognitive Continuum Theory and Dual-Processing

Earlier in this chapter, automatic, System 1 thinking (in terms of *dual-process theory*; e.g. Stanovich, 1999) was addressed as intuitive judgment and as being in opposition to RJ. RJ 'blocks' the critical thinker from jumping to a conclusion that is 'automatically generated' by intuitive judgment, makes us take our time with our thinking and allows us to consider the nature, limits and certainty associated with the information being thought about and applied. There is nothing anyone can do about intuitive judgment – that's why it's automatic; System 1 thinking will always tell you what it thinks at any given time. We need to be willing to engage RJ when we face a scenario that we want to think about critically. The point is, you can't turn intuitive judgment off. It's always there; and because it's not a one-or-the-other type of situation, it's useful to think of reflective and intuitive judgment as working on a continuum. According to cognitive continuum theory (Hammond, 1981, 1996), at one pole you have RJ; at the other you have intuitive judgment, referring to automatic cognitive processing that generally lacks effort, intention, awareness or voluntary control – usually experienced as perceptions or feelings (Kahneman, 2011; Lieberman, 2003). Intuitive judgment has also been referred to as the 'the absence of analysis' (Hamm, 1988) and as 'trusting your gut'.[8]

Thinking is never purely reflective, nor is it completely intuitive (Cader et al., 2005). For example, no matter how much time you spend reflecting

---

[8] The phrase 'trust your gut' has become part of the pop culture zeitgeist, particularly in business and commerce domains. As we will see in the chapters that follow, intuitive judgment is often right; but when it's wrong, it's *very* wrong. Sure, the beauty of intuitive judgment is that it's fast and often accurate; but, in situations where the outcome is important – say the difference between making and losing money in business settings – wouldn't you think it worthwhile engaging RJ rather than simply relying on your gut? I've written a piece on this in the past and, of course, I got interesting feedback from those who work in business settings. A typical response was 'if going with your gut is so wrong, then why does it pay off so often?' First, I wonder how often is 'so often' – particularly in comparison with instances where RJ was engaged. Second, I think people often miss the point I'm making: I'm not saying intuitive judgment is always wrong, I'd just be a lot more confident with my decision after engaging RJ in light of what my gut will inevitably have told me. In this sense, perhaps, there is an important distinction between *trusting your gut* and *going with your gut*. Trusting your gut implies that there is no need for RJ. Going with your gut is something you might do once you have appropriately engaged RJ. Sure, some might argue that this is purely semantics, but there is a practical distinction. So, my recommendation is don't trust your gut when a situation requires CT; instead, engage RJ first and if, after your application of CT, your conclusion confirms your gut, then 'go with it'.

Reflective Judgment

and reading new information, it's not possible for your decision to be completely reflective and void of intuition – your existing knowledge, experiences and/or emotions will bias you in some way. So, instead, the thinking behind your judgment lies somewhere in between these realms of reflection and intuition – the combination of the two often described in the field as *quasi-rationality* (Cader et al., 2005; Dunwoody et al., 2000). Quasi-rationality is adaptive in the sense that one may, on some occasions, reflect more on their judgments than use intuition or vice versa. The proportions of the reflective and intuitive thought 'mixture' are dictated by one's expertise or existing knowledge (which are notably distinct – see Chapter 4 for further discussion) regarding the nature of the situation or task, for example, with respect to the complexity, ambiguity and presentation of the situation/task structure and its content (Hamm, 1988). The ability to adapt our thinking in a 'quasi-rational' manner is both practical and important because we face countless decision-making situations each day – some that require very little reflection, some that require deeper, more reflective consideration and some that require a 'delicate balance' of both (Langley, 1995).

Arguably, being able to distinguish these contexts is a CT skill unto itself! Indeed, this concept is so important that it warrants its own chapter; thus, the following chapter will discuss the 'when and why' of thinking critically. But first, to conclude this chapter, I reiterate, CT is *a metacognitive process consisting of specific skills and dispositions that, when applied through purposeful, self-regulatory, reflective judgment, increase the chances of producing a logical solution to a problem or a valid conclusion to an argument.* Yes, it is a long, abstract definition and I'd love to shorten it and use more accessible language; but, at the end of the day, it's long and abstract because it's a complex process, and I want to be sure that people are clear on it. What I need to be clear about – for my own thinking – is that people who want to truly learn how to think critically are not going to be able to do it after reading a definition. Instead, the definition provides an outline of what it is and of what it consists (i.e. skills, dispositions and RJ). It takes instruction and practice for it to develop. Not everyone will understand CT from their first encounter with the definition; but, hopefully, one can come to understand it and its nuances and intricacies following sufficient instruction. One could argue that the entirety of this chapter is a definition of the term. I can see that. Indeed, my goal for this chapter has been to explain

CT as thoroughly as possible, within the confines of succinctness, conciseness and accessibility. The remainder of this book aims to add 'flesh to the bone' in terms of diving a little deeper into many of the concepts introduced in this chapter, and further develop the thinking around them for a more thorough understanding and appreciation for what it means to think critically.

CHAPTER 2

When and Why Do We Think Critically?

Now that we have a better understanding of what CT is and how it's achieved, a logical progression in thought might lead you to question when and why we think critically. We have addressed the latter to some extent in the previous chapter – citing the many benefits of applying critical thought. However, it is worthwhile further considering this issue, particularly in more personalised contexts.

Considering the fact that you are reading a book on CT and other associated concepts, you might get the impression that the author of such a book would be advocating that you should *always* apply CT. I am not doing that at all. Why? Simply because it's not feasible. Instead, I argue that you should only think critically about issues you care about or are important to you.[1] The when and the why are, arguably, the same in many contexts – you apply CT when you care and because you care.

The issue of 'caring' is important because it excludes judgment and decision-making in day-to-day scenarios that are not of great importance and do not warrant CT. Imagine critically thinking about every decision you make! If we were to wake at 7 am and think critically about all of our decisions, not only would we achieve very little in our mornings, we probably wouldn't make it past noon from exhaustion! We want to conserve time and cognitive resources and avoid cognitive load (Sweller, 2010) and decision fatigue (Baumeister, 2003). Imagine critically analysing and evaluating your morning sequence of tasks: making coffee, eating

---

[1] Notably, there are even some scenarios that might be important to you that will not require CT. One of my favourite examples is that of a nurse who instinctively goes to catch/support a falling patient, in which case the speed of such an incident makes it nearly impossible to reflect upon the potential options associated with the problem situation (see also Chapter 10 with respect to *naturalistic decision-making*). Going with your gut and catching the patient is the only real option. However, exceptions like this may be a result of the nature of the situation, that is, a task (as is the case here of catching the patient) as opposed to a cognitive process per se (e.g. Cader et al., 2005; Hammond, 1996). A similarly simple way of looking at this is as us, as individuals in our own contexts, not always being afforded time to think before acting.

breakfast, brushing your teeth, dressing and getting yourself transported to work or school. None of these actually require critical thought, particularly if you do all of them the same way each day, in which case intuitive judgment and heuristics (i.e. experience-based plans that act as mental shortcuts for quick decision-making) will suffice in leading your judgments and decisions. Sure, if you discover that you're out of milk or are forced to take a different route to work in the morning, your protocol may require subtle amendment, but not so much that you have to sit down and really think about it. It's simple problem-solving at most, not CT. Of course, problem-solving is an important application of CT, but in many contexts, it doesn't have to be – much like in this one.

As I alluded to in my first book, there is a famous chain of coffee shops that used to boast an amazing possibility of thousands of permutations of beverages from which their customers could choose. Imagine stopping on your way to work – perhaps making coffee at home isn't part of your 'getting ready' protocol, or you, in fact, ran out of milk (thus amending your protocol with a simple solution to the problem). Would you look at the vast menu and eliminate, one by one, each beverage before deciding on the perfect one for you? No, of course not. It would be a waste of your time and energy. You select the drink you want based on your already established preferences. Alternatively, you might be influenced by the person in front of you who orders something that looks or sounds particularly enticing. Either way, you're going with your gut in a scenario like this because, ultimately, the decision doesn't matter. It's just a cup of coffee. If it was a health insurance policy, your perspective might change; but, the worst-case scenario here is that you don't enjoy your drink.

Applying Critical Thinking to Things You Care About

As someone who loves coffee, of course I'm a little disappointed if I don't like my order. But, a bad cup is not going to ruin my day – I don't *care* that much about it. If a topic, issue or decision to be made isn't particularly important to you or your life – if it doesn't warrant the time and energy necessary to appropriately consider – then you don't care enough about it to apply CT, and that's fine. 'Importance' is subjective and essentially boils down to what one cares about (e.g. issues potentially impactful in one's life). I don't think critically about what kind of coffee I'm going to order, what I'm going to eat for dinner or what film I'm going to watch on television – these decisions are not likely to have large impacts on my life;

Applying Critical Thinking to Things You Care About   25

so, I'm not going to waste the energy.[2] But, then, the question becomes, *what do you care enough about to spend your time and resources thinking critically about?*

My perspective generally splits off in two directions when presented with this question. First, I worry that people may not care enough about things they should. For example, if they don't fully understand the importance of the decision space within which they're working, they're probably more likely to go with a conclusion or solution that's 'good enough' (see 'satisficing' in Simon, 1957). Likewise, if they overestimate the strength and accuracy of their intuitive, gut-based decision-making (see Chapter 1), they're going to be less likely to sit down and truly consider their thinking. With that, though people don't (and shouldn't) think critically about everything, they typically at least consider the implications of each somewhat important decision they make (i.e. quasi-rationality) – well, I'd hope so anyway! You might call this conscientiousness or something similar, but at the end of the day, it doesn't require much cognitive effort.

Second, people often poorly conceptualise what is meant by 'care' in the context of why or when to think critically. This may be in reference to what 'care' operationally means (e.g. in comparison to concepts such as 'passion', which we'll discuss later in this chapter) or what it means relative to other people. For example, everyone is different in terms of what they care about, why they care about it and even what they don't necessarily care about but rate as important anyway (e.g. the work conducted as part of employment may not be something the individual cares about per se, but as the quality of the work they complete has implications for their status in their job, they likely rate it as important – akin to extrinsic motivation).

Context is key here, as it is whenever CT is applied. For example, if you're struggling with finances and one of your larger appliances stops working – say a washing machine – you will probably care more about what to do about it than if money wasn't a concern. For example, would

---

[2] This may be one of the reasons why we engage such a lack of CT in online settings. Think about it: you're on social media, you see a post and in the thread of comments, there are countless people saying 'ignorant things'. You might take it seriously, because you care about the topic. The other person might not – they're just giving their two cents. One issue with social media situations like this (and the real-world in general) is that CT is not a prerequisite to give your opinion. Social media simply provides you a larger platform and further reach to give that opinion. Another issue is, *why should you care about what some non-expert person – that you may not even know – thinks about a topic?* If you care about a topic, see what a credible source thinks.

26 When and Why Do We Think Critically?

you consider trying to fix it yourself? You might find yourself learning new skills in an effort to save some money. But what if you're still not confident even after reading up on it and watching 'how to' videos? Do you call a repair person? Do you live near a laundrette? Of course, the added chore here might place extra stress on you during what is already a stressful time because of your struggling finances; anyway, are either of these solutions more cost-effective – in your particular context – than just buying a new, albeit cheaper, machine? With that, it may be the case that the new machine may have a shorter lifespan than a more expensive, better-rated one. Maybe you'd splash out and buy a more expensive option and look at it as a worthwhile investment, even though it would further deplete your already suffering bank account. I can't tell you the right answer, because it depends on your own situation. This is a situation where you need to genuinely think for yourself. On the other hand, if money isn't a concern (or a care), you might simply go for the most reputable washing machine on the market with little thought behind it.

Burden and Value

Likewise, if topics such as politics, children's education or healthcare policy are ones in which you are not particularly interested, then it's probably not really important for you to dedicate time and effort to evaluating arguments regarding these. This may also strike you as surprising – that a book on CT and associated concepts seems to be advocating apathy towards what many might consider rather important topics and isn't recommending becoming more socially aware, active and engaged. This isn't the case; rather, I'm saying *be practical*. If such topics and issues are not things you care about, are interested in or find personally important, why bother? Consider this notion for two interconnected reasons.

First, people are more likely to actively search out information regarding the issues they care about than they are to seek information on those they don't; thus, if and when they do engage the latter, then it's more likely to be on a passive basis, such as through listening to the news or other forms of media. Of course, media presentation of 'important' issues is generally quite brief and incomplete (i.e. there's always other news to which to attend), thus facilitating a person's bias, emotion and pre-existing schemas to fill in the blanks as necessary and potentially misrepresent the actual information. The other thing about news and media worth noting here is that it's often the case that more bad news is reported than good. Human bias towards negativity is not a new concept in psychology. Sure, we may

Applying Critical Thinking to Things You Care About   27

not want to engage with negative events or news, but behaviourally we are inclined to do so – for a variety of reasons, be it concepts associated with schadenfreude,[3] morbid curiosity and/or, perhaps to some extent, as a means of self-preservation and learning of what to be wary. Given this propensity to focus on negative news (see, for example, de Hoog & Verboon, 2020; Soroka et al., 2019; Trussler & Soroka, 2014), it's no wonder that this is what generally makes headlines; simply, bad news sells.[4]

Second, some of that previously mentioned surprise may stem from the notion that there potentially exists apathy towards topics that *you* might consider important (e.g. politics, healthcare, education). Believe me, I know what you're talking about – it's tough trying to promote CT to people who believe they don't need it. But, that's just it – your surprise (or maybe even anger or outrage) results from *your* care about these topics. Remember, everyone is different; and so there is subjectivity here with respect to importance and care.

For example, consider the phenomenon of virtue-signalling. The concept has evolved from originally referring to costly behaviours representing a commitment to a belief system (e.g. fasting for religious reasons) to having a new, often negative, connotation: publicly expressing opinions or values to demonstrate one's good character or moral correctness with the (implicit or explicit) intent of enhancing social standing (notably, the signalling no longer requires much 'cost'). I'm not a big fan of the term, particularly with respect to its evolution – 'virtue-signalling' implies that the person is actually expressing a *virtue*. However, if an individual posts an article online supporting a certain view, though they may receive a large deal of support, it does not mean that the opinion or perspective is virtuous to everyone, let alone 'correct' (e.g. being pro-life as opposed to pro-choice or vice versa). The assumption behind the individual's action might be that (a majority of) people share the same perspective, even when they may not (e.g. *false consensus effect* or consensus bias); so, what is virtuous to the individual may not be the commonly shared perspective

---

[3] In this context, schadenfreude might refer to comfort or pleasure derived from other's misfortunes, perhaps as a mechanism of social comparison.

[4] I reached a point in 2011 – in the midst of an economic crisis following the 2008 financial crash – where I made the decision to avoid watching the news altogether, simply because I deemed it potentially harmful to my mental health. It seemed all the news in Ireland focused on the economy, job losses, politics and the sad anecdotes of Joe Everyman. Fast-forward a decade and we've since encountered world-impacting political turmoil, a pandemic and, as always, war. I still heard about all of these, at length; I just didn't actively seek such news out – unless it was directly important to me. I wasn't missing out; rather, I chose to 'curate' the information that I processed – not in a biased manner per se, but rather in an evaluative manner.

that they assume. As a result, I would argue a more accurate phrase would be *value-signalling* (i.e. the 'signalling' of material that the signaller values) because it does not require others to hold the perspective dear or even agree with it for it to be of some value (to the signaller at least). Regardless of how it's labelled, acknowledging that not everyone cares about the same things you do is important. Moreover, this will impact the use of CT by individuals at different times and in different contexts.

Care versus Passion

Of course, what you value is likely something you care about. But, this *care* might not be the type that is linked with CT; rather, it might be a more 'passionate' type of care – a concept alluded to earlier in the chapter. This distinction is of utmost importance for understanding the nature of when and why we apply CT. Though for quite a while I've advocated the perspective that people should only apply CT to issues they care about, I have noticed its contradiction of another important message that I often convey: 'leave emotion at the door', as emotion is an enemy of CT. That is, if we want to be able to think critically, we must remove our emotions from our thinking (as much as possible) – a perspective consistent with a large body of research on the negative impact of emotion on decision-making (e.g. Kahneman & Frederick, 2002; Slovic et al., 2002; Strack et al., 1988), higher-order cognition (Anticevic et al., 2011; Chuah et al., 2010; Denkova et al., 2010; Dolcos and McCarthy, 2006) and cognition more generally (Iordan et al., 2013; Johnson et al., 2005; Most et al., 2005; Shackman et al., 2006). Surely, though, if we care about a topic and choose to apply CT, doesn't the emotional bias we have – the foundation of our care – similarly bias our application of CT?

The short answer is yes – but that's assuming passion is still playing a role in this conceptualisation. If we truly *care* about a topic, we will conduct CT to the best of our ability, making sure to apply the CT skills of analysis, evaluation and inference; ensure a positive disposition towards the fundaments of critical thought; play devil's advocate; judge the information reflectively; and, as best we can, leave the aforementioned emotion at the door. Of course, this might just be wishful thinking on my part. Moreover, what I propose here is not easy, especially with the emotional slant of care influencing CT at each and every turn. But, if we truly care about our thinking, applying CT in this manner will facilitate better solutions to problems and valid conclusions to arguments.

With that, we are still yet to define what we actually mean by care – the type of 'care' that is integral for CT. Apart from its other meanings, care can be described as *a feeling of* 'concern or interest; the attachment of importance; and serious attention or consideration applied to doing something correctly or to avoid damage or risk' (Dwyer, 2023). Consider this description in comparison with an often similarly thought of, though meaningfully distinct, concept – such as passion: 'an intense, driving or over-powering feeling or conviction; emotions as distinguished from reason; a strong liking or desire for or devotion to some activity, object or concept' (Dwyer, 2023).

Though the description of care implies that there is an element of emotional involvement, it isn't pointed in a particular direction in terms of bias (as might well be the case in terms of passion). Rather, the feeling is one of concern, interest and importance regarding a topic, followed by attention and consideration – both of which lend themselves to the fundaments of CT. In this light, care can be argued as more of a dispositional or self-regulatory factor than emotional bias, thus making it useful to the application of CT. With respect to passion, emotion's involvement is explicit, for example, with respect to concepts such as desire and devotion. However, what may be most important to consider, in this context, is the description of 'emotion distinguished from reason', that is, acknowledging the reliance on emotion over and above reason – the latter often goes hand in hand with describing what is meant by CT. Thus, perhaps *passion* is a better fit for what is meant when one might think of care from an emotional standpoint, albeit, possibly, a more extreme version.

With that, I'm not saying passion is necessarily a bad thing. It can be a positive driving force – a great motivator for facilitating individuals to achieve their goals. However, for the purposes of CT, it's best to remove 'passion' and emotion from the process and focus on the less biased features of 'care' (as much as possible, given that no thinking is completely void of emotion; consider again *cognitive continuum theory*). So, when we apply CT, it should be to a topic we care about; but, it's important that we distinguish the emotional features of care from our perspective when engaging the otherwise useful features of identifying concern, interest and importance for subsequent attention and consideration.

Does Time of Day Matter?

Thus far, our tackling of the questions of why and when we think critically has largely led to the same answer for both: *because we care* and *when we care*. However, I'm sure there are people who would like a more direct answer, particularly for the latter. As I've often been asked to simplify descriptions of CT in the past, I've also been asked to provide simplified tips for enhancing CT, one of which has been to 'do it in the morning'. I got a hard time from one of my colleagues about this comment, who, like me, is rather pedantic about accuracy and clarity (hence the issues often faced by academics in trying to oversimplify research for lay audiences). My colleague suggested that my comment did not account for circadian rhythms and that morning wouldn't necessarily be the best time for everyone to engage CT. This is a fair point, so I will elaborate further here to ensure clarity and accuracy of the statement. Assuming you went to bed on time, had a decent sleep and were up at a normal time in the morning (let's say 7 o'clock), then an optimal time for engaging CT would indeed be in the morning. This is not because of the time, the sun in the sky or because you just pounded two cups of coffee (though that generally helps me – placebo effect probably); rather, it's because of the amount of rest you received relative to the amount of decisions you've made thus far in the day and the cognitive load placed upon you.

I recall the sitcom *How I Met Your Mother* and the character Ted Mosby's motto regarding no good decisions being made after 2 am. Sure, the reasoning behind such a motto might be different in our context, but the rule remains a good one, because we are faced with countless decisions each and every day. Even the automatic, schema-based ones regarding coffee (as described earlier) take their toll. Now, imagine being presented with an important decision at 2 am. I'd recommend putting the situation out of your head (as best you can) and simply going to bed. Deal with it in the morning when you are rested and fresh (i.e. *sleep on it*). It's similar reasoning as to why a large body of research suggests that you shouldn't go food shopping in the evenings; simply, you make poorer decisions when you're tired and then couple that with an increased likelihood of hunger – alongside being in a food store that's specially curated to manipulate or 'nudge' you into making specific purchases (e.g. see Thaler & Sunstein, 2008). Of course, we all do it from time to time; and typically, we come home with a chocolate bar or a bag of crisps that we didn't need.

Of course, some people will read this and immediately recoil at the thought of engaging CT in the morning, having always considered them-selves 'night owls'. I ask this cohort of readers some important questions: do you typically get up during traditionally 'normal' hours in the morning, or are you more of a midday riser, going back to bed, then, around 4 am?

If the latter, fair enough – again, it's not about time per se, but rather the amount of rest you got coupled with the amount of thinking/decision-making you've engaged thus far in the 'day'. On the other hand, you might get up at 7 am every day and still classify yourself as a night owl. I ask you, then, is this an artefact of necessity or routine? By necessity I mean is it the case that you only have time enough to yourself to engage things like CT at night? If you have a full-time job, kids or some other responsibility that limits your time, then it may just be that you're a night owl because you have no other choice. This is a shame, because I'd be confident that your thinking would be better if you did it soon after waking. With respect to routine, it may be that you have developed into a night owl over time – perhaps you once were out of necessity, and though you may no longer need to, you still do it out of habit. The reasoning doesn't particularly matter. I'd recommend the same – I bet you'd be better after some rest. Of course, if it's a necessity issue, I understand that there might be little you can do to amend the situation – but try nonetheless. If it's a routine issue or a mindset of sorts (e.g. taking some kind of pride in being a 'night owl'), people are not likely to amend it, even though they can, because people don't like change – but that's a whole other story (which we'll discuss in Chapters 4 and 6).

Concluding Thoughts

All in all, there is great overlap in the answers for when and why we should apply CT. We should apply CT *because* it facilitates a more complex understanding of information (Dwyer et al., 2012; Halpern, 2014), better judgment and decision-making (Gambrill, 2006), less dependence on cognitive bias and heuristic thinking (Facione & Facione, 2001; McGuinness, 2013), and becoming more informed and more active citizens (Andolina et al., 2003; Barton & McCully, 2007); increases the likelihood of academic and employment success (Bezanilla et al., 2019; Butler et al., 2012; Dwyer, 2017; Ennis, 2018; Holmes & Clizbe, 1997; National Academy of Sciences, 2005); and is important for social and interpersonal contexts where decision-making and problem-solving are necessary (Ku, 2009). Perhaps the simplest reason of all is that we should apply CT *because* there are topics and decisions that are important to us and we care about them. Likewise, we should apply CT *when* there are decisions that are important to us and we care about them. Moreover, it's likely the case that we'll produce better thinking when we're rested and free of cognitive burden.

CHAPTER 3

Knowledge Doesn't Exist
The Nature of Certainty and Problems with 'Theory' and 'Proof'

In my first book on CT, I started with the first few chapters focused on the cognitive mechanisms that facilitate it. I thought of these as foundational and necessary to discuss in order to fully grasp what is meant by CT. I still believe that they are, indeed, foundational; but, perhaps there was an element of 'alright already, when do we get to the CT?' As you can tell by this book, we got straight into what CT is in Chapter 1. The discrepancy is largely down to each book's purpose. The purpose of the first was to provide clear conceptual perspectives and practical guidelines, whereas the purpose of this book is to provide an accessible discussion of the nature of both CT and the information we think about, as well as how these can be appropriately applied in our modern world.

Where does that leave foundational cognitive processes, such as memory? This time around, I'm going to treat them a little differently. This time around, you need to understand CT before you can truly understand memory, comprehension and how they're represented, that is, as *knowledge* – alongside some of its existential quirks, as alluded to in this book's namesake. So, let's briefly run through these foundational mechanisms for context, before getting into knowledge. With that, please acknowledge that the brevity with which we treat these processes here by no means diminishes their importance to thinking and, indeed, CT. Without processes such as memory and comprehension, CT wouldn't be possible.

When we perceive information from our environment, we can attend to it through executive functioning and process it through working memory, where the information is manipulated as necessary, used in the short term and, potentially, stored for long durations (i.e. long-term memory). What we hold in these memory stores and the manner in which the information is organised and constructed relative to other information (i.e. encoded) dictates how it is remembered and comprehended (i.e. understood).

That's it. Hooray! We now have knowledge.

32

Knowledge Doesn't Exist

The information a person has assimilated and stored in long-term memory is what we refer to as their knowledge. But there's a problem with the way in which we conceptualise this idea. Once stored, that information can be re-engaged, reorganised, amended and adapted as appropriate. So, if knowledge can be changed, is it really knowledge?

Think back to Chapter 1, where we discussed RJ and its epistemological function – RJ refers to understanding the nature, limits and certainty of *knowing* and how this can affect how individuals defend their judgments and reasoning in context. Essentially, we must think about knowledge before we can use it in our CT. So, what is the nature of knowledge, what are its limits and how certain can we be about any given piece of knowledge?

My epistemological standpoint – concerned with such questions about the nature, certainty and limits of knowledge – has developed over the years, through lessons learned as a researcher and efforts to become a better one, as well as observations from cognitive psychology. As we addressed earlier, from a cognitive psychology perspective, we engage a piece of information, process it and once it is stored within long-term memory, we treat it as knowledge. However, that piece of knowledge doesn't necessarily have to be 'correct', 'true' or 'factual' to be stored as such – and this can be for any number of reasons (e.g. as a result of being misinformed; assimilating a gist or incomplete story; or misrepresenting belief as evidence).

Essentially, what we store as 'knowledge' and how we express it is simply information – be it accurate or otherwise. This concept may differ significantly from what is commonly accepted as 'knowledge' (and perhaps this is the crux of the issue), that is, as something more akin to fact-based or 'true' information. Moreover, knowledge can 'change' – and I don't mean this in some kind of 'fake news', postmodernist, existential, living in a simulation, 'Oprah told me to live my truth' kind of way.[1] Knowledge can *literally* change.

---

[1] The notion of following or living 'your truth' is nonsense (and potentially dangerous) in this context. I understand that when people of notoriety recommend this approach to life, they typically mean it in the sense of 'being yourself' or being true to oneself. This is advice that you likely received at some stage in your life. I know I'll recommend it to my children – indeed, this is an important aspect of mental well-being. However, there is an unfortunate opportunity here for taking this advice out of context. Regardless of the absolutism of knowledge in terms of 'truth', as we are exploring in this chapter, it remains that there is no such thing as *your* truth, only *the* truth (for as long as it is the truth – that is, until it is advanced upon or falsified in light of credible evidence). Anyone who tells you different is trying to sell you something. The concept of 'your truth' is simply a biased perspective on how you see things, what you believe and what you think you know. If we all engaged our lives according to our own subjective views of reality, then there would be eight billion different realities happening on Earth at this very moment. We know this is not the case, given that we all share a reality. Sure, we can have different perspectives on things, but that doesn't mean others have to buy into yours or your 'reality'. Again, there is no reliability in a sample size of one. If you

Knowledge Doesn't Exist

34

One of my favourite examples of this is that it was once believed that all swans are white. Then one day, a black swan (*cygnus atratus*) was spotted and 'knowledge' had to be amended. The original perspective was *falsified* (e.g. see Popper, 1934/1959). More recently, in 2006, 'knowledge' once again required amendment in light of scientific advances – there are now eight planets, as opposed to the nine we once thought we knew, following Pluto's reclassification as a dwarf planet. The more 'knowledge' we obtain, the more advanced our understanding; and, thus, amendments may be required. Simply, new knowledge may overwrite old knowledge. Thus, those 'facts' that we might hold as near and dear, like the number of planets in our solar system, are subject to potential change. As a result, the 'truth' of 'knowledge' can never be absolute – we can never be 100 per cent certain.

Is It *Really* 'Just a Theory'?

When I pose the question to some of my classes, 'what is a theory?', most of my students (regardless of age or educational level) respond with an explanation that is akin to 'a reasonable, educated/informed guess'. Consistent with this perspective, the phrase 'it's just a theory' is one I'm sure you have heard thrown around from time to time – be it in reference to one's humility regarding their own perspectives or an attempt to denigrate another. These common perspectives are both incorrect and a cause for concern considering that we're dealing with a pretty foundational concept that has great implications for how we approach the nature of thought and knowledge.

While many conceptualise a theory as a reasonable, educated guess, what they're really describing is a hypothesis (i.e. a proposed outcome, explained on the basis of limited evidence or a thread of logic as a starting point for further investigation). A theory is much more concrete than an educated guess. It's an established model for explaining how a certain phenomenon occurs, based on repeated observations time and time again.

You are likely familiar with the 'law of gravity' – a crude description of, simply, what goes up must come down. I call it crude not because I have any real doubts about gravity, but rather because calling gravity a 'law' is a

---

genuinely care about a topic, ditch your subjectivity, your feelings and your experience and search for objective evidence. Sure, it may be time-consuming, but that's part of the reflective nature of judgment-making within CT – sifting through the 'noisy' information (e.g. see Chapter 9).

misnomer. Gravity, as I imagine many readers will know, is actually a theory. *But why?*

Gravity is the leading *theory* for why objects accelerate down towards the Earth (at 9.81 m/s^2). Even though it's 'only a theory', if I'm holding a cup in my hand and release it, I'm going to bet my house that the outcome will be that it falls to the ground and that 'gravity' will work just fine, as expected – today, tomorrow and for the foreseeable future. However, we can never be 100 per cent certain; and there are various reasons for this.

First, what if our understanding of gravity is incorrect? Of course, I'm not saying it is – I'm not a physicist; I have no expertise in this area (a concept that is important to consider when evaluating credibility and one's own perspectives); but just as an example – *what if?* What if there are, as of yet, unobserved characteristics of gravity beyond our current conceptualisation? What if there's more to it than we think? You might say, 'surely we would have seen such characteristics by now?' Well, the same could be said about being able to count planets! Remember, neither of these examples/potentialities are necessarily a function of *being wrong* about a phenomenon; rather, they are a function of *learning more*.

Second, as neither you nor I can see into the future, we cannot guarantee – with *absolute certainty* (no matter how sure we think we are) – that something will happen or that some knowledge will always be the case. However, we might have a strong theory as to what will happen (e.g. the cup will likely fall to the ground). Our prediction is one of extreme confidence – because gravity is a strong theory. But, what happens if an asteroid hits the Earth, knocks us off axis, changes our polarity and/or plays games with the electromagnetic forces associated with our planet? Perhaps 'gravity' will then behave differently and we'll need to conceptualise it differently. Thus, gravity will cease to be *gravity* as we know it. With that, if this was the case, we would all likely be dead and so wouldn't need to reconceptualise anything; but, I think you get the point. Of course, this is extremely unlikely; however, there is still the possibility, no matter how minute; and as a chance exists (regardless of how minute), that means that we cannot be 100 per cent certain of the original premise. Again, this talk of gravity is a rather extreme analogy for my point; but it does provide what I think is a thought-provoking example for consideration.

Let's dig deeper into what theory actually refers. As before, we conceptualise it as an established model for explaining how a certain phenomenon occurs, based on repeated observations time and time again – an explanation of observed regularities. The theory of gravity is such a strong one because it has been observed time and time again, since its establishment, without ever being *falsified*. Notably, this is a fundamental reason why replication in research is so important. When research is replicated, it means that similar findings are yielded that do not falsify the original findings. In this sense, it facilitates reinforcement of a theory. It is also why any one piece or even bodies of research cannot 'prove' a theory true; rather, replication provides further evidence to support a theory – it strengthens a theory. The term *prove* is also of utmost importance to our consideration of the limits of knowledge and further informs us about its fickle nature.

'Proof': The Dirtiest Word in CT

Think back to when you were in school. Did you ever end an essay with the claim that you had proven something through your four-page epic? Yeah, me too. If I knew then what I know now. C'est la vie.

Of course, as an educator, I try my best to teach my students from common mistakes, as well as my own; so I warn them about 'proof' and the word's variations in my CT classes, explaining that points will be deducted if I see it in their writing. Though that may seem harsh, I'm not being pedantic or 'nitpicky', because the issue of 'proof' is at the heart of CT.

Proof is often described as evidence establishing a fact or the truth of a statement – indicating a level of absolutism. For example, we sometimes hear of 'undeniable proof' in certain contexts. 'Proof' and 'proven' have infiltrated minds in ways that make people *sure* of certain phenomena. If it seems like I'm slapping a negative connotation on it, that's because I am – 'proof', 'prove' and their variations represent the dirtiest word in CT. Consider one of my favourite examples: *how many tubes of a certain toothpaste have been sold based on its advertisement as 'clinically proven' to whiten teeth?* Have you bought such a toothpaste? Did it work for you? Maybe it did; but maybe it didn't. So, what happens in the case of the latter – what happens if it doesn't whiten your teeth? Is that not proof that it doesn't work? No of course not, because this is not a black-and-white case (pardon the pun). If the toothpaste doesn't whiten your teeth, that doesn't mean it doesn't work for others. Likewise, just because it works for some people – maybe even most – doesn't mean it will work for everyone. What happens if it whitens teeth in 95 per cent of people who try it? Though that may suffice in terms of reaching the threshold for statistical or clinical significance, is it enough to satisfy the parameters of 'proven'? Of course not – that's why 'proven' is a fallacious use of the term.

Simply, the phrasing implies that it's guaranteed to work. But, if all it takes is one black swan to disprove the claim that all swans are white, then one case of non-effect of the 'clinically proven' toothpaste should disprove that claim too. However, that doesn't mean the toothpaste isn't useful to others. With that, we wouldn't be having this discussion if the word 'proven' hadn't been used.

The problem with the word, in this example, is that it implies that the toothpaste will work for everyone, not just 'most people'. Of course, the phrasing here is likely a product of the marketing team – well, I'd hope so anyway; I can't imagine any self-respecting scientist using the word 'proven'. Notably, it's marketed this way because people like certainty.

The Psychology of Certainty

People feel safer when they are decisively assured. They don't like to be confused or uncertain. Uncertainty can be frightening. With that, people often *create* an understanding to combat this uncertainty (see Chapter 4 for more on this concept). Moreover, people are cognitively lazy and engage a cognitive miserliness (e.g. for reasons discussed in Chapter 2 regarding decision fatigue and cognitive load). So, accounting for these two phenomena, people tend towards embracing nice, neat little packages that more easily facilitate how they engage the world (e.g. like schemas) – the toothpaste either works or it doesn't (hence the label 'proof'). People don't want to hear that something will only work under certain conditions or in certain contexts – that's too much to think about. More importantly, that does not sell toothpaste.

Of course, like our previous point about coffee, who really cares about toothpaste? I mean, I'm sure dentists and people with teeth issues might; but, how likely is the average person to apply CT to toothpaste? Sure, this question might just be an artefact of my own bias – my priorities for toothpaste are that it's minty and designed for both fresh breath and whitening. That's as far as my consideration of toothpaste goes. If I had specific dental needs, I'd probably ask my dentist. But, that's not the case – hence my lack of caring, in context. With that, this is just one example – the core notion extends beyond toothpaste. What about when the stakes are higher, say, in the case of a 'simple proven treatment' for a serious illness? If the claim itself lacks credibility, what else about what is being provided as part of this treatment is suspect? Simply, the concept of 'proof' can be very dangerous, and education needs to better address this.

38 Knowledge Doesn't Exist

The primary strategy I used in my critique of proof in the toothpaste example was that of falsification – a concept introduced in our discussion of theory. Falsification can be said to date back to ancient Greece. Though no first-hand written legacy of Socrates exists, his student Plato avidly relayed his mentor's teachings throughout his own works. It is from this that we are provided with the 'Socratic method' and, at its core, the *elenchus*, which refers to the procedural refutation of a claim based on in-depth examination. The falsification of a claim through this form of examination often leads to the realisation that the original claim requires refinement in order to make it 'true'.

Though debate exists over whether the Socratic method actually leads to the attainment of knowledge or is used simply to make another's argument look foolish (i.e. the negation of information as false 'knowledge'), from a scientific perspective, it should be regarded as the former. That is, through the *falsification* of a claim (which may have been previously accepted as true; e.g. 'X is Y'), new knowledge is created (e.g. 'actually, X is not Y'). For example, acknowledgment that the Earth is not flat was just as important as the discovery that the Earth is round. Simply, a finding that indicates the truth of a null hypothesis is still a valuable finding and is in itself new knowledge. This latter point is important to consider, particularly in the world of publishing research and the tendency to 'chase statistical significance' (i.e. because null findings are often perceived as more difficult to get published).

This notion introduces another important concept regarding falsification. Consider the nature of science – and, more specifically, the nature of controlled comparisons. For example, we might hypothesise that some phenomenon or manipulation will have an effect – we can call this the experimental hypothesis (or in the case that there's a relationship between variables, the alternative hypothesis). On the other hand, we must also consider that there will be no effect (or no relationship), that is, the null hypothesis. Once we collect all of our data, we do not use it to confirm that the experimental or alternative hypothesis is true; rather, we use it to *disprove* the null hypothesis (i.e. 'disprove' is an acceptable term, as it reflects falsification). So, what 'the science' is actually telling us isn't that something happened (e.g. some therapy or educational programme worked); rather, it's saying it is *not the case that nothing happened* – that is, falsification (*not the case*) of the null hypothesis (*nothing happens*).

One of the primary reasons that science has developed in this way is because we recognise that it might be that some other variable – unbeknown to all involved – is influencing change across the testing scenarios.

Knowledge as 'Theory', Not 'Truth'

This could be anything – time of day, temperature or, in the case of individual differences among human participants, age, level of education, amount of caffeine consumed – you name it! Of course, good scientists design their experiments in ways that limit, as much as possible, outside variables and confounds (i.e. there could have been a reasonable impact) from influencing the protocol; however, there is no way to ensure that there isn't *some* confound. Moreover, such science also accounts for individual differences. For example, though some study may report that a particular therapy was found to be beneficial – on a statistically signifi-cant basis – that doesn't mean that each and every individual on that therapy's trial showed improvement. With that, if the number of people on the trial was increased or, perhaps, a different random sampling of the people was used, the data might yield something different (e.g. a null effect or even the opposite effect) – hence the need for replication. The point is, such research doesn't prove anything, because it can't; but, what it does do is either (1) reinforce the evidence base for a theory or its development or (2) provide evidence disconfirming some theory or hypothesis. This is not to say that research is pointless because it can't prove anything – far from it! Rather, it adds and adds to our *current* knowledge base. It also highlights how unattainable proof actually is once you consider that, arguably, the most credible source of evidence (i.e. research) can't generate it.

Knowledge as 'Theory', Not 'Truth'

Over two millennia after Plato's initial reports of the Socratic method, associated falsification processes remain an integral function of good thinking. Perhaps the reason for such focus on falsification is that, according to the logician and philosopher of science Karl Popper (1934/1959) – akin to the example regarding the null hypothesis – we simply cannot prove things 'true' – only false. We can only *disprove*.

According to Popper, knowledge is theoretical. That is not to say that there may or may not be something that is knowledge; rather, what we think we know may or may not be the case. Essentially, all that we hold as true is not proven fact but simply the current best working model for how things are – they are *theories* and not laws. No amount of consistently occurring outcomes can prove a theory – they simply suggest, at best, that the theory is likely not to be false. On the other hand, in order to falsify or disprove a theory, it only takes *one* occurrence of an outcome that directly contradicts the theory to prove its generalisability false (e.g. the observance of a black swan). Important to note here, this does not necessarily mean

40 Knowledge Doesn't Exist

that one research study can disprove a well-established theory. For example, that one study might be poorly designed, conducted, analysed and so on. Just as a theory is well established by research over time, in order to disprove it (i.e. without objective observation of its falsehood, as in the case of the black swan), an equally well-established body of research needs to indicate otherwise. For example, in the case of homeopathy, it is not the case that medical experts said it's nonsense and we all just went along with it; no, it was researched thoroughly and, subsequently, concluded to have no significant efficacy.[2] That's why it's nonsense.

From Popper's perspective, knowledge develops based on the process of eliminating falsified theories. Following this process, there may be only one or even a few theories that are still open to falsification; but this does not mean that one of these theories is true (e.g. the one that is 'true' may not yet have been discovered); rather, one better fits the problem situation it was designed to solve. The manner in which theories develop and adapt (i.e. 'to fit') is what we perceive as our improved understanding of the universe; and, as a result, the problem situations we face also adapt, develop and become more complex, in line with our theories.

For example, consider the previous example regarding Pluto's reclassification as a dwarf planet, leaving us with eight 'traditional' planets in our solar system. I can think of two very distinct reactions to this news, which I do believe reflect two different types of people in the world: (1) 'science is amazing because it's always developing – we've now reached a stage where we know so much about the solar system that we can differentiate celestial bodies to the extent of planets from dwarf planets, floating in space, millions and millions of miles away from us!' and (2) 'I don't understand why these scientists even have jobs – they can't even count'. The first perspective is consistent with that of an individual with epistemological understanding – in this context, that previous understandings of models and theories can change, not necessarily because they were wrong but, rather, because they have been advanced in light of gaining further evidence. The second perspective is consistent with that of someone who has failed to engage epistemological understanding, does not necessarily see that the change might reflect progress, might be resistant to change and might grow in distrust of science and research in light of these changes.

---

[2] I would argue that if homeopathy was actually useful (beyond eliciting a placebo effect), it would have been adopted into actual medical practice long ago – if for no other reason than financial gain. That is, if it worked, then there's money to be made. But, it doesn't work; so, the only people who do advocate it are those with a lack of medical/research understanding and snake oil salespeople preying on those with, you guessed it, little medical/research understanding.

Implications

Of course, the latter point is of great concern to the field of CT (and, indeed, educational circles around the world), because of fears associated with such growth and unwarranted cynicism (e.g. to some extent consistent with the manner in which conspiracy 'theories' (conspiracy beliefs is a more accurate description) are developed, rationalised and maintained; e.g. see Swami and Furnham, 2014).

Implications

A theory is a much stronger notion of 'truth' than many in the larger population may think – it's much more than a hypothesis and certainly stronger than an educated guess. Thus, it should not be cast aside as if it were. However, just because *you know* that a theory is an established model for why or how a given phenomenon occurs doesn't mean that everyone else does. Be cautious in interpreting how people throw the term around and be sure to seek clarification! Likewise, be cautious of how the word 'proof' and its variations are used. The use of terms like these might seem like minor issues, but their implications are impactful with respect to how you or people with whom you engage approach the building of understanding.

With that, truly understanding the notion of theory – and, indeed, the nature of science and falsification, isn't terribly reassuring with respect to our attainment of the *absolute* truth of things. It seems we may never reach it. However, what should come as reassuring is that this is nothing new – this has always been the case; it's just that now you might be more aware of the notion than you might have been before.

As alluded to earlier, prior to the Enlightenment, it was widely believed that the Earth was flat. Though it may seem to us silly that this was actually believed (i.e. to most people anyway, bar some conspiracy 'theorists'), generations from now, people might view one of our near-and-dear beliefs as equally preposterous. If you ask me, there's something equally frightening and exciting about this proposition.

Overall, the concept of 'knowledge' – as commonly considered akin to fact-based or 'true' information – can be reasonably argued as not existing. If there's nothing absolute, if we can't prove things, then how can we know *real* truth and, thus, possess *true* knowledge? Of course, there are caveats to this. First, for example, it can be reasonably argued that every piece of information is either untrue (i.e. misinformation) or *currently* true (e.g. gravity being the currently best explanatory model for why 'what goes up must come down'); that is, it's reasonable to classify 'current truth' as knowledge. Second, there are some things we can truly know – those things that are blatantly wrong! Similar to both Socrates and Popper, though a proposition cannot be proven true, through our investigations, we can 'prove a claim false' – we can disprove it akin to rejecting the null hypothesis. Thus, though we may not know what is true, we can know what is false. However, I must also admit – consistent with the same logic as earlier – who is to say that what is false now may stay false? That is, what happens if what was disproved was just poorly conceived? Once clarified and remedied, then it might better fit a theoretical model that is observable and replicable – then, would it cease to be false? That seems reasonable – it's kind of like recognising your mistake and, proverbially, 'going back to the drawing board'. But, then, if a bad idea has been amended, is it truly the same idea (akin to the Ship of Theseus[3])? Such is the nature of uncertainty.

Okay, so knowledge – as we commonly understand it – may not exist. But, apart from being an interesting philosophical/psychological consideration, how does that affect you in your everyday life? Well, knowing about this notion, alongside related concepts, may help you better interpret the information that you're provided and make better decisions in light of it. You know that knowledge can change as it's advanced. Saying 'knowledge doesn't exist' (though sensationalised as it might be, admittedly) isn't an indictment of science, research and epistemology, it's a celebration of them and ways in which we *advance* knowledge. You know that when someone says 'evolution is just a theory', it's not just an unwarranted perspective – there's strong research behind it; and so, you're not as easily deterred by such statements, because you have such epistemological understanding. You also know that when someone states 'my theory', they're really just talking about personal experience or anecdotal evidence – and that's by no means on par with that of a theory that is established by research. Likewise, you won't be taken in by verbal acrobatics regarding some product's proven benefits. You'll engage these scenarios with more caution. The more opportunities like this, where you engage your epistemological understanding, the more opportunities you will have to practise RJ and, likewise, CT. Moreover, truly understanding to what theory and proof refer, as well as the mechanics behind falsification, is a fantastic way for individuals to begin embracing the concept of intellectual humility,

---

[3] The Ship of Theseus is a philosophical paradox in which the titular ship is preserved by the Athenians. One by one, the wooden planks are replaced as they decay over time. Though there are various versions of this paradox dating back to the time of Plutarch, the core question is, after all the planks have been replaced, is the craft still *Theseus's* Ship?

through engaging epistemological consideration regarding the nature of knowledge and the concept of certainty (Dwyer, 2017).

One final note to consider in this context is that another, less than desirable implication might be that some individuals read this and take it as justification for reinforcing their own unevidenced worldviews. That is, 'if knowledge doesn't exist, then what I believe is just as valid as whatever anyone else proposes'. This is not the case at all. Again, *absolute* knowledge does not exist – and that's on a theoretical basis; I don't see anyone jumping off the Brooklyn Bridge (an analogy my father would often use to query my susceptibility to undesired conformity) to test the theory of gravity. What theories suggest are the best explanations for given phenomena – that's not equal in credibility to what you believe to be true. Beliefs, conspiracy 'theories' and magical thinking are not substitutes. Knowledge not 'existing' in the manner people commonly conceive of it does not give you licence to apply erroneous thinking processes and expect that others should entertain them. Your personal worldview does not trump our shared reality.

With that, the premise that nothing can be proved is not to say that reality is subjective or that facts are relative to each and every individual (i.e. it's also not a licence to propagate previously falsified or evidence-lacking information). Again, we cannot prove, but we can disprove; and, on top of that, the information we, as a larger population, typically hold as 'absolute' is generally so well corroborated through countless repeated observations that we must consider the related outcomes as 'extremely likely', at the very least.

Potential Criticisms

I wrote a piece not long ago in light of a comment a fellow academic made that 'the methodology a researcher uses to conduct their study should be dictated by their epistemological standpoint'. I assumed they misspoke because that's not right at all, at least not from a CT perspective. The research methodology you use should be dictated by your research question or purpose. Perhaps they meant the epistemological standpoint *of the research question*?

I'll admit that I took for granted the notion that the research question/purpose dictates the methodology used, because it was one of those 'day 1' kinds of foundational lesson I received early on in my research education. As a research methodologist, I have studied and utilised a wide variety of methodologies and approaches from various traditions; so, it's not like I'm naïve to other approaches and perspectives – I wouldn't have further

44   Knowledge Doesn't Exist

engaged what this said fellow academic had I been. That said, this one was new to me.

So, I did some further research on this specific issue and found that there is indeed a cohort of researchers who believe just as my colleague said. From an epistemological standpoint, this is troublesome because what it yields are groups of researchers who will only ever conduct one type of research (unless their epistemological standpoint significantly changes over time). Of course, I've seen this kind of thing a lot over the years – some researchers only conduct qualitative and some only conduct quantitative. I probably just assumed that they were expert in the methods they used and so gravitated towards that type of research (or, not a criticism, maybe they didn't have expertise in other skill sets, for whatever reason). Either way, though I'm aware other epistemological standpoints exist and that these have influenced how methodologies are developed, I never really considered that the issue regarding 'which methodology to use' would be anything other than one of the research question.

I say all of this because I conduct both quantitative and qualitative research, trying to infuse a mixed-methodology approach into my studies as much as appropriate. *Which do I prefer?* Whichever one helps me most appropriately answer my research question. I have problems with both approaches, but having such issues is a good thing. It means that you recognise their limitations, which allows you to make corrections or accommodations for them. With that, I typically conduct more quantitative research – but that's not down to preference; it's down to how my research goals and purposes are developed, thus influencing my research question, which subsequently influences the methodology I use. Of course, you might be reading this and thinking, *well, there's the answer – 'it's down to how my research goals and purposes are developed'*.

I received some interesting feedback on the piece I wrote. One comment came from a qualitative researcher who, like my colleague, believed that the methods used should be dictated by perspective and suggested that I may have a biased one when it comes to epistemology. This might be true – if it is, you will likely see it in light of this full chapter on the subject, alongside the point I make regarding 'it's down to how my research goals and purposes are developed'. For example, from this commenter's standpoint, a researcher might be a positivist, interpretivist, a hypothetico-deductivist, a post-positivist or some other '-ist' on the list of epistemological perspectives.

Now, I've come across all of these different perspectives in the past, but I've never really put much faith into them – don't get me wrong, I agree with each perspective in different ways, so it's hard to say I have *no* faith in them, but, likewise, it's hard to adhere to just one perspective. Like any good psychologist would question, *why does it have to be one or another? Can't it be some shade of grey?* That's just what I see my perspective as being – a collation of appropriate propositions from each. The use of the word *appropriate* here is important because what further impacts my reluctance to take on one of these stances is that each is fundamentally flawed in important ways. Perhaps this is the core reason for my lack of 'faith'. So, I reflected and, in doing so, I took a step back and looked at the field more broadly. I thought about the *other* way of considering epistemology – not about how we come to gain knowledge but, rather, *what is knowledge?* This questioning is what led to the writing of this chapter.

So, if you're the type of person who argues that you need to start with an epistemological perspective, I'd say that's flawed thinking; instead, let the research question guide you – but, I'll play along anyway. My perspective is that knowledge, with absolute certainty, does not exist. In my reading, I've seen perspectives similar to mine described as 'radical scepticism'. Please don't call it that – there's nothing radical about it. If anything, it's practical. The purpose of CT is practical – it is to question. That's what the epistemological understanding that I've been discussing throughout this chapter is doing. It acknowledges that there are advances in 'knowledge', that there's potential for change and that every day we make progress in learning more; but, at the same time, our tools and methodologies are imperfect, and we as researchers must constantly fight back against our own biases as well those from the environment. So, how can we ever know something for sure? We can't – and if you think we can, perhaps that's a symptom of the arrogance inherent within human cognition and the manner in which we personalise our thinking. With that, however, the inquisitiveness, curiosity and intellectual integrity and honesty associated with being a good thinker and researcher are what drive us forward to contribute to the world around us. So, regardless of your epistemological perspective, always consider the words you use, their connotation and both your and others' understanding of them, as well as your basis for knowing.

CHAPTER 4

Understanding the Flaws of Experience and Memory

A traditional behaviourist perspective of psychology would argue that human beings are born as a tabula rasa – a blank slate; and the more we experience and learn, the more we fill this previously blank slate. As behaviourism evolved into the field of 'learning psychology', we better saw the development of cognitive architecture from antecedent (i.e. stimulus) into a black box (information processing – as briefly addressed in Chapter 3) and the subsequent outcome (i.e. response). Simply, from the most traditional of behaviourist perspectives, everything we learn is a result of experience and, indeed, who we are is a result of this learning. It's no wonder that many developmental psychologists metaphorically speak of young children's minds as 'sponges' soaking up everything – they are filling up with knowledge. Likewise, from a philosophically phenomenologist perspective, everything we are is a result of experience. We are our memories and our memories are constructed in light of experience. So, how is it that experience is potentially detrimental to CT?

First and foremost, we are not blank slates. If we have learned anything from the nature–nurture debate, it's that *both* sides influence us on a variety of levels – not just the nurture aspect inherent with the blank slate analogy. Many traits are inherited; and biology plays major roles (i.e. nature) in the way we engage our existence, both in isolation and in interaction with the environment. Be that as it may, experience – another take on 'nurture' – plays a significant role in this context.

Second, with respect to how experience can be detrimental to CT, we must recognise that experience is a rather philosophical way of saying 'remembering how something happened'. Not only can the information we store as knowledge in memory be inaccurate (as discussed in the previous chapter), the manner in which we process it to get it to that 'knowledge' level can also be inaccurate, as can the manner in which we retrieve it – concepts that we will explore later in the current chapter. Specifically, this chapter will focus on ways in which our memory-based processes and the manner in which we think about such processes can deceive us. Such topics for consideration include experience, misremembering and cognitive bias. For example, consider our treatment of intuitive judgment in Chapter 1. We discussed it as automatic, gut-level decision-making that should be avoided in scenarios that require CT. When we make decisions based solely on experience, that's essentially the same thing – the application of intuitive judgment – going with your gut in light of what feels right on an experience-based level. Now, that's not to say that experience is likely to be wrong – much like it's not necessarily the case that intuitive judgment is going to be wrong. However, if we truly care about our CT, we'll avoid basing our decisions exclusively on experience-based thinking.

Experience versus Expertise

As might be the case for many families, an older member of mine likes to pride themself on how much they know in spite of their lack of both schooling and reading (perhaps resentfully perceiving both as pointless endeavours, given their lack of opportunities for it) – citing *life* as their primary educator. As this individual is in their seventies, I typically hold my tongue for the sake of harmony during family get-togethers. With that, this person holds a common perspective – albeit an extreme version – that life experience is the best teacher, and that, essentially, a more mature individual – with rich life experiences – is more knowledgable than someone in their twenties or thirties, maybe even forties, regardless of their level of education.

Now, there is a difference between older and younger cohorts in their approaches to intellectual endeavours – not necessarily because of experience per se; rather, because of other associated variables. For example, let's consider some research I conducted a few years back on CT in educational settings with a more 'mature' cohort. Though this mature cohort (mean age of forty-two) achieved significantly higher gains in CT following CT educational training in comparison to more 'traditional' college students (mean age eighteen–nineteen-year-olds), their CT scores were significantly lower than those of the younger, traditional students at baseline (Dwyer & Walsh, 2019), thus, to some extent, debunking the concept of 'life' experience being a driving force for CT. The findings suggested that whereas improvements from pre- to post-training may have been facilitated by an enhanced approach with respect to autonomy and responsibility (i.e. which is generally consistent with mature students), the lower CT scores

48   Understanding the Flaws of Experience and Memory

at baseline may have resulted from mature students being more 'set in their ways', for example, with respect to their experiences (and associated beliefs, biases, routines, heuristics, etc.) prior to engaging CT training.

Nevertheless, just because someone went to college and got a bunch of paperwork doesn't mean they got a quality education[1] or that they're a critical thinker – indeed, the lack of CT among individuals leaving third-level education has been a concern in the field for a number of years. On the other hand, experience can be a great teacher. You may not experience CT training, but you might develop some skills through trial and error or pick up some good advice through the years (of course, you might also pick up some bad advice).

Indeed, education itself is an experience. Everything we learn is through experience. However, *over-reliance* on experience – that which is learned from one's own perspectives or sources lacking either credibility or corroboration from established justification – is a mistake (e.g. having a few poor healthcare experiences leading one to distrust doctors in general). Unfortunately, such over-reliance often stems from people's confusion of experience for expertise.

Though experience is, arguably, the critical component of expertise, the latter is reserved for domain-specific tasks. People don't typically develop expertise in multiple domains. That's why it's so important to embrace uncertainty and caution in our thinking – because more often than not, we are not the expert source of information that we need for important decisions.

Sure, people may enjoy *proficiency* in various areas, but it's not likely that they will be expert in them all or even multiple ones. Likewise, it may be the case that you don't develop expertise in any area – and that's not a criticism. Your life experiences may not have afforded you opportunities to do so. It may also be the case that it wasn't necessary for you to do so. Moreover, expertise requires very specific dedication to a particular area, and some people's varying interests may not facilitate that.

What is problematic, though, is how we often misconstrue and/or misrepresent such perceived proficiency – be it in ourselves or others. For example, I know a family with two sons. One son was very good in school, but their weakest subject was maths. On the other hand, the

---

[1] By quality education, I do not mean from where their 'paperwork' (i.e. diploma(s)/degree(s)) came. I would argue that a quality education is not dictated by where you went but rather the work you put into it and what you got out of it, regardless of the institution's name. Sure, the institution's name may play an important role in the job you eventually get, upon going out into the working world. But, in terms of education, you could have gone to the 'best' school in the world, but if you didn't put in the work that you're capable of doing or simply just did 'enough' to get by, then you didn't get a quality education – rather, just very fancy paperwork.

second son's best subject was maths. At surface level, one would assume that if they couldn't solve a particular maths problem and had to go to someone in this family, they should go and ask the second son (given that this was 'their' area). However, the reality was that even though maths was the first boy's weakest subject, he was still much better at it than his brother, even though it was the latter's 'best subject'. Remember, the first son was very good at school. The family played on this misrepresentation – always going to the second for advice on maths-related problems. Whether or not this was actually misrepresented as a schema for who is better at maths or that they recognised that this was a means of boosting the second son's confidence I can't be sure. However, it does well to exemplify a form of misrepresentation people commonly make.

With that, just because an individual is proficient (or even an expert) in one domain does not guarantee expertise in another – no matter how *experienced* they feel themself to be in it. For example, I like to consider myself as having some level of expertise in psychology – particularly higher-order cognition (with specific focus on CT), hence my initiative to write at length about it. On the other hand, I have read at length about quantum physics and have been doing so for years. But, if you asked me to teach it, I couldn't; I mean, I could – I could fake it, but I shouldn't; and then this becomes an issue of intellectual honesty and integrity (which will be discussed further in Chapter 5). The point is that though one may have expertise in one field, it does not mean they will have it in another; but that little digression does introduce a relevant point to the overall chapter: *what if an individual 'fakes it' but doesn't realise that they are faking it?* That is, what if an 'expert' really isn't an expert, but they're none the wiser? Indeed, what if someone mistakes their personal experience as a sufficient basis for important decisions?

A useful example for elaborating on this concept is the *Dunning–Kruger effect*, which refers to the tendency for low-skilled individuals to overestimate their ability in tasks relevant to said skill and highly skilled individuals to underestimate their ability in tasks relevant to said skill[2] (e.g. see

---

[2] In the context of experts underestimating their skill set, this finding is consistent with the aforementioned concept of intellectual humility; but it's also associated with the concept of epistemological understanding, as discussed in Chapter 3. That is, when we truly understand the body of research and literature on a particular topic – as an expert would – we are also aware of the gaps of knowledge, the things we don't know. Such uncertainty plays into this 'underestimation'. Moreover, there is a psychological phenomenon known as 'impostor syndrome' that links in with this concept. Though further research on impostor syndrome is warranted, it was something I observed frequently during my PhD candidacy, and following its completion, colleagues and myself, most of us in our twenties and straight out of undergraduate and/or Master's degrees, would feel almost fraudulent in discussing our work or even being considered for a doctorate. Contextually

50   Understanding the Flaws of Experience and Memory

Kruger & Dunning, 1999; Mahmood, 2016). Furthermore, experience is often found to be unrelated to the accuracy of expert judgments and can be negatively correlated with accuracy (Goldberg, 1990; Hammond, 1996; Kahneman, 2011; Stewart et al., 1992). This may be a result of overconfidence (Kahneman, 2011) or, simply, large amounts of experience in doing something or things wrong (Hammond, 1996). The notion of 'having much experience in doing things wrong' is by no means new – and it's not to say that all such outcomes are 'completely' wrong (e.g. yielding outcomes that are, at worst, tolerable or, at best, adequate, akin to Nobel Prize winner Herbert Simon's (1957) perspective on *satisficing*, where people generally settle for a decision or solution that is satisfactory, or simply 'good enough'). For example, you may have conducted a task for thirty years the same way and never experienced a 'negative' outcome; however, there may have been a different way to carry out the task that was more efficient (faster, cheaper, more productive, etc.) or that yielded a 'more positive' outcome.

The Personalised Nature of Experience …

Another problem with relying on experience is its personalised nature, as alluded to earlier, with respect to the manner in which experience is inherently biased. Consider any high school class you enjoyed. Were there any students in that class who didn't enjoy it? Likewise, maybe that same student loved a class that you absolutely abhorred. They're the same classes, but two different experiences of them. Should I trust your experience or the other person's? *Neither* is the correct answer, because all either one amounts to is anecdotal evidence and that's not a very credible source (again, see Chapter 5 for a discussion on credibility). Simply, personal experience is based on a sample size of one, which does not yield reliable data – even if it's your own experience. Again, you must acknowledge that you could be subtly biased in a wide variety of ways that, cumulatively, create a very specific perspective on that experience. So, we cannot generalise one person's experience to the larger population. If I really want to know what that high school class was like, I'd want to assess the perspectives of everyone who was in it. From a class of thirty, numbers are now on

---

speaking, we're talking about, arguably, young, high-achieving people that – though they've worked hard and long to achieve a level of expertise – are self-aware enough to recognise that their relative youth, work ethic (i.e. there's always more to be done) and recognition of what they don't know makes it hard to accept that they may have already achieved the level of expertise to which they, for so long, have been aspiring. Simply, experts are more likely to know what they don't know.

The Personalised Nature of Experience . . . 51

my side in terms of getting a good perspective on what the class was like. That is, if I only have the experiences of a few people, the best I can do is make a *hasty generalisation* (i.e. prematurely drawing a conclusion without sufficient evidence). With thirty, though I'm aware I'll encounter very distinct experiences, I'm more likely to have sufficient data within which to identify common themes and similar recollections of events. Where there is a high degree of replicability in the data (i.e. a high level of overlap in recollections of events and how they happened), I can draw some 'more reliable' conclusions about the class. For example, if twenty-five of the thirty loved the class, I'd be more reasonably inclined to believe that it was a good class. On the other hand, though, if it was a fifteen/fifteen split, I might be inclined to try and collect more data (e.g. see what the classes from the year before and after thought as well) or conclude that maybe the class 'wasn't for everyone'.

The issue of bias plays an important role in the recollection of experience, as well as how we might approach topics, problems or other CT-relevant scenarios. Remember, an experience is the perspective of one person – with their own beliefs, attitudes, values, passions and desires at play under the surface. Indeed, the reliance on experience in decision-making is its own typology of bias – *experience bias*, which is essentially a cognitive error in which we take what we perceive, believe or have encountered as fact or as how such events play out a significant amount of the time[3] (for a list of some more commonly engaged cognitive biases, see Table 4.1). Though this is a rather simple description, it is a very complex psychological phenomenon in terms of all the social-cognitive mechanisms at play, including, for example, false consensus, egocentrism, theory of mind and open-/closed-mindedness.

Despite this, people have a tendency to put great value into the notion of experience. Again, it may be that they are not aware of research suggesting otherwise (or in some contexts, they may distrust research), in which case their lack of more credibly sourced knowledge influences their faith in and/or over-reliance on experience. We can see aspects of this each time someone talks about 'studying at the university of life', starts a sentence with 'well, when *I* . . .' or engages declinism (i.e. talks about the good ol' days, when things were better).

---

[3] On a macro level, it can be argued that every bias *is* an experience bias in the sense that biases are developed *through* experience; however, the distinction here, in this particular bias, is that the nature of experience, in general, is the erroneous source of belief as fact.

Understanding the Flaws of Experience and Memory

Table 4.1 *Common cognitive biases*

Bias	Description
Self-serving bias	We attribute successes and positive outcomes to our own doing; but, when we face failure and negative outcomes, we tend to attribute these events to other people or contextual factors outside ourselves. For example, have you ever done poorly on an exam because your teacher hates you? Maybe you aced the next test because you studied really hard despite that teacher? Both scenarios reflect a self-serving bias and work to maintain a positive self-image.
Curse of knowledge and hindsight bias	When you develop understanding of a new piece of information, it becomes seemingly obvious to you. You might easily forget that there was a time you didn't know this information, and so you assume that others, like yourself, also know this information. However, it's often an unfair overestimation of others to assume they share the same knowledge. Similarly, with respect to *hindsight bias*, once we have knowledge of the details of some event, it then seems obvious that it was going to occur all along. *I should have seen it coming!* Notably, these biases are also similar to the aforementioned *false consensus effect* and the *availability heuristic* (i.e. a mental rule of thumb whereby people base a judgment on the ease with which they can bring relevant information to mind, e.g. some recently encountered information, like an example).
Optimism/pessimism bias	We have tendencies to overestimate the likelihood of positive outcomes, particularly if you are in good humour, and negative outcomes, particularly if you are feeling down or have a pessimistic attitude. Consider the expression 'hope for the best, prepare for the worst'. Depending on your mood or emotional state, this expression can be interpreted as either conscientious, organised advice (positive effect) or perhaps as a defence mechanism (negative effect) against a setback. Notably, this bias again highlights the impact that emotion can have on one's thinking – remember, 'leave emotion at the door' as best you can.
Sunk cost fallacy	Though labelled a fallacy, 'sunk cost' is just as much in line with bias as faulty thinking, given the manner in which we think about winning, losing and 'breaking even' (e.g. we typically believe that when we put something in, we should get something out, for example, time, effort or money). When we lose, obviously, we get nothing in return for our efforts – a sunk cost, similarly, refers to something lost that cannot be recovered. Given our aversion to losing, we irrationally cling to the idea of

The Personalised Nature of Experience . . .

Table 4.1 (cont.)

Bias	Description
	'regaining', even though what has been lost cannot be recovered. For example, in gambling, this is similar to making a bet and 'chasing' after it, perhaps making another bet to recoup the original (and more) even though, rationally, we should consider the initial ante as lost.
Negativity bias	Negativity bias refers to our irrational weighing of the potential for a negative outcome as more important than that of the positive outcome. The bias is not dissimilar to the aforementioned *pessimism bias*, but it's subtly distinct. It also works according to similar mechanics as the *sunk cost fallacy* in that it reflects our aversion to losing. We like to win, but we hate to lose even more. Consider also our previous discussion on why 'bad news' sells.
Decline bias (aka declinism)	You might have heard a member of an older generation who prefaces a grievance with 'well, back in my day' before following up with 'how things are getting worse'. Declinism refers to bias in favour of the past over and above 'how things are going'. Again, people typically don't like change – even when the majority might view the change as positive. People take comfort in the familiar because it makes sense to them. The world is easier to engage when things make sense to us.
Fundamental attribution error	The fundamental attribution error is a bias where we attribute outcomes to observable characteristics of the event (e.g. attributes of a person) and fail to acknowledge the situational variables. Consider one of the best textbook examples: you are driving behind a car that is swerving a bit and unpredictably starts speeding up and slowing down. You decide to overtake them (so as to no longer be stuck behind such a dangerous driver) and as you look over, you see a female behind the wheel. You might conclude that their driving is poor because they're a woman (i.e. applying a stereotype). What you fail to see is that the driver has three children yelling and goofing around on the back seat, while she's trying to drive one to football, one to dance and the other to a piano lesson; plus, she's had a particularly tough day and now she's running late with all of the kids because she couldn't leave work at her normal time – all situational variables. If you or I were that driver, we'd judge ourselves as driving poorly because of these reasons, not because of who we are (e.g. a single observable characteristic).
In-group bias	Consistent with the *self-serving bias*, we tend to be kind to ourselves in our judgment-making, and this also applies to those we hold near and dear, those who we perceive as

54 Understanding the Flaws of Experience and Memory

Table 4.1 (*cont.*)

Bias	Description
	similar and those who we consider as part of our 'group'. In-group bias refers to the favouring of someone from one's own group. Sure, you might think that you're impartial and fair, but we all succumb to this bias in light of its evolutionary advantages (e.g. consider kin selection) and humanity's penchant for grouping and categorising things (and people).
The Forer effect (aka the Barnum effect)	The Forer effect refers to the tendency for people to accept vague, ambiguous and general descriptions as uniquely applicable to themselves without realising that the same could be used for just about everyone else (arguably akin in some ways to the false uniqueness effect). Horoscopes are a prime example.

To reiterate, much like our previous discussion on intuitive judgment, this is not to say that what experience tells us is always wrong – much like such gut-level decision-making, it's often right. Experience and gut-level intuition will tell you not to put your hand over an open flame; it will tell you to look both ways before you cross the road; it will tell you many important things to which you should listen. However, in situations where CT is required, when you need to take a step back and reflect on the issue, it is important to recognise that your experience is biased, is largely anecdotal and is based on a sample size of one. If you care about your decision, do not rely on experience.

However, context is again key here. What *kind* of experience are we talking about? Are we talking about the lessons you learned during that summer backpacking in Cambodia? Are we talking about the time you got a black eye for being too mouthy in the wrong company? Or are we talking about that twelve-week course you took in health literacy? The nature of the experience plays a role in its credibility. What you learned backpacking in Cambodia may be largely useless – highly philosophical and only personally relevant to you. On the other hand, you might have learned a very important lesson in social dynamics from that shiner you got. Likewise, that module on health literacy may have been the first step you took into a new career that eventually led you to expertise in a health-service field. The point is, experience is most definitely useful and important because it is what allows us to learn, given that learning *is* an experience. When we are able to parse the emotion and the bias, as best we can, from our recollection of experiences, we can retrieve very useful information that can be applied in our CT. This may come across as obvious, but it is important to be able to distinguish experiences in terms of what we've explicitly learned (as in the hypothetical health literacy module), what we've implicitly learned (as in the physical altercation in the car park) and what we're interpreting as usefully applicable (as in our Cambodian holiday).

So, yes, experience can be useful. It's not always right, so we best not use it in isolation, in contexts that require CT. I know I have reiterated this multiple times, but that's because I genuinely cannot stress it enough. Why? As addressed earlier, be it for the reason of false consensus, egocentrism or any combination of the slew of social/cognitive reasons, *do not* confuse it for expertise. We cannot generalise our personal experiences to the larger population. Our own personal experience is not good enough – be it with respect to sufficient knowledge or objectivity. If we want to develop our experience in a manner that facilitates some level of proficiency (or maybe even expertise), we must do so in light of evidence, humility and openness to differing perspectives.

... And How It Affects Memory

One of my favourite films, *Lost Highway* (written and directed by David Lynch), focuses on a husband and wife whose house is broken into, and the two are filmed while they sleep. Upon watching a video of this with the police – left to them by the perpetrator – they are asked if they own a video camera (very much dating this film). They respond 'no', because the husband likes to 'remember things his own way'.

The truth is, we all like to remember things our own way, and our brains do this for us. As discussed earlier, we are biased in terms of how we experience events; but, we are also biased in terms of how we remember things. We don't consciously do this; it's simply a function of our cognitive processing. When we remember an event, it's not just what happened but everything that goes with it – for example, what we thought was the key focus at that moment, what we felt at that moment, the smells, the sounds and the context (e.g. what else was going on in our lives at that time).

For example, and similar in a way to the aforementioned movie, I knew a guy whose girlfriend's place was broken into and one of the things stolen was a special necklace that was gifted to her by a family member. He managed to track down a shop that sold the same necklace and jumped

56 Understanding the Flaws of Experience and Memory

at the opportunity to replace it for her. Of course, she was very appreciative of the gift. However, he noticed, months later, that she never wore it. When he questioned her about it, she told him that every time she saw it, it wasn't a gift she saw – be it from him or her relative; rather, it was a reminder that someone broke into her home and took something from her. She didn't see a necklace, a gift or the love that it represented – she saw loss, intrusion and violation. Her feelings associated with the experience (i.e. the break-in) were able to change the way in which she remembered something else (i.e. the necklace).

A similar, albeit distinct, example is as follows: I recall the 'where were you when JFK was shot?' question getting thrown around to adults when I was young. I can't recall why I would be aware of this, as a kid; but perhaps that's telling about my great interest in the subject area we're considering. As I got older, 'where were you on 9/11?' became my generation's version. I actually asked a final-year class of mine this, only a couple of years ago, and one hand went up. The student answered, with a confused look on her face, 'I was one'. Perhaps, that's *also* telling about the subject area we're considering.

In any case, I used this moment in class to make a point about memory. I grew up in New York and was living on Long Island when 9/11 happened. I remember everything about that day. I was in high school; and at 10 am we went to homeroom. The guy sitting in front of me turned around, asking if I had heard that some guy flew a plane into the World Trade Center. I remember thinking that it was probably a small, single-engine plane, perhaps a flying lesson gone wrong. Shortly after, an announcement on our PA confirmed that not only had a plane flown into the World Trade Center, a second one had just done likewise – and that it appeared to be an attack of some sort. I recall students crying, leaving for the office to make some phone calls (having family members working in the city). I recall that all classes had been cancelled and though we could leave, those waiting for buses – as I was – had to wait until the buses had been checked for explosives. We actually waited for most of the day and ended up going home only about an hour earlier than normal. We had not been allowed to watch the news on TV at school and, as this was in an era pre-camera phones (let alone smartphones), no one saw any of it until they got home. My parents were in our den watching the news. Different angles of what had happened kept cutting into the live feed. I watched for about an hour before Mum and Dad decided we should get out of the house and go to get some food. We went to our usual spot – an Italian restaurant less than ten minutes away from the house. It was empty apart from staff.

. . . And How It Affects Memory   57

I suspect they were surprised to see anyone come in. It was a quiet meal, apart from speculation regarding what was actually going on. We finished up, went home and went about our typical pastimes. I went to my room and threw on the Mets game. They had a jet fly-by in honour of both the victims and the efforts of New York's finest and bravest. Then I went to bed.

Arguably, that's a pretty thorough relay of events for a random Tuesday in September. Of course, it wasn't just any Tuesday – it was 9/11. As a New Yorker, how could I not remember that? Sure, I remembered it. The problem is, I didn't remember it correctly.

On the twentieth anniversary of 9/11, I read an article that commemorated that very baseball game – the ceremony, the score and the highlights. However, that game took place over a week later than I remembered – when Major League Baseball reconvened after cancelling all games in light of 9/11. No such game took place the night of 9/11. So, what did I do that night? I can't remember.

That was an emotional day, even for people who didn't lose anyone. I could only imagine how they felt. There was fear, anger, confusion – and uncertainty in general.

Consistent with our previous discussion on uncertainty, people generally don't like to feel that way – they don't like to be confused; so, to combat that uncertainty, we provide ourselves simplified explanations. Think about ancient times and how people weren't yet able to explain the sun's movement (or, more accurately, our movement around the sun); so, without understanding things such as orbit and gravity, civilisations simply attributed such action to some form of intelligent design – a deity if you will. Such explanation made life easier for many – filling in the gap of uncertainty with an explanation. Of course, it made life much worse for those who were sacrificed on top of a temple built in honour of said heliocentric deity, who might not allow the sun to rise again without the spilling of virgin blood – but, that's a different story! Nevertheless, we fill in the gaps.

Despite having made great advances in science and understanding, it remains that we intuitively fill in our 'knowledge' gaps when they arise. I couldn't remember what I did the night of 9/11; but, I know I typically watched sports and I know that the game in question made me feel better about things. So, let's just fill that knowledge gap in with a relevant, though comforting, memory.

What I just described is an example of the *misinformation effect*. Since the 1970s, Elizabeth Loftus and colleagues (e.g. see Loftus, 1974, 2005;

58   Understanding the Flaws of Experience and Memory

Loftus & Palmer, 1974) have conducted a large body of research on false memories (i.e. a memory of something that didn't happen or happened differently to how it was recalled) and the misinformation effect (i.e. diminished recall accuracy due to subsequent competing information). One of the more famous studies in this field involved showing participants footage of a crime and subsequently asking them questions about what they watched on tape. Findings revealed that not everyone remembered the same things as they happened and that people were rather easily manipulated into reporting false memories based on the manner in which they were interrogated about the footage. Indeed, findings from this body of research are a main reason for why eyewitness testimony no longer holds up in court as well as it once did. With that, the examination of such phenomena began well before the seventies, back during the development of very important theories on memory and knowledge construction.

For example, Bartlett (1932), who is often cited as being one of the first people to describe the concept of cognitive *schemas* (i.e. mental frameworks for how we interpret the world around us), found that individuals misremembered information from a story they read years beforehand, but did so in a manner that drew links – almost like educated guesses – between the correct and incorrect information. The story in question concerned Native American folklore regarding ghosts. Some individuals reported that the story from Bartlett's study was about people fishing – it wasn't; but, because people in the actual story were in a canoe, it's not an entirely ludicrous guess for a person to make, or, perhaps, even a group of people. For those individuals, they could remember that the setting was a boat, but beyond that, they couldn't exactly remember – too much time had passed. So, their schemas (regarding boats) helped them fill in their gaps of knowledge.

Not dissimilarly, think about famous children's books. Was the *Berenstein Bears* a popular series of children's books when you were young? No, of course not. It was the *Berenstain Bears*. Did you know this, or were you one of the many who misremembered it? Perhaps you have seen this presented before as one of the many examples of the *Mandela effect*.

Misremembering Mandela

The *Mandela effect* refers to an internet phenomenon that has done the rounds for the past few years or so, regarding the misremembering of an event or artefact (typically pop culture-oriented), by a large group of people, in the same way; wherein, groups of people very clearly remember something one way or another (e.g. *Berenstein Bears* versus *Berenstain*

Bears). A more thorough, clearer definition is not provided because the Mandela effect isn't really a *thing*. I'm being gracious even referring to it as a phenomenon.

The 'effect' was named as such based on the discovery that many individuals online reported recalling Nelson Mandela having passed away in prison during the 1980s, when he, in fact, served as President of South Africa from 1994 to 1999. Other common examples include misremembering famous quotes from films (e.g. it's 'Magic Mirror on the wall . . .', NOT 'Mirror, Mirror on the wall . . .'; it's 'No, I am your father', NOT 'Luke, I am your father') as well as names/spellings of various pop culture characters and brands. According to numerous 'postulations' online, the various occurrences of the Mandela effect result from the creation of parallel universes (that, in some speculations, have been generated by CERN (European Organisation for Nuclear Research)), similar to the film *Sliding Doors* (e.g. imagine what would happen if you *didn't* get on to that train as opposed to what happened given that you did, i.e. where both realities co-exist). Specifically, the Mandela effect is often explained via pseudoscience as a distinct effect in which such occurrences result from movement(s) between parallel universes.

In light of a piece I wrote on the Mandela effect, I have been contacted by numerous people over the years to discuss the effect, be it for a quote or to take part in podcasts, given my 'expertise' in the area. I generally take part because I look at such opportunities as ones in which I can discuss CT. However, I always make it clear that I am not an expert on it because the 'Mandela effect' isn't really a thing, and that people have simply misconstrued misinformation effects as more sensational phenomena, relatively speaking, than they actually are (i.e. in reference to their explanation being more sensational than a misinformation effect, which in its own right is fascinating). But, I am happy to be interviewed about it given my background in cognitive psychology and higher-order thinking. Plus, explaining this is actually pretty fun – I typically discuss various examples of the 'effect' and elaborate on why people might misremember them.

For example, with respect to the fictional bear family addressed earlier, 'stein' is a common feature of many surnames and 'stain' is not. Thus, it's not surprising that, in many cases, when we speak about this family of bears, Beren*stain* is what gets misread or misheard, and Beren*stein* is what gets assimilated, pronounced, repeated and remembered. Moreover, Mandela didn't die in prison as an anti-apartheid activist – he lived until 2013 and, as addressed earlier, was the President of South Africa before that. However, Steve Biko was also a South African anti-apartheid activist

60   Understanding the Flaws of Experience and Memory

imprisoned during the same time as Mandela (and, arguably, was as famous as Mandela at the time, if not more). In this context, the only difference was that Biko died in prison and didn't go on to become South Africa's president. I reasonably speculate that his was the death many people recall.

Of course, some people – like me – find the explanations to be the most interesting aspect of this. Sure, they're not always 100 per cent complete explanations, but they do tend to lead thinkers down the right path. On the other hand, some people don't find these explanations as interesting as the alternative – the potential for parallel universes, in fairness, render phenomena like the misinformation effect mundane in comparison. Thus, some people will gravitate more towards what seems more interesting and more complex – like they want it to be true (e.g. wishful thinking and, in some cases, 'magical' thinking). Unfortunately, this is not a particularly good strategy if good decision-making is your aim.

Consider Occam's razor, which is a problem-solving principle that states: *among competing hypotheses, the one with the fewest assumptions should be selected.* The principle is commonly interpreted as meaning the 'simplest solution is typically the best', though that's incomplete. Perhaps a more accurate description is that, all things considered, solutions that require less complexity often work best (e.g. there's less room for things to go wrong). If we're considering 'popular' accounts of the Mandela effect in this context, not only do we have to evidence the existence of parallel universes (though this is not completely impossible), but we also have to evidence that such universes can interact and that there is a mechanism that allows for them to do so within a temporally equivalent fashion. Again, I'm not a quantum physicist, but that sounds pretty complex to me. However, the fact that people can be mistaken (as per the nature of memories) – and for reasons that can be identified with relative ease by people expert in relevant fields – misremembering (even on a large-scale basis) just seems like a much more palatable explanation for the 'phenomenon' than the Mandela effect. With that, it may be that some people find it easier to 'buy into' a parallel universes perspective because they are more familiar with it from pop culture (e.g. comic books and films) than the cognitive psychology explaining misinformation effects. Moreover, the possibility of misremembering may not sit well with some individuals, so they might eliminate that as a possible explanation (i.e. biases associated with 'I don't like it' or 'such a prospect frightens me'; thus, 'let's ignore it').

To conclude this section on the Mandela effect, I just want to clarify that I don't think that this particular pseudoscientific bastardisation of

Concluding Thoughts 61

how some people interpret the world is a genuine concern of ours – it can be fun and interesting to look up various instances in which people misremember information from, for example, famous events, products and films. However, I put it under the spotlight here because it exemplifies a variety of cognitive mechanisms that warrant discussion, such as dismissing the notion of a reasonable, science-based explanation and, instead, putting faith in pseudoscientific rubbish because it provides a sensational, perhaps 'more interesting', explanation. Additional dangers associated with nonsense like the Mandela effect is that people will bestow credibility upon such assertions because (1) they are sometimes, in some ways, based on actual science, and because, consistent with the prior discussion, (2) their *life experience* doesn't necessarily equip them with the capacity to differentiate between evidence-based and spurious information.

With respect to the first additional issue, for example, quantum physicists have indeed theorised the potential existence of multiple universes based on mathematical models. However, there is not yet concrete evidence for this that, likewise, disproves other leading models regarding the structure/nature of the universe. Nevertheless, such concepts have been postulated, in an earnest manner, by genuinely credible sources. An unfortunate outcome of this is that people who believe in things like the Mandela effect will latch on to developing ideas and manipulate that knowledge base to represent/explain whatever they want it to. Of course, such practice can be dangerous when the stakes are higher than those associated with the 'Mandela effect'.

With regard to the second issue, I refer back to earlier portions of this chapter – biased experience is not a credible source of information from which to work. You are likely not an expert in quantum mechanics (if you are, send me an email – I'd love to chat!); so, you don't have the expertise to truly evaluate the veracity of such claims. Thus, my recommendation is that you either take a course on quantum physics (i.e. assuming you have the care in which to apply to this topic) or you apply CT and come to recognise the flaws in thinking associated with concepts like the Mandela effect.

Concluding Thoughts

A critical thinker reads between the lines in the case of the *Mandela effect* and looks for a more logical explanation; and one is easily found (a great example of *Occam's razor*) – the Mandela effect is likely nothing more than a product of false memories, a product of the misinformation effect.

62   Understanding the Flaws of Experience and Memory

In turn, this exemplifies how fragile our memory systems are – the way we remember things is covered in a film of emotion and bias. Thus, when we recall our experiences and apply them to our decision-making, we must acknowledge that they are at best imperfect, incomplete and not as requisitely thorough for important decision-making, let alone credible, as for application in CT. Yes, we can learn many useful things through experience that can aid our CT. Hopefully, your reading of this book is one of those experiences! However, we must also acknowledge that such reading is a very personalised experience – how you interpret what is stated, what you remember and how that makes you feel will dictate how you use the information presented here.

CHAPTER 5

Evaluating Information Sources and Credibility

When I first started lecturing, I had two major fears. First, I was afraid that I would run out of material to discuss way before the scheduled finish. Back then, my lecture slots were scheduled for approximately fifty minutes. *What if I only had enough for thirty minutes? My students will think I don't know enough to talk about the topic!* The truth is, if I went short, students would only be delighted to leave early. In addition, if I was able to convey all I wanted to in less time than I initially thought it would take, that just might be a strength (e.g. by being succinct and concise). Moreover, if I did finish early, having that additional time would facilitate me in presenting more examples of the concepts I was discussing – and examples are vital for facilitating student understanding. As it turned out, I never really had a problem with talking, so this fear was a bit on the unsubstantiated side of things. If anything, I would have struggled staying within the scheduled time! The second fear, however, was a more realistic one – and anyone who has ever taught a class, I believe, is likely to have had this particular fear as well, at some stage of their career: *what if someone asks me a question to which I don't know the answer?*

With that, my belief here is just that – a belief. I have no evidence for it. I haven't surveyed teachers about their fears; I've read no papers on this phenomenon. It's just a belief I have in light of over fifteen years' experience in teaching (consider the discussion from Chapter 4 in light of this statement). Regardless, it's just a belief. Sure, it might be true; but, such a possibility does not suffice in terms of substantiating it. The source of my statement requires evaluation in terms of its credibility. That's what this chapter is all about.

Now, back to the question. In my early years of teaching, I spent great amounts of time not only on the slides I presented (which I still do) but also on developing scripts for what I would say, so as to ensure I never left anything so vague that a student would quiz me on it (again, this was probably less to do with a lack of knowledge regarding the topic and more

64 Evaluating Information Sources and Credibility

about 'impostor syndrome', as discussed in footnote 2 in Chapter 4). I was as thorough as possible. Of course, these were useful exercises and reinforced in me the importance of being thorough, a trait I still value quite a bit. However, the value I put into being thorough is no longer a result of fear. I recall a conversation I had in my early teaching years with two colleagues at similar stages in their careers, wherein we discussed what to do when asked a question to which we didn't know the answer. I laugh to myself now as I relay to you the most interesting solution posed during that conversation: *smile and nod before responding that the question is very good and very interesting – so much so that the class' homework will be to write a half-page answer. It might be the case that students will no longer ask 'tough' questions after that.*

But, doesn't dodging questions like that defeat the purpose of education – deterring students from asking the 'tough' questions? Of course! Sure, efforts should be made to be as thorough and clear as possible, so that students won't have too many questions; but as someone who values CT, I want students to ask the tough questions when they have them.

Despite its somewhat humorous nature, this was not an acceptable solution. Over time, as I became more comfortable and confident in my teaching, as well as diving deeper into my research on CT, I learned that it's okay to say 'I don't know'. Set an example for others by showing them that it's okay to be uncertain – this is the nature of RJ.

In retrospect, I recall some of my undergraduate lecturers – across disciplines – being posed with questions and then rambling on and on with some waffle that was barely relevant to the question. That did not reinforce my confidence in them. If anything, I probably thought less of them in terms of their verbal acrobatics. If you don't know the answer, say so. If it's an interesting question, be a role model and say that you will find out for them and discuss it with them in the next class. Additionally, open the question up to the class for discourse. Encourage collaborative CT! Try to avoid speculating; and when you do, preface the assertion by advising students that you *are* speculating.

Show them that we don't know everything and that, if it's important, it's worth putting the work into finding out the right answer. Saying 'I don't know' isn't a sign of ignorance, it's a sign of intellectual integrity, honesty and humility – core features of CT. Moreover, it shows that you are an information source that is credible.

Of course, it's no longer the case that people get their information primarily from teachers, books or even the news (well, 'traditional news' anyway). Vast changes have occurred in the past quarter of a century or so

Evaluating Information Sources and Credibility 65

with respect to how we access information. Our modern world and developing technologies have made it much easier to transfer information. Unfortunately, it has also become much easier to propagate misinformation and *disinformation* (i.e. intentionally inaccurate information). On the surface, disinformation might seem more sinister, given that it represents efforts to purposefully misinform; however, *misinformation* is, arguably, just as bad given that people very often don't know that the information they're spreading is wrong. Consider, for example, the Momo hoax in 2019.

For background, the 'Momo challenge' was a game involving the texting of social media[1] profiles, which would send back disturbing picture messages aimed at persuading recipients to self-harm or, perhaps, worse. In some instances, it involved unsolicited messaging of children through hijacking child-appropriate videos on YouTube, via the Momo picture messages. The 'game' had, apparently, already been linked with approximately 130 suicides in Russia. This, of course, led to uproar among parents who came across such news, and they posted warnings online and notified their friends and their children's schools. This is how I ended up finding out about the Momo challenge.

The good news was that none of this was true – it was all a hoax; but, that also represents the big problem here. Someone created the story of the game – not the game itself – as a sort of urban legend. The individual(s) who first reported the game – those behind the hoax – were propagating disinformation. On the other hand, scared parents and teachers were propagating misinformation. Though I recall being slightly amused at the time that so many people were duped (as a result of not applying CT), it's really not funny at all. Though everything turned out alright, the implications of not applying CT – in a mass population scenario – can yield disastrous outcomes. For example, only months later were we globally faced with COVID-19 – representing a scary time, not just in terms of

---

[1] Throughout the remainder of this book, reference to and examples from social media will make quite a few appearances. As this is the first meaningful mention of it in this book, I think it's important to be clear from the get-go: I am not 'anti-social media', despite the many examples I use that may portray it in a negative light. Sure, social media has a variety of associated, negative effects on thinking (which will be discussed); but, it also has a number of positive outcomes – and not just in terms of 'thinking' as we discuss it here. Those positive outcomes are why I'm on social media (and probably why you likely are too). The point is, we can't be looking at social media as 'good' or 'bad'; rather, it exists and we need to accept that. More importantly, it exists as an environment in which many people engage. As social media facilitates an interpersonal 'connectedness' among people from all over the world (beyond which we've ever before seen), it should come as no surprise that many of the examples we engage in this book come from a social media context.

fear of a spreading disease but also in terms of spreading misinformation and disinformation.

At the end of the day, the distinction between misinformation and disinformation may not matter much (depending on the context), given that both information types are, simply, inaccurate. Critical thinkers must be aware of such inaccurate information and the manner in which one can identify such inaccuracy. Understanding the sources of information and the credibility each type of source holds is of utmost importance for evaluating an argument's strength and plausibility of the information conveyed.

In Chapter 1, we discussed the CT skill of evaluation, which refers to the assessment of a proposition's, a group of propositions' or a full argument's strengths and weaknesses. Through evaluation, we can assess a variety of issues – credibility being one of them. It can be argued that the issue of credibility might be the most important aspect of evaluation, given that the information we rely on to make our point represents the foundation of our arguments and rationales; so in order to construct a critically thought out argument, we need to trust in the information we use. Assessment of the information's sources – their credibility – is vital. Thus, the aim of this chapter is to present a broad scope of the sources we can use to gain information (i.e. personal experience/anecdotal evidence, common sense/belief statements, research findings, expert opinion and statistics) and discuss each source's strengths and weaknesses.

When I teach credibility in my CT classes, I start by presenting these five broad sources and ask students to rank them in terms of which they think are most credible. I always find the answers and their rationales quite interesting. When the students are right about which are most credible, their rationales are typically correct as well. But, when they get the ranking wrong, the rationales make clear the types of issues we need to be concerned about when thinking about what CT is and how we do it. Some of these issues will be addressed later on, but for now, it is worth noting that I advise students, after this exercise, that it can be argued that three of these sources are *roughly* equal in terms of credibility (depending on context): research findings, expert opinion and statistics – these being the most credible of sources. The remaining two, personal experience/ anecdotal evidence and common sense/belief statements, are the least credible and should be avoided in situations that require CT – for reasons soon discussed. With that, regardless of strength, all five have their limitations; and these limitations require consideration in order to optimise our justification in context.

Personal Experience/Anecdotal Evidence

As we discussed in Chapter 4, experience can be a great educator. When you boil it all down, learning – be it in the classroom, through reading or otherwise – *is* experience. It is the experience of engaging with information and storing it for later recall and application. However, relying on experience in contexts wherein CT is necessary would be a bad move. To reiterate, one might have learned inaccurate information as true, recalled an experience from an emotional perspective or, simply, just have had a lot of experience doing the wrong thing (Hammond, 1996; Kahneman, 2011).

As a large portion of Chapter 4 dealt with issues regarding the limitations of experience, we'll keep this section brief. Simply, the major issue with personal experience, in the context of credibility, is that all it really amounts to is anecdotal evidence (and that experience might not apply to others) – essentially, the same as telling a story. Stories and narratives can be woven in a myriad of ways, depending on their purpose, and can be very powerful in persuading people of our points of view. I've used countless anecdotes throughout this book thus far (and will continue to do so for the remainder of the book) because they are so useful. Anecdotes breathe life into explanations, giving them a 'concreteness' that allows people to better understand how things might unfold in real-world scenarios. However, when I present such anecdotes, just as with other researchers who use them, I do so to either set the scene (i.e. and not to convince you of some particular premise) or to clarify what I mean by some kind of abstract notion, through an example that is corroborated by research (i.e. presenting a finding, describing it and then exemplifying it). I don't make them the basis of my argument.

So, in your CT, anecdotal evidence *can* be used to exemplify an abstract concept, but only if it is coupled with corroborating information from a credible source. Simply, one should not use anecdotal evidence, *exclusively*, as the justification of a claim. Anecdotes and personal experience represent a weak source from which to base an argument since they are not necessarily reliable or generalisable to larger populations.

Think about a poor experience you had at a restaurant, where you might have had terrible service alongside bland or cold food. You might feel so strongly about your poor experience that you feel compelled to leave a review online; but, then, you're surprised by how many people have left great reviews (legitimately). How could this be? There are many reasons why: the day of the week, the time of day, the waiter/waitress serving you,

68 Evaluating Information Sources and Credibility

or the main chef might have been on holiday or not feeling his best that day. The possibilities are endless.

To really know if the restaurant is a 'one-star dining experience', as you may have felt like you wanted to rate it, you'd need to go many times, at different times, on different days. I'd be more inclined to listen to the person who has been there twenty times than someone who has only gone once. But, of course, if your first experience at the restaurant is poor, you're not likely to go back – I don't blame you. However, your perspective might be very different if your first experience was good – as were your next ten. Maybe your twelfth experience is a poor one. You probably wouldn't just quit going after that one bad meal, having had eleven nice ones there before. You're more likely to give the restaurant the benefit of the doubt and try it again. Again, context is key. The point here is that a sample size of one (in this case one person or one visit) cannot be generalised to the population at large because everyone has different experiences.

I've had some backlash from students on this in the past. As in the previous chapter, some people often over-engage in experiential perspectives, in that because they feel they are unique individuals, that somehow gives them the freedom to create their own reality and build their own, as Oprah might say, 'truths'. That's not how it works. Sure, you have the right to believe whatever you like; but when you then try to convince other people of your truths, the people you're trying to convince, likewise, have every right to dismiss it because we, collectively, have a *shared* reality – not just your 'truth'. If 98 per cent of people like a restaurant and disagree with you, they're not trying to 'invalidate' your experiences or your feelings, they just have a different perspective. If it's the case that you are 'a unique individual, with different experiences', that's fine – but acknowledge the fact that this is the same for everyone else who speaks from experience, even if it is counter to yours; hence the irrelevance of one's personal experience – it can't be generalised to larger samples. Thus, if CT is your aim, be objective and avoid using these experiences and anecdotes as foundations for your argument.

Common Sense/Common Belief

In a way, it can be argued that common sense/belief statements are slightly better than personal experience statements or anecdotal evidence, simply because you're increasing the sample size. Then again, just because a majority believes something doesn't mean it's true. That 'majority' might be a particular cohort ill-equipped to be offering advice on a specific topic. For example, the majority of the population are not medical doctors; so, it's not really a smart move taking medical advice based on common belief – especially if it's contrary to medical advice.

On the other hand, it can be argued personal experience is a better source of credibility than common sense/belief statements when making personal decisions, because it's specific to the individual, who has a better understanding of one key facet – context. Nevertheless, I don't recommend either source for use in CT; but, for those interested in which of these weakest sources is if any way 'better', my answer – consistent with the previous rationale – is, *it depends*.

Moving on, common sense/belief statements might also be a little dangerous because there's the added element of social pressure. It kind of reminds me of the saying 'just because everyone is running towards the cliff, you look like the crazy one for going the other way'. With that, I'm also cognisant that people with conspiracy beliefs also use the same saying as a kind of mantra for 'engaging their interests' (we'll discuss conspiracy beliefs in greater detail in Chapter 9). Nevertheless, I purposefully present this relevant saying here because that's what common beliefs are – ideas and concepts that we encounter on a regular basis; and we often hear them reflected in such common sayings/adages. They might refer to concepts the wider population holds true (without much consideration) or perhaps an old adage your mother used to repeat to you during childhood, maybe as a kind of teaching tool.

Of course, the problem with common beliefs is that they're not always correct. For example, you've probably heard the old adage that 'opposites attract'; but research disputes this *complementarity hypothesis*, indicating instead that, most often, we like people who are similar to us and dislike people who are different. So, we can see here that scientific research findings are sometimes at odds with common belief. Likewise, common beliefs can be at odds with one another. For example, in this case, 'birds of a feather flock together', another common adage, directly contradicts the common saying regarding opposites attracting each other. Notably, this common belief *is* supported by research. Despite 'birds of a feather ...' being evidence-based, I'd argue that you should probably find a different source for your justification, or, follow it up with a reference to the corroborating research.

But, then, why do we have these sayings and adages, if many of them can't be trusted? Consider again how people don't like being uncertain or confused by certain events. People like nice, neat little packages that wrap up complex events into something that they can comprehend. I recall the sitcom *Scrubs* from the early 2000s – at the end of each episode, the main protagonist, JD, would narrate a short summary of events into a nice, neat little abstraction that was easily understood. Arguably, this technique is used for the audience to get the 'moral of the story' from each episode and more readily see JD's character development throughout the show, as he comes to learn more about himself. It's a clever narrative technique, I suppose, but it essentially serves the same purpose as the common sayings we develop – to help us understand a phenomenon more easily, even if it is just on the basis of belief.

Notably, this section has exclusively discussed only common beliefs thus far. With respect to common sense, it must be noted from the outset that the concept is one of those that though we have the term common sense, we've been rather poor at appropriately defining it. One definition that suffices, to some extent, is that of being a type of 'quasi-rationality' (Dunwoody et al., 2000; Hammond, 1996; as discussed in Chapter 1). However, given that no form of thinking is ever purely intuitive or purely reflective, it can be reasonably deduced that this description of common sense can refer to all thinking; and, obviously, that's not a great distinction. Perhaps, a more productive outlook on common sense may, indeed, stem from this quasi-rational outlook, but that the combination of intuitive and reflective judgment is a bit more defined; for example, common sense may be more adequately described as a form of thinking that, though not critical, is not entirely bereft of RJ. Simply, let's consider it a step above what we might commonly think of as intuitive judgment. With that, such status does not ensure accuracy, but it does imply that you gave it at least some consideration. However, common sense approaches to complex problems and questions may not be so common and, instead, may require much more reflection and, in turn, CT. Yet, when CT is not feasible and expertise is not available, we have a tendency to refer to shared beliefs and common sense that plausibly explain the situation, solve the problem or answer the question – to some degree.

Let's revisit the 'sun god' example from earlier, in a context where these integrated concepts of common belief and common sense very clearly overlap. Hundreds of years ago, before the spread of the enlightenment, science and developing an understanding of the workings of outer space, humans commonly attributed the workings of celestial bodies, like the sun and the moon, to various gods. Of course, most of us look back on these people in history and wonder how they could be so foolish. The fact is, these people were not foolish or stupid, having accomplished many great

Research 71

things – things that required intelligence. Their problem was that they had no domain-specific expertise on which to rely. Sure, some civilisations developed such expertise sooner than others, but the means of transferring such knowledge was not easy either. Given the barriers to gaining the requisite knowledge, our predecessors needed to develop their own explanation in light of this knowledge gap (again, humans do not like uncertainty or confusion; and so, we fill in the gaps as necessary). The most plausible explanation in our pre-science civilisations was that when we – the apex of all living things in the known world – were not able to explain something 'bigger' than all of us, it was likely that we were not the apex, that there must be something bigger and better than us – something that we have not yet encountered. Common sense led them to the most plausible answer they could develop – there must be beings out there more powerful than us, gods that control the skies, the stars, the winds, the water, you name it. As so many bought into this plausibility, it developed into a belief, despite them never seeing any real evidence of it. Sure, they believed they had evidence – the sun goes up and down, the tides come in and out, wind blows in different ways – but their understanding of such phenomena was incomplete and inaccurate.

With that, common sense, consistent with common belief and, perhaps, a touch of egocentrism, led to the concept that, like us, these gods could be happy or sad and that we could affect that – eventually leading us to human sacrifice. So much for common sense and common beliefs. Again, people might laugh at these older civilisations, but we still do the same things – obviously not on the scale of ritual murder (although that's not entirely unheard of); we still make mistakes based on the mechanics of *believing* something because it seems plausible (i.e. makes *sense*) and because we don't have (or don't understand) other means of explaining it.

To summarise this stance on common sense/belief, just because many believe something to be true doesn't make it so – without appropriate justification. The notion of appropriate justification provides a fitting segue into a discussion of the final three information sources, all of which are typically considered as credible. Of course, there are caveats to this, which will also be explored.

Research

Evidence-based research is the gold standard of credibility. When we use it as the basis for our decisions, we are using something that is not based on feelings, beliefs or biases; rather, we are dealing with objectivity. Of course,

72   Evaluating Information Sources and Credibility

this does not necessarily mean that all research is of adequate or even good quality. For example, in Chapter 3, I questioned some researchers choosing a methodology for their studies based on their epistemological views rather than what the research question dictates. Thus, I might find myself questioning whether or not such research that they have produced could have been conducted in a more appropriate manner.

Consider a more specific example of this: imagine a piece of qualitative research wherein fifteen individuals are interviewed and, following analysis of their data, the researchers make certain conclusions about the nature of things – perhaps some generalisations within their interpretations. Of course, many readers will know that the purpose of qualitative research is not to make generalisations – it's not designed to do that. If you want to make generalisations, you should not be using a qualitative approach. However, if your epistemological slant is consistent with a qualitative tradition but you're interested in inferences consistent with generalisations, then you're at a bit of a fork in the road. Either you adopt a new methodology (and learn how to conduct it well to facilitate your research interest) or you limit the type of research questions and purposes that you can reasonably pursue. Unfortunately, there are fields of research out there that don't understand this issue of what dictates methodology, and so they will conduct qualitative research and make implications to much broader contexts than they should. This is not good research practice, and is only one example of research that is not of 'good quality'.

When evaluating research, you must ask yourself whether a study was limited in some respect, for example, the design, sample assessed, measures used or even the conclusions drawn (obviously, just citing the news report or article you encountered that drew your attention to the research or even reading the study's abstract to ascertain findings are insufficient in this context). For example, I used a fictional study in one of my class exercises wherein it was found that dogs enhance their owners' mental well-being. This prompted a series of questions, including, *were dog owners compared with people who do not have dogs on mental well-being?* Alternatively, it may be the case that dog owners were already scoring high on mental well-being, prior to owning dogs. Maybe that's why they decided to get a dog in the first place? Moreover, we must ask if this is an issue of cause or correlation. Could this hypothetical finding regarding higher mental well-being stem from something other than owning a dog? Maybe it was their caring nature and nurturing emotions that led them to get a dog that impacts their well-being?

Still, the nature of research is that it's based on credibility. Bodies of research are conducted on single topics – not just one single study. They are replicated to assess the credibility and generalisability of findings. Thus, if you question the credibility of one study, see what other studies on the same topic say. Evaluate their methods and conclusions as well. Of course, no study is perfect, but if a large body of research indicates the validity of a certain phenomenon (e.g. as can be evaluated through systematic reviews and meta-analyses), it would be reasonable to incorporate these findings into your decision-making. However, if you find yourself siding with an idea that's only supported by one study or is substantiated by a suspect methodology, you may want to reconsider your stance.

Expert Opinion

Consistent with our discussion in Chapter 4, if a genuine expert with relevant qualifications in a particular field tells us something about that topic, we should be inclined to believe them – simple as that. Though you might be surprised by a book on CT recommending blind belief in a person's opinion, there is more to it than that. Of course, you should see what other experts and research in the field say about the topic, but if all the information you have available to you is from that one expert – go with it. They are the authority. Notably, authority is a good thing in this context. Expert opinions are a strong source of information because experts have to maintain their reputation in order to continue being seen as experts. The person has the authority in this role because they worked to get there, based on credibility and reputation. If they weren't credible, they wouldn't be seen as an authority on the matter. Terms such as 'authority' and 'expert' sometimes have a negative connotation in modern society, perhaps because of ill-formed perspectives on 'being an individual' and 'questioning everything'. You could question everything, but as we discussed in Chapter 2, you would sure be tired after a few hours of it. An important part of CT is knowing what to question and when. Of course, if you care about a topic, you should question it. But, if you have very little expertise in that knowledge domain, going with what the genuine experts say is a prudent and practical route.

Early in my career of researching and teaching CT, I would advise students to do their own research – and I meant this in two ways. First, as these were students in a traditional university, chances were that they would conduct their own actual research at some stage – be it as part of an undergraduate project, a Master's dissertation or even at PhD or postdoctoral level. This concept was not a stretch of the imagination. Second, there are varying degrees of the extent to which research can be conducted. You can conduct actual research through collecting data, analysing it and getting it published through the peer-review process (such as through primary research). You can even read thirty peer-reviewed journal articles on a topic and write a review of the field and its findings (such as through secondary research). However, anything less than that is kind of a stretch in terms of 'doing your own research'. For example, as per that last example, you could just read those papers to inform yourself about the topic – your purpose for doing so might be to help you make a decision (as opposed to writing a review and directly engaging the field). I would call that educating oneself, definitely. But research? No, probably not (i.e. without the forced effort to evaluate, such as through the act of writing as in the previous example). However, 'educating oneself' is definitely a requisite part of the CT process – for evaluating the strengths and weaknesses of relevant information.

Unfortunately, 'do your research' has become a meme for something different over the years – a battle cry for cynics who lack faith in experts and authority thinkers. Sure, sometimes you should question authority and 'experts' (as discussed soon), but one thing is for sure. If you have no research methodology training, you will not be able to conduct research appropriately – moreover, the body of work that you would need to conduct to even bring you par with the expertise level of a genuine expert (or experts) would take years, if not decades. 'Do your own research' is not feasible. The best you can do is to read enough to sufficiently inform yourself. Watching five 'documentaries' on YouTube is not going to cut it. The information you engage needs to be credible, and what is credible is the research conducted by the experts and published in reputable, peer-reviewed journals – not some website or random publication no one's ever heard of outside of your 'community'.

Perhaps, such aforementioned cynicism of expert opinion results from the nature of 'opinion'. Generally, the 'opinions' expressed by true experts are developed based on research findings. Mostly, these opinions are not opinions in the traditional sense (e.g. based on attitudes and feelings); rather, they're simplified interpretations of what their data and the data from the field suggest. Maybe a better way of considering expert opinion is as expert interpretation or perspective.

Notably, expert opinions may differ from others in their field, but that's okay. Debate is part of the scientific process. Likewise, expert disagreement may be due to different research perspectives. For example, a social psychologist may focus on the 'nurture' influences of aggression, whereas a neurobiologist may focus on the 'nature' aspect. Both will identify

Expert Opinion

different contributors to aggression, but they are also both likely to acknowledge the existence of each other's perspectives. That's what credible researchers do.

However, some 'experts' may not practise such intellectual humility or even have credibility. You might have noticed that I often preface expert with words such as 'actual', 'true' or 'genuine', and this is purposeful. Consider again one of my previous examples. It's one thing for me to get up and present to audiences information on cognitive psychology, the psychology of education and CT – given that they are my areas of research. But, it's another thing for me to advise audiences, in a similar manner, about quantum mechanics (as in our previous examples) or, a little bit 'closer to home', on psychiatric matters. Of course, if I'm provided a platform and have been introduced as 'Dr' or 'PhD' or whatever, audiences are implicitly primed to believe that I'm somewhat of an authority on anything that I speak about in my communication. Obviously, this is not the case. But, this is how the human brain works. Even if I made it clear to the audience that I'm not an expert in quantum mechanics or psychiatry before speaking about either, the nature of schemas will still implicitly influence audiences to believe I somehow know more about the field than anyone else who is just simply interested in it.

Unfortunately, from time to time, people take the platforms that they are provided and exploit them to spread what they *believe*, regardless of whether or not it's from a place of genuine expertise or complete misinformation. For example, you might have a controversial topic being debated on a live TV show, in which case you have 'person A', who is pro-X, and 'person B', who is anti-X. They debate and hijinks ensue. On the surface, that's what people see. However, it's often the case that 'person A' might be a credible researcher and/or scientist – a true expert on the topic; and 'person B' might be a social media influencer, politician or famous person of some type (but not a researcher). I can't fathom why television programming allows for this other than the fact that it might inflate ratings, but it is suspect at best in terms of credibility. But hey, ratings are ratings. Essentially, they are painting a picture for the audience that this celebrity is in some way an authority on a topic in which they are not expert.

Sure, the influencer and celebrities are to blame for accepting – but do they necessarily know any better? They might genuinely believe that their perspective is just as important as the experts'. Besides, exposure is good for them and they're getting a chance to value-signal (see Chapter 9). However, I think the producers of the broadcast are mostly to blame,

76 Evaluating Information Sources and Credibility

because they're actively taking part in creating what could well be a false debate – which is not of benefit to the wider population.

Consider a further example regarding the global warming 'debate'. I use the term *debate* quite liberally. Now, I'm not a climatologist or a researcher of environmental systems, but I know those that are or are involved in related fields agree, on an approximately 98 per cent basis, that man-made global warming is real and is happening.[2] Consistent with an example from a segment on John Oliver's *Last Week Tonight*, when global warming is presented in the news or on talk shows, they typically treat it as a genuine debate, with one person saying 'yes, it's happening' and another on the other side saying 'no, it's not'. Such presentation subtly manipulates viewers into believing that, on the 'one v one' basis presented, there is real debate as to whether or not global warming is happening. John Oliver humorously brought out ninety-eight scientists on to the stage to 'debate' two as a means of representing what this 'debate' actually looks like. Of course, consistent with our discussion from Chapter 3, we cannot be *absolutely sure* that global warming is happening with certainty (at least, not entirely consistent with the manner in which it has been conceptualised); however, based on the staggering agreement of 98 per cent of experts (I say staggering because I struggle to imagine 98 per cent of people agreeing on *anything*), I'd imagine myself foolish to not align myself with their perspective – they have a very strong theory.

Overall, expert opinion is strong in credibility; however, it is up to that expert's audience to evaluate the credibility of the 'expertise'. If you are sceptical of the expert, check their credentials and compare their advice to other experts in the field. Consider again that just because an individual is an expert in one domain does not guarantee expertise in another, no matter how *experienced* they feel themselves to be in it. Moreover, consider the expert's level of humility in their relaying of information. If they're willing to admit gaps in knowledge or that they don't know certain answers, that's the true sign of comfort and confidence that develop alongside expertise. I'm more likely to believe *that* person. Unfortunately, human cognition makes it so that we implicitly side with the person who is assertive, confident and has all the answers to the

---

[2] I'm cognisant that just by my addressing this, some readers will jump to conclusions about my political leanings. Unfortunately, the notion of 'global warming' has become a very political topic. First, I say, check out Chapter 9 for a better understanding of my view on politics. Second, it doesn't matter how much some people want to make things political, this has little to do with politics and everything to do with science.

Statistics

questions – an intuition many of us have, which, if we apply to our decision-making, may well come back to bite us at a later time.

Statistics

Statistics are one type of output we get from doing research (i.e. quantitative research). The type of statistics reported also often tell us something about the type and quality of the research. When presented with statistics, we should ask, 'what is the purpose of these data, and what is the goal of reporting them?' Every statistic is simply a number. This is actually what makes it such a strong form of evidence – it is objective. The great strength of statistics is that numbers don't lie, but as we know from a previous example, the people who interpret numbers can. Again, credibility – in this context that of the statistician – is a core focus of CT. Moreover, it's not that people who misinterpret statistics in their reporting are purposefully lying; rather, it's just that statistics are not always easy to interpret (again, the importance of expertise).

It doesn't help either that human beings are terrible natural statisticians (see Kahneman, 2011; Tversky & Kahneman, 1974). For example, statistics are another arena in which causation and correlation must be carefully considered. *Did B directly happen as a result of A, or is it the case that the two of them just happened to be linked in the sense that 'every time we see an increase in B, we see an increase in A'?* To some, this is obvious. To others, not so much. But, these are very distinct concepts. Though we use and report on correlational statistics in some types of research, we must also make a point of considering the nature of these in our interpretation. One of my favourite examples of what I mean by this is the strong correlation between Nicholas Cage film appearances and drownings from falling into swimming pools between 1999 and 2009. Of course, common sense will tell you that neither of these influenced one another, in a causal way, despite being strongly correlated statistically. Another of my favourite examples is in reference to the illusory correlation, where little Johnny believes he has a superpower because, following his wishes for snow before bed, he awakes the next morning to a school closure due to dangerous weather. We're not surprised when children like little Johnny conclude things like 'I can make it snow', but we expect better from adults, many of whom use the same logic as Johnny.

These examples are humorous, but let's apply the same fallacious thinking to practical, real-world issues where there's more at stake. Imagine that 100 per cent of sex offenders were found to consume 'X'.

78 Evaluating Information Sources and Credibility

Many individuals would instantly jump at the opportunity to call for bans on 'X' without ever truly considering the intricacies of the relationships. When I tell you that 'X' refers to water, then you're more likely to see the error in your decision-making. Obviously, the drinking of water plays no role in sexual offence – everyone needs water to survive. But, what happens if 'X' or water is replaced with 'product Y' or (let's call it) 'Yeolig'? Because you don't know what Yeolig is (I just made it up), it's not as easy to see the flaw in judgment, thus increasing the chances of jumping to a conclusion based on a potentially spurious correlation (see also the *dihydrogen monoxide parody* for a similar example). Another example of how statistics are difficult to interpret comes from one of my class exercises: 'dog owners have significantly lower cholesterol levels than those who don't own dogs' (before getting into the example, note that the reason we know that this is a statistical issue is because of various terms used, for example, 'significantly lower' and 'levels'). Now, I don't know if this proposition is actually true – it represents yet another fictional example to make a point in an introductory class; but with that, people were inclined to believe it. *Why?* Must be something about dogs. One of my favourite common guesses is that maybe they release some kind of pheromone that has cardiovascular benefits for humans. But, imagining that this proposition about dogs impacting cholesterol is actually true, using Occam's razor, a good thinker might look at the relationship and say, 'well, dog owners must walk their dogs, and physical activity is good for keeping cholesterol down; so, it's likely that it's the walking rather than anything about the dog per se'. Obviously, the proposition takes a bit of 'unpacking' for us to draw a reasonable conclusion about it.

One final example regarding difficulty in interpreting statistics comes from the advertising world. Think of a commercial you might have seen with a persuasive celebrity advertising Shampoo X as the best on the market, with 90 per cent of women agreeing. Upon hearing 90 per cent, my eyes immediately divert from that beautiful shiny hair wafting in slow motion to the bottom of the screen at the actual numbers. Years ago, companies didn't have to provide these numbers. Then, mandatory provision was legislated. Of course, it was barely legible. Then, in some markets, a minimum font size was legislated. Why does that matter? Well, because 90 per cent doesn't tell us very much. What if that was only nine out of ten women? That's a pretty small sample size and, thus, not generalisable to the broader population. If it was 90 per cent of 800, then I'd be impressed. Sure, it's the same proportion, but the larger sample tells us a little more about another question we should be asking – *which women?* To which women does this advertisement of '90 per cent of women agree' refer? We don't know if they all purchased the shampoo from the same shop, how they were selected, if they're all around the same age, same ethnicity, same demographic, etc. In the case of only ten women, maybe they surveyed women from only one shop that had a sale on that shampoo that day. Maybe the survey team chose these particular women because they were observed to be carrying that particular shampoo out of the shop. The variables and questions are endless. However, when the sample size shoots up to something like 800, it's more likely that we'll see a more diverse sample of women and that the survey took place in multiple locations. Sure, it's not guaranteed, but it is more likely – and so, we should be more confident in the findings. Next time you see such an ad, be sure to look at the bottom of the screen and see what information is provided to you about the statistics regarding the claim.

Concluding Thoughts

Overall, a pattern emerges across these five informational sources. No source of evidence is perfect. If we care about the decision with which we're faced, we will engage research, expert opinion and statistics with care, ensuring some level of consistency across the body of research in that field. Personal experience and common belief are poor routes to take if CT is our goal, because there's no assurance that they have grounding in an evidence-based approach. In many cases, there may be research that debunks such beliefs and experiences. Sometimes, there may be research that supports them; but then why bother reporting anything but the research? It depends – some people just want research-based justification, so in those cases, give them that. However, if you're trying to change someone's mind about something, who isn't really research-minded, perhaps using all sources of justification at your disposal is a good idea. This notion will be explored further in the following chapter.

Is it easier making decisions based on experience and common beliefs? Of course, but then no one said CT was easy or that it's supposed to be easy. Perhaps that's why a lack of CT has been such a concern. CT takes time, regardless of whether you use common belief/sense or personal experience-sourced information alongside it. Sure, such examples might be more persuasive than others – and that's important in certain situations. However, if this is for your own decision-making, why spend more time than necessary in humouring information that lacks a basis in evidence? Go straight for a source derived from research and use your valuable time well.

CHAPTER 6

Changing Minds

People love to be right (though they hate being wrong more; e.g. see Kahneman, 2011; Thaler & Sunstein, 2008). However, 'being right' just for the sake of it is not – and shouldn't be – the primary focus of CT; rather, it should be about deciding what to believe and what to do. With that, critically thinking for the purpose of 'being right' – to find the truth – can be a positive thing, particularly in educational settings, that is, for making good personal decisions, disseminating accurate information and teaching others. On the other hand, wanting to be right might lead us down some less than desirable paths. For example, if being right is our goal, might striving to attain that goal potentially cloud our judgment (e.g. in cases where CT might recommend abstaining from a decision for the time being)? Likewise, assuming being right is our primary goal, is it possible that we might cease thinking about a topic once we believe we are correct? In this case, doubting our 'correctness' might be what keeps us engaged in CT.

Eigenauer (2024) discusses this in terms of various fact-finding strategies. For example, in some healthcare settings, such as radiology, there is a tendency to engage the 'satisfaction of search' error, which occurs when a search for abnormalities or issues of concern cease upon finding the first one. Likewise, he refers to 'makes-sense epistemology', wherein instead of engaging the information and reflecting on it in light of reading more on the issue, an individual will hear or read the information in question and, if it sounds plausible or 'feels right', they will adopt it as fact (akin to satisficing).

One of my favourite examples of such 'fact-finding' strategies regards relying on news headlines to inform us: in 2012, a UK news source reported that flip-flops cause cancer. I often report this headline in my CT classes and ask the students to discuss. 'Maybe there's some kind of chemical in the plastic or rubber that flip-flops are made from?' is a frequent response in class. Not a bad guess, I suppose; but, eventually someone will come up with the correct answer: 'flip-flops expose your feet to the elements, and as we typically wear flip-flops in the sun, our feet are exposed to harmful rays'. That's pretty much what was reported in the article – it has nothing to do with the flip-flops as such,[1] but rather whether or not we remember to apply sunscreen to our feet. It seems so obvious, but we don't recognise it that way because that's not how the information is presented. In fairness to the news outlet, this is addressed in the article, but not before the sensationalist headline 'grabs you' (of course, this is a common strategy for selling newspapers). But, what if someone didn't read the full article? The only reason I read the article was because the headline piqued my scepticism. I imagine there are many who encountered the headline, didn't read it and now many of those people might go around falsely believing flip-flops are dangerous (and, perhaps, still not adequately applying sunscreen to their feet). Nevertheless, the headline reports information and if it seems reasonable, we're inclined to accept it – an issue magnified by the fact that it's being reported by a news outlet, which many will implicitly believe based on some bastardised few of credibility (see, again, Chapter 5). Remember, at the end of the day, newspapers exist to sell papers – translating the news comes second; and if they can sell more papers by making the news sound more sensational, they will. That's not a criticism per se; they're businesses – they're in the business of selling news. An unfortunate by-product, though, is that their audiences are required to think a little bit harder about what they read.

You might see the flip-flop story as a humorous anecdote and accept it as a reasonable example in our discussion, but fail to see the importance of it in situations that require CT. What I mean by that is, if you're anything like me, you don't care about this particular finding. You may not care about flip-flops – in which case you might have been one of the many who didn't read the article in full. I don't care about flip-flops; I don't often wear them – not even on sun holidays. So, for me, this example represents just that – an example. However, there may be a variety of knock-on effects from it that could impact or influence you in meaningful ways. Let's consider another example.

---

[1] Coincidentally, a few years after this headline was reported, one flip-flop manufacturer was found to be using materials that were classified as hazardous. So, as it turns out, the commonly used explanation in my class turned out to be right in the case of this particular manufacturer (*see how 'knowledge' can change?*). As such, I feel compelled to provide this extra nugget of information as a sort of caveat to my example. Nevertheless, the point of the example remains – and at the same time teaches us something about applied epistemology!

Diet soda has long been the subject of debate with regard to the inclusion of aspartame as an artificial sweetener. Like in the previous example, it is widely thought to cause cancer. Indeed, I remember hearing this when I was in my early teens and advising my mother that this was the case. She actually listened to me and, as a family, we stopped buying diet soda (going full sugar instead). Upon looking into this deeper – and not just on the surface headline level, even though it seems legitimate – it turns out that you would need to consume *a lot* of aspartame-laden soda, on a daily basis, for there to be a reasonable risk of cancer. Of course, there remains a risk, albeit negligible, depending on how much diet soda you consume; but, isn't there a risk associated with many things we consume? In this context, think about the health risks of switching to full-sugar soda, as we did.

This is where the knock-on effect that I previously mentioned comes into play. Let's say your doctor advises that you are overweight and your health is at risk. You will need to exercise and improve your diet. So, you make amendments to your diet. However, removing coffee (which many enjoy with sugar) and soda might be one step too far. Is it not reasonable to risk the effects of aspartame – in moderation – in light of the very real risk of obesity-related health problems of which your doctor has advised you? Some will; some will not. Personally, in light of knowing the finer details of aspartame use, I would quickly switch to diet soda and 'risk' the aspartame. It's not like I'm drinking six litres of it a day. But then, if you are drinking six litres of it a day, maybe soda really is something you might think about trying to remove from your diet. Again, context is key.

Taking into account these examples of gut-level acceptance of information, if being right about the information is our goal, then it seems like we do cease thinking about a topic once we believe we are correct or feel like we 'know' a sufficient amount about it. The obvious problem with this is that all many people will need to do is simply *believe* they're right and then that's it. The manner in which people typically engage in political discourse is a good example of this (see Chapter 9 for further discussion). Of course, belief in one's 'correctness' does not necessarily make it so. Couple that with not having adequate epistemological understanding and you will have people who simply stand by their beliefs without sufficient justification. How do we correct these perspectives? That is, *how do we change other people's minds?*

I'm often asked this question by students in my CT classes and it is a great question – and a very interesting one to consider. I think about it often and, even though I do, it remains a question I stumble about with every time I try to answer it. I never seem to readily have an answer! Of course, 'it depends' is the obvious starting point here; but, there are so many routes to go down in order to arrive at a comprehensive answer, which is inevitably summarised as 'it's not easy'.

To clarify, *how do we change other people's minds?* is not the same as asking *how best to persuade people* – there's a large body of research examining various peripheral persuasion techniques (persuasion that relies on incidental cues, as opposed to central route persuasion techniques that focus on the argument at hand), whether they're used for a benevolent purpose (e.g. getting people to choose healthier eating options; see *nudge theory* (Thaler & Sunstein, 2008)) or for reasons more aligned with the persuader's self-interest (e.g. marketing a new product for public consumption). See Table 6.1 for a list of commonly used persuasion techniques.

No, the question at hand is more about when *we* have critically thought about something and developed a reasonable conclusion, based on credible, relevant, logical evidence, and see value in changing the minds of *those who haven't* thought critically – or, worse, those who believe they have thought critically yet are still wrong. Now, this is not to say that we can't use persuasion techniques in this context (e.g. as a last resort (from the perspective of CT) in cases where changing minds is of utmost importance); rather, it may be a more noble endeavour to facilitate others to use CT and help them change their minds for themselves (e.g. teach a man to fish versus give a man a fish). Of course, that might just be a bit of wishful thinking on my part. With that, perhaps a more accurate way of looking at the question is, *how do we convince others that we have debunked erroneous information to which they subscribe?*

Being Practical

Before getting into any situation where you try to convince someone that their perspective is wrong, I urge you to be practical. Sometimes, even when you know you're right, it's just better to leave it. Question yourself: *does it matter that I change this person's mind?* Broadly speaking, I ask myself what I'd be getting out of entering into such a dialogue prior to deciding whether or not to engage. For example, what's the point of arguing with every person on social media with whom you don't agree? What are you actually gaining from this? Sure, we can all get baited from time to time – it's a frustrating endeavour. Do you really need this aggravation in your life? Of course not; so, *why bother?* Self-regulation is important here and a vital aspect of RJ.

Changing Minds

Table 6.1 *Common persuasion strategies*

Strategy	Description	Example
The bandwagon argument	The argument that something is true if a majority believe it. This argument can be presented in two distinct, but similar, ways: (1) you will be left out if you don't believe/act in a certain way – consistent with 'the fear of missing out' and (2) if a majority believe/act in a certain way, then it follows (incorrectly) that they can't be wrong.	*Everyone else is doing it, so why don't you?*
Use of pity	An appeal for compassion.	Using impoverished children (e.g. a photo, video or even the idea of them) to promote one's perspective.
Scare tactics	Using emotion, such as fear, in a manner that trumps the efficacy of a reasoned argument.	Instead of presenting disease rates resulting from a particular activity in writing, images representing the effects (e.g. a diseased liver or lung) are likely to be more persuasive.
Card-stacking	The use of an unbalanced and biased argument that purposefully omits important counterpoints.	Advertising a consumable as 'low in fat', which implies that it's a healthier option, relatively speaking, when, in fact, it might be higher in calories than other options not 'low in fat'.
Circular reasoning	A proposition that assumes the very conclusion it is attempting to conclude.	*We need to cut spending as too much money is being spent.*
Speaker effect	Relying on certain characteristics of the argument's communicator or representative.	Using a popular celebrity to advertise a product (e.g. a talented basketball player to sell sneakers), an attractive communicator (e.g. good-looking politicians and clothing models) or a communicator with observable credibility (e.g. a medical specialist).

Being Practical 85

Table 6.1 (*cont.*)

Strategy	Description	Example
Slippery-slope argument	A form of reasoning (often fallacious, but not always[2]) that concludes that if a specific action is taken or an event occurs, other negative consequences will follow.	If event X were to occur, then event Y would (eventually) follow; thus, we cannot allow event X to happen.
Conveying similarity	Drawing parallels between the persuader and the audience (to exemplify their similarity), prior to making their pitch.	We both enjoy X and Y. Have you tried Z? I love it and I think you will too.

I recall, not long after getting my PhD, going on a current social media site (which was still relatively new at the time) and advising a friend of a friend that their psychology-related conspiracy belief was unfounded, taking the time to point by point correct each of their spurious propositions. Sure, I did it partly as an educational endeavour, but I also did it because I took what was said as an insult; thus, in a way I probably felt I was 'defending my field of work'. In hindsight, though, who really cares what this person thinks? I sure don't, but I engaged anyway. Like I said, we all get baited from time to time; but I suppose such is the case in light of Lowenstein's (1996) 'hot–cold empathy gap', wherein we might see slips in self-control due to underestimation of arousal effects. That is, when we're 'cold' we recognise good decisions, as you would hope many of us do. However, we fail to appreciate how much our desires, level of arousal and contextual factors play on decision-making when 'hot'. Thaler and Sunstein (2008, p. 42) provide a nice example of this: 'Tom is on a diet and agrees to go out on a business dinner, thinking he will be able to limit

---

[2] The slippery slope argument is often perceived as fallacious primarily for reasons of relevance (e.g. such arguments typically avoid response to propositions pertinent to the 'here and now') and certainty (e.g. it's not possible for us to see into the future and guarantee that the subsequent event will occur). However, neither point necessarily makes this 'if, then' conditional proposition illogical or even unreasonable to suggest – it just requires assessment of plausibility. For example, it may be possible to assess the likelihood of an event occurring in light of some previous event. If there's a good chance of it happening, then the 'slippery slope argument' isn't illogical. Of course, the more 'stops' we make on this trip down the slippery slope, the less likely the outcome, and the often chain-like way such scenarios are set up is likely why the slippery slope argument gets a bad name. However, if A leading to B is 90 per cent likely (based on a credible evaluation) and the outcome is of importance, then it's not unreasonable to use this strategy in a CT context. With that, by integrating B into the argument, then CT will need to be applied to that as well.

86   Changing Minds

himself to one glass of wine and no dessert. But the host orders a second bottle of wine and the waiter brings out the dessert cart and all bets are off.'

Long story short, I didn't change the person's mind. In fact, I think I only reinforced their belief in what they posted – an example of the *backfire effect*, which refers to the strengthening of opposing beliefs and attitudes in light of one's efforts to intervene (Cook & Lewandowsky, 2011; Lewandowsky et al., 2012). For example, one might get defensive about being told that they're incorrect and, thus, 'double down' on their stance, regardless of truth. Likewise, situations like this might reflect a prior commitment bias (e.g. see Staw, 1976). Ever notice how, before the arrival of video review in sports, referees never changed their minds? That's because they don't want to look weak in their decision-making. If they look weak on one occasion, then players will think they can get them to change their minds in future situations regarding controversial calls as well. People are like that in real life too.

So, with respect to my experience on social media, time was lost in checking and rechecking my updates, alongside crafting responses. All I had to show for it was aggravation. I didn't even care about this person – I think I had only met them in real life once before (and never again thereafter). What was to be gained? If 'nothing' is the answer in situations such as this (apart from some feeling of self-righteousness), then don't bother. If you're on social media and find yourself engaging simply for the purpose of 'being right' in a public forum, then that might be more of a 'you issue' than being about educational purposes or anything related to CT. Self-validation probably isn't a good enough reason to risk the time, effort, cognitive resources and frustration. Save your cognitive efforts for things that matter.

On the other hand, there are times when you might come across an individual in a position of power or influence who might have an inaccurate perspective on something of importance. In situations like this, you might take the opportunity to try and change their mind as their thoughts or actions might have direct influence on you or someone you care about. This recommendation is made consistent with what seems to be emerging as a kind of mantra of this book, *depending on the context*. For example, imagine your boss at work is making amendments to how things are being done and some of these amendments could potentially affect you in a negative way, such as pay, scheduling or workload. You happen to be aware of credible research that suggests that such amendments are, indeed, a bad idea. Depending on a range of factors, it may be a good idea for you to present your boss with this research (which may end up benefitting you) or it may be a very bad idea in that your boss interprets this as you second-guessing them (which may end up hindering you). Such potential outcomes should be considered because though they may seem obvious, they may not be to everyone; I have genuinely heard of individuals complaining to their *spouse's* bosses about working conditions – this should be taken as an example of when *not* to engage. Alternatively, you might see that a close friend or family member is on the verge of making a very poor decision with important implications – this might be a more reasonable context to engage with offering evidence-based thinking.

Perhaps this is the most 'practical' stance to take – assessing whether or not the incorrect standpoint is actually hurting anyone else. If I knew someone who believes that the world is flat and is unwilling to change their mind over it, what am I gaining by arguing with them? From a cost–benefit perspective, the ideal outcome is that they do change their mind – and if they do, great. But, what does that really achieve? If they're happy believing whatever they believe, good for them. Of course, if they have kids (whose education in which they will inevitably have a role), that's not great; but it probably won't affect *me* in any meaningful way. Alternatively, the situation changes drastically if this person is, say, your child's school-teacher – their misinformation is now impacting your child, and so this is problematic. It would make sense to intervene in this context.

Being Right Is Not Enough

Moreover, just being right isn't enough in many cases. Looking back at the example of my experience on social media, what good is being right when the person you've 'educated' *still* thinks that they're right and you're wrong? What if they don't want your education? Success depends largely on the nature of the individual you are trying to educate – and not just in terms of who they are in relation to you. Rather, consider the allusion to the two different earlier scenarios: how can we change the minds of (1) those who haven't thought critically, and (2) those who believe they have thought critically yet are still wrong? Though similar, the subtle difference between the questions is important, because it results in two different answers.

How Can We Change the Minds of Those Who Haven't Thought Critically?

To reiterate, people generally do not like change, and that certainly applies to their thinking as well. Once people process information, it's quite difficult to remove that information's influence. For example, when misinformation is processed *prior* to the accurate information, even if the accurate information is believed, the misinformation is likely to 'stick' in some manner, perhaps as a result of reinforcing familiarity with the misinformation (e.g. *how do you debunk erroneous information without addressing it?*; see, for example, Cook & Lewandowsky, 2011; Lewandowsky et al., 2020).

This concept is by no means new and makes sense from a cognitive standpoint. For example, consistent with our discussion regarding knowledge construction, when we process novel information, we integrate it with pre-existing information, thus amending schema architecture in our long-term memory store. We are organising the information based on relevance, consistency, narrative congruence and a variety of other features. The manner in which we organise it is how we understand it; and because of efforts made to integrate it through ongoing schema construction, we are essentially adapting the information (both novel and pre-existing) to accommodate the addition. Everything we take in requires constant updating, which perhaps explains, to some extent, reluctance to engage further, rather effortful, amendment.

Imagine that you are told that certain information you assimilated a year ago is wrong. To rectify the issue, you essentially have to reverse-engineer or maybe even deconstruct this schema and re-evaluate any relevant information since integrating the misinformation.[3] Now, let's say this information isn't terribly important in terms of its impact on you as a person. It may be the case that, relatively speaking, a year isn't that long for you (e.g. depending on your age or the meaningfulness/importance of the information), you don't often deal in topics relevant to this erroneous information or you're simply very open-minded to thinking and rethinking about particular topics – all of which might enhance the likelihood that you will engage the potential of changing your mind. Alternatively, if we raise the stakes a bit and say that the information you were told was wrong relates to a worldview that is important to you or is one you've had for many years, changing your mind is a less likely outcome (i.e. consider the *worldview backfire effect* – Cook & Lewandowsky, 2011).

---

[3] We don't perceive this happening of course, but we see the effects in various ways. For example, learning that X isn't true might affect how you perceive Y and Z, which you had previously learned/believed shared a relationship with X. You might notice this inconsistency immediately or it might not dawn on you until some time later when Y or Z come to mind. Will you then question your understanding of Y in light of what you learned about the erroneous X, or will you fail to see that the link you thought was there no longer is?

Being Right Is Not Enough 89

Either way, it's tough to reconstruct your existing schemas to accommodate new information that may debunk your beliefs. Many may choose to ignore this new evidence. Some will accept it and try to accommodate the new information, but find that it impacts how they perceive other 'knowledge' as well (as in the case of footnote 3). These impacts may be positive, but they could also be negative (e.g. frustrating), thus making 'mind-changing' all the more difficult. Of course, they may welcome the new information and happily make efforts to reconstruct their perspectives. You never know.

In terms of longer-held beliefs, if you were even open to the notion of changing your mind (dictated by bias), you would have to re-examine a vast majority of what you have learned over the years because your worldview is now under fire. If you are wrong about *this*, then it follows that you might question *other things* that you could be wrong about – not only because of precedence but also because of the bias your initial (erroneous) worldview has applied to your engagement with novel information throughout your life. If our worldviews are in question, uncertainty increases – and, consistent with our previous discussion, human beings don't like uncertainty.

Of course, human cognition is an amazing thing. Now, 'amazing' doesn't always mean 'good' in the world of CT. We have developed cognitive safeguards to help protect us against opponents to our mental well-being. Our worldviews are an important aspect of such well-being and, so, we have cognitive strategies to protect them.[4] For example, when faced with questioning of a worldview, we engage confirmation bias. Engaging confirmation bias is easy to do and, often, we don't even know we're doing it – let alone being in a situation where we're under duress in some kind of philosophical cornering. Just the way you type something into a search engine implies some level of bias. Remember, what you search for is what you get. One of my favourite examples of this was where one individual posted a request for help on social media regarding what to do after searching online for evidence supporting their perspective, finding

---

[4] Another related way in which we cognitively protect ourselves is through rationalisation. This is an interesting one because it not only accounts for us being wrong but justifies our being wrong through manipulated logic – and even though some part of us knows we made a mistake, we use the logic to deceive ourselves, to misinform ourselves that there was a reasonable rationale behind the mistake. We all do this; so it's important to self-assess upon making such mistakes. If we can identify the deception, we can learn from our mistakes. However, if we succeed in our self-deception and fail to self-evaluate, we can end up constructing schemas and heuristics that reinforce these mistakes again in the future. Once reinforced, as cognitive structures, such thinking can be hard to change or overcome. This will be elaborated on later.

none and, instead, finding evidence indicating that their perspective was wrong. The best advice was, obviously, that they should probably change their perspective.

But, even if you are *willing* to change your mind, it's not necessarily easy – for the very same reasons addressed earlier; it may very well be the case that there are 'artefacts' of that erroneous information that remain stuck in your knowledge store. Another interesting example is that of the *sleeper effect*, which refers to the engagement of information from a source that lacks credibility. Even though we know the source lacks credibility, over time, it's not the source that we remember, but the information; thus, when that information is retrieved bereft of its source, we are then more likely to use it, because we forget it lacks credibility. Much like the *availability heuristic*, we are sometimes at a loss for useful information in real-world settings if we have not recently engaged information pertinent to such situations. For example, have you ever got into an argument with someone and after all is said and done, you keep thinking of things you wish you had said to them? As you probably had not planned to get into an argument, you probably were not thinking of these issues; and, thus, the information necessary to verbalise your issues was not likely readily available for retrieval in the moment. On the other hand, if you purposefully started the argument, it's more likely that you had such information available because of your initiation of it – it was on your mind. Likewise, think of all the conversations you've had with people where either you or the person that you're speaking with has brought up some research but failed to recall either who conducted it or from where it was learned: 'I heard that research was conducted on . . .' or reference to elusive '*they* did research' on whatever. It may be a legitimate point, but its credibility is decreased because of a failure to adequately source it.

Consistent with our discussion thus far, research in this area has long looked at the power of belief(s) on cognitive processing, as well as the sustainability of this 'power'. According to Cook and Lewandowsky's *Debunking Handbook* (2011) (see also Lewandowsky et al., 2012), a common solution strategy is to remove the influence of erroneous information by providing, educating and adding correct information; but, this strategy is in itself erroneous in many contexts, given various backfire effects and because, more broadly, such strategies ignore, to some extent, the implicit workings of bias. Instead, Cook and Lewandowsky recommend three routes towards successful debunking.

First, the position you are trying to teach must focus on the core evidence rather than misinformation. Though you should refute the

Being Right Is Not Enough

incorrect information (even though such refutation can reinforce the misinformation through effects such as familiarity), the primary focus must be the accurate information. Second, any mention of said misinformation should be prefaced by an explicit warning that the following information is erroneous. Finally, the refutation should include alternative explanation(s) of the supporting propositions presented within the original misinformation.

Accounting for these three routes, a procedure takes shape: (1) emphasise your claim; (2) present evidence for the claim while reinforcing it; (3) address the misinformation as a myth; and (4) explain how the myth is erroneous, while keeping the truthfulness of your claim centre stage. Though these are useful recommendations based on extant cognitive research, arguably they don't completely address contexts wherein people simply disagree and subsequently disregard your position in favour of their own. For example, consider my earlier recommendation of being practical and not engaging in debate when it's not worth it – others with 'differing' views to you might be, likewise, practical – which brings us to our second question.

How Can We Change the Minds of Those Who Believe They Have Thought Critically, yet Are Still Wrong?

Changing people's minds is not easy; and it's even more difficult when the person you're working with believes they have critically thought about something (e.g. consider again people who believe they have 'done their research'). The truth, it seems, is that there's little you can do about that – it simply boils down to the person you're trying to educate, their disposition towards CT and situational variables (e.g. when I'm tired and/or hungry, the last thing I want to do is engage in any meaningful thought). With that, let's consider an example where the individual in question is well fed, well rested and happy to engage in argumentation. If the individual you're trying to educate is lacking in disposition towards CT, it's certainly going to be hard to change their minds. But, if they do possess these specific inclinations, it's more likely that, through their willingness to think critically, they will at least amend (if not altogether change) their perspective to be more consistent with your, already critically considered, view. Of course, this might well be easier said than done, and what I've suggested here could very well be the exception. Again, it may be the case that both sides are 'practical' and agree to disagree.

Changing 'Hearts and Minds'

Consistent with one of the persuasion techniques presented in Table 6.1, conveying similarity, one useful piece of advice regarding changing minds might be to create an emotional connection with the individual for them to be open to what you have to say. This advice is consistent with research from social psychology, which suggests that we typically gravitate towards and like people who are both similar and familiar to us. As such, it's reasonable to suggest that building such a connection will increase the potential for the person to like us and, thus, enhance the likelihood they will, at least, take on board our perspective.

In making such a recommendation – to create such a personal/emotional connection – two further important considerations are yielded. First, the recommendation implies that perhaps we should use emotion to battle emotion in CT. That is, if people make poor decisions or spread misinformation as a result of emotion-based thinking, then are critical thinkers not just as welcome to use the same methods in their arsenal? Of course, I'm not saying that we should substitute CT with emotion-based thinking; rather, should we not utilise (or even exploit, in some contexts) our understanding of human emotion to elicit CT? If it's for the right reasons, I certainly think it's a fair utilisation. Alternatively, some might argue that we *can* substitute CT with emotion-based thinking in cases where nothing but emotional statements has been presented as a rationale. Though I would generally disagree with this strategy from a CT standpoint, perhaps it is warranted in situations where it's likely to work and there's something important at stake. This perspective is not new. For example, according to Hitchens' razor (named as such after Christopher Hitchens), 'what can be asserted without evidence can be dismissed without evidence'. So, in this context, if an emotional, heartfelt stance is made, then it can be refuted through an equally emotional and heartfelt objection (i.e. assuming that there's no empirical evidence to refute).

There is certainly value to this razor (i.e. it is up to the person making the argument to find and present appropriate justification, not their audience – consistent with the *burden of 'proof'*[5]); however, in terms of CT, if you truly care about the topic, just because the other person failed to think critically doesn't excuse you to do likewise. For example, it might be the case that neither of you are correct. It's much like the old adage *two*

---

[5] In the context of argumentation, the burden of 'proof' (ugh, that word again) refers to the responsibility of the individual who makes a claim to evidence the claim when requested.

wrongs don't make a right. Again, though, if it's for the right reasons, the issue is important and you have credible evidence to further support the claim, then the utilisation of such an approach seems warranted.

The second consideration is more specific to clarifying what is meant by creating that emotional connection. Though doing this might well increase the likelihood of changing someone's mind, it does not guarantee it (as is the case for most things, as we've discussed throughout this book). Moreover, I would argue that it's not just *any* emotional connection that's created but, rather, a specific one – one of trust. Just because an emotional connection is created between debaters doesn't ensure that the person whose mind you are attempting to change will trust the logic behind your stance.

For example, I have friends and family who will question my logic and who will disagree with me – perhaps *because* we are emotionally connected (e.g. as a result of enjoying a pre-existing social dynamic). On the other hand, some of my loved ones will strongly trust in my perspective on a majority of things, as I might strongly trust in theirs. With that, I have close friends and family in whose perspectives I would most certainly not trust. So, maybe a more accurate description of the solution is not that an emotional connection is created; rather, a connection of trust in reasoning is created. A connection of trust in reasoning isn't necessarily blinded by emotional, gut-based thinking; rather, it's based on a record of credibility. For example, we may encounter people on a day-to-day basis that we like or don't like, either of which does not matter (i.e. the emotional connection isn't key); however, we can consider previous encounters with this individual and whether or not they have an established record of credibility and, perhaps likewise, CT. For example, there are some intelligent, good thinkers out there who I do not like on a personal level. Regardless of my feelings for them, I would likely trust the conclusions they draw from their reasoning.

Broadly speaking, it might be that strategically utilising emotion may facilitate the changing of a person's mind, when necessary, as may establishing trust (e.g. credibility). Such perspectives are consistent with research that suggests that successful mind-changing is linked with both the patterns of interaction and the type of language used, such as on social media platforms (Tan et al., 2016). However, it's also worth noting that this largely happens in situations where such individuals are open-minded and willing to change (i.e. consistent with a positive disposition towards CT), which may not always be the case when you're attempting to change someone's mind in real-world scenarios. With that, depending on the real-

94   Changing Minds

world situation you find yourself in, those who typically apply CT – who you may typically 'trust' – also may not be applying it in that specific context. Remember, regardless of how commonly one practises CT, it may well go out the window for them when dealing with a controversial or sensitive topic that has personal meaning for them.

A few years ago, news broke out of a scandal occurring over half a century ago involving a vulnerable cohort of people. The nature of the scandal is not important; rather, the strategy decided upon for 'easing the scandal's effects' is what is notable, as it could have yielded some potentially harmful outcomes (though unintentional) to some members of said cohort. I saw this as an interesting opportunity to learn something about CT, and so I presented an argument on my personal social media regarding the potentially harmful effects of the solution strategy and encouraged discussion in the thread below. Notably, the scandal did not affect me or any of my loved ones in any way – I had no 'chips in the pot', so to speak; thus, it was easier for me to write this in an objective manner, void of bias (as much as it could be). After about a week, I went back to check the responses – I didn't care about likes or shares, only active engagement through comments. Eight individuals left comments, of whom six were other academics. Altogether, only one person agreed outright with the premise presented and only two other individuals provided commentary pertinent to the proposition of considering an alternative solution strategy (i.e. only three of the eight provided commentary *relevant* to the argument). Of course, eight participants is not a particularly healthy sample size. Moreover, it could well be that many more read the post and chose not to add a comment (despite my encouragement), in which case it could have been that, actually, a majority agreed with me or, alternatively, an even larger majority disagreed with me (maybe they were being practical). Regardless, analysing the numbers was not my aim. Instead, I was more interested in *why* people would either agree or disagree, that is, the rationale behind their perspective. I wanted to see the threads of logic and the types of argumentation that people would use. Of course, I anticipated differing viewpoints – this was a highly sensitive topic – it was the reasoning that interested me. From this exercise, I recognised that when faced with a 'sensitive' topic that may affect people on differing personal levels, those who usually think critically (i.e. based on the number of academics who left comments and their successes in academia) can, in some situations, fail to engage the inferential logic within a debate and, instead, engage the information presented from an emotionally charged perspective.

Similarly, my wife once engaged a post on her own social media feed in which a former researcher, who promotes science education and research, argued that females are, on a large scale, very often subject to misogyny in the STEM (science, technology, engineering and mathematics) fields through incessant 'mansplaining'; and, subsequently, she encouraged her female 'followers' to share their experiences. My wife is an engineer and has often worked in male-dominated offices. She shared her experiences of a pleasant work life (without any experience of sexism), as had been encouraged by the poster; acknowledged that hers was but only one experience; then addressed the initial claim by stating that there could be a potentially damaging effect to the promotion of females in STEM fields by painting the picture for younger female followers that such fields are rife with misogyny; and finally recommended that another method of encouraging female involvement in STEM might be useful. The poster responded to my wife, among other commenters who reported similarly pleasant experiences, in a dismissive manner and advised my wife, specifically, to 'check her internal misogyny'. The poster then argued that my wife's anecdotal evidence was not credible and that only empirical, research evidence should be considered.

Of course, I agree with the poster – anecdotal evidence is not credible, and only empirical, research evidence should be considered; however, she failed to initially present any credible research either (see, again, Hitchens' razor). Moreover, the poster specifically asked for personal accounts, and when she got a good few, like my wife's – contrary to her beliefs – she dismissed them, 'moving the goalposts' along the way. My wife did not engage any further. She recognised that the type of response she received, despite coming from a learned individual who likely engages CT on a regular basis, was one infused with too much passion and emotion – suggesting that engaging further with someone emotionally fuelled might well be a futile waste of energy.

To reiterate, these two anecdotes (yes, I'm aware of the irony) reinforce the notion that everyone is susceptible to the negative effects of emotion on CT. It doesn't matter how often you engage CT, there will be times when your gut takes control. Moreover, people blinded by emotion aren't necessarily lacking in CT – they may just not be engaging it right at that moment. Though they may be otherwise credible sources of information, when emotion creeps in, CT is evaded. If that's the case, they probably are not likely to change their mind. Open-mindedness and willingness – required for mind-changing – are not likely in such cases.

Rationalisation: Who Are You Trying to Convince, Me or Yourself?

Changing one's own mind – like changing others' – is not an easy task. We will get into that a little bit later, but one specific way in which we do change our own minds (easily and often) isn't a particularly useful strategy for CT – rationalising our decisions and actions. We've all rationalised bad decisions – be it buying something you couldn't afford or didn't need, doing something you knew was wrong but wanted to do anyway or opting out of something that you should have done. We always seem to find a way to justify our decisions. However, we don't really succeed in justifying the decisions; rather, we deceive ourselves into *believing* that there's a solid logic behind them. Often, we're completely oblivious to this deception; and other times we know – deep down – what we are doing. This distinction is reflected by two types of rationalising: prospective and retrospective. *Prospective rationalising* refers to rationalising a decision before making it, whereas *retrospective rationalising* refers to rationalising a decision after the fact.

So, why do we do it? If you've noticed themes forming throughout this book, you can probably guess the twofold answer to this question. Arguably, there's a different answer for each type of rationalising, but I consider it one twofold answer because they're so interdependent. To elaborate, in the case of retrospective rationalising, the answer is that *we don't like to be wrong*. In the case of prospective rationalising, *we are emotional beings that typically act on gut-level intuitive judgment*.

The two are interdependent in the sense that it's about protecting our ego, protecting the manner in which we perceive ourselves and how we feel about ourselves – our self-schemas – and, as a knock-on effect, our concern for how others perceive us. In this context, a fitting way of considering rationalisation is as a defence mechanism used to facilitate what we want or how we want to feel, while at the same time preserving positive self-perception – and again, perhaps, others' perceptions of us – in light of a poor decision we've made based on gut-level thinking.

Take, for example, a prospective rationalisation: 'I know I can't afford this coat, but I never buy myself anything nice and this is something I really want.' In this case, our gut is telling us what we want. Our RJ should be asking questions like 'Do you even need a coat right now? If so, is there a more financially suitable option?' After our gut wins, we often reflect a bit on it after the fact. We might feel a bit guilty. We reiterate the rationalisation. However, if the rationalisation was truly *rational*, it's likely

Rationalisation

that we would have elected to return the coat or not buy it in the first place. But, we don't do that; we maintain the deception.

With respect to retrospectively rationalising a decision, it's not that we knew we were making a poor decision in advance (though that poor decision might have been emotional or gut-level in nature); rather, it's about 'saving face' – protecting our self-perception. For example, you know you've made a bad decision when you directly experience the negative outcomes. 'How could you be so foolish?' We don't want to be perceived as foolish – be it by others or by ourselves; so we explain, as reasonably as we can, why that decision was initially made (e.g. finding a scapegoat: 'Yeah it ended up being wrong, but had it not been for X, Y or Z, then the mistake would never have been made!').

The concept of rationalising decisions can sometimes be closely related to the concept of cognitive dissonance (i.e. having thoughts, attitudes or beliefs inconsistent with your actions). My favourite example of cognitive dissonance, in this context, is that of smoking. In our modern world, smokers know what smoking does. It's expensive and it decreases your life expectancy. They know this. Even if they state that they want to quit, it's tough. So, they rationalise why they're still smoking – 'I'm addicted; I tried quitting once, but the withdrawal was too much for me.' Some smokers just like it too much and don't want to quit – 'I'm still young and have plenty of time to quit before there are any real health risks.' It seems there's a rationale for every choice and every attitude, even if the rationale isn't that rational – even if we know better.

Rationalising our decisions boils down to engaging emotion during the decision-making process. What do we want? Are we right to want this? If 'yes' to the latter, then no harm. If 'no' to the latter, then we often revert back to the first question and say 'we want it' – and that's our decision made. But, at the same time, we don't want to give in to it because when it comes to decision-making, we want to feel justified and we want to be right, and, likewise, perceived as such. Emotionally based decisions do not facilitate this the way logic does, because a logical decision is one based on evaluating inferential relationships among various objective justifications. In context, emotionally charged gut-level processing is only concerned with what you want.

However, the use of emotion can be dressed up – semantically, for example. Intuitive judgment is evolutionarily adaptive and is often a useful cognitive tool to have in our arsenal, so much so that some schools of thought celebrate it as a 'go to', as previously discussed. We often romanticise the concept in popular culture. Similarly, think of times you've heard rationalisations that suggest 'it felt right' or 'something inside me told me this was the right way to go'. These are common justifications, but nevertheless completely illogical for important decisions. Simply, this is *emotion* dressed up as something many people value – *gut-based decision-making*. Even this explanation serves as an example: 'who would you rather listen to, someone who lets emotion steer their decision-making or someone who always goes with their gut?' Of course, we know these are the same thing; but, the latter sounds far more attractive and is perhaps why so many seem to have embraced it. It's because someone who goes with their gut sounds like someone with assuredness and confidence, someone we can trust. Of course, intuitive judgments are often right and, perhaps, this further facilitates continued belief in this perspective; but, that's not sufficient when it comes to CT.

One final consideration regarding rationalisation is that, sometimes, the person *doesn't really want to* be right. Again, that comes down to disguising our thinking. In such cases, we rationalise when we know we are wrong so that the poor decision doesn't seem to result from poor thinking but rather from a forgiving line of reasoning that is disguised as logic. For example, 'I bought this new tablet because my other one is going to die soon and this one was on sale.' It's forgiving because, as we're generally kind to ourselves (i.e. biased in favour of ourselves), we provide a reasonable justification (or two in this case) but, at the same time, 'accidentally on purpose' omit relevant information and/or reasoning (e.g. 'though it was on sale, there were still cheaper options that would have sufficed' or 'do I really need a tablet when I have a phone and laptop?'), which we know, deep down, will likely debunk the logic behind our actions. This form of rationalising is essentially confirmation bias. Notably, acknowledging the potential for confirmation bias, in all our important decision-making, is a very useful mechanism for decision-making. That is, acknowledging what we want or feel when making a decision can facilitate us in addressing such emotion honestly and could enable better reasoning. For example, start by asking yourself, *what do I want to happen?* Then proceed being mindful of said desire.

Changing One's Own Mind

When was the last time you changed your mind about something? I'm not talking about what takeout you're getting or which album by The Clash is your favourite – I mean something ideologically 'big', maybe even controversial. This is another one of those questions I ask in my CT classes. Unfortunately, very few hands ever go up. How can we expect to change other people's minds if we're not willing to change our own? If we are willing to engage all of the information presented in this chapter, how can we not be better able, if not at the very least better willing, to reflect on our own thinking and amend it, as necessary, from time to time?

So, again, when was the last time you changed your mind about something big? It doesn't matter what it was – the content isn't important – rather, what mechanics or logic led you there? Just as it's difficult to change other people's minds, it's hard to change your own, given all our emotions and biases, as well as making sure that our willingness and dispositional inclinations (e.g. open-mindedness and perseverance) can overcome such boundaries.

A few years back, when I saw the lack of hands go up in class, I shared a personal example with this particular cohort of students – how I had changed my mind about a certain controversial issue – because it was of topical relevance (as it still is at the time of writing). I'm not going to mention the topic here because (1) I don't want to come across as preachy on the issue, (2) it might bias you and your reading of this book in some way (which I don't want) and (3) because the topic is not relevant to the points I'm trying to make here. In any case, later that week, I shared it on my blog. The students took it on board and little was said to me about it after class, other than that they enjoyed the debate I created around it as a class exercise. Comments regarding the blog were very different.

The topic in question is largely political in its implications (hence my second reason for not identifying it) – and, as I've alluded to before, I don't like politics (again, see Chapter 9 for a detailed discussion). Nevertheless, feelings one way or another typically align with one political perspective or the other. I must admit, though, that this may be why I find the topic so interesting. The comments back were a mixed bag; of course, those who disagreed called me this, that and the other. Those who agreed lauded me as a true voice of reason. I didn't care about either. These responses were not surprising given that I had refuted the former's and confirmed the latter's already existing beliefs. I was more interested in if I changed anyone else's mind – be it to see things from my perspective or maybe even have the logic backfire altogether. I genuinely don't know if I did change anyone's mind, but I wanted to provide a schematic or a template of some sort for how I did it for my own change of mind. I mention all of this because I urge you to take some time, on a regular basis, to question yourself on why you take certain sides on certain issues. Does the schematic you inevitably end up constructing facilitate a genuinely logical support of your perspective? Is it based on belief? Is it emotionally charged? Is it a rationalisation? Simply, ask yourself why you believe it. Then, ask yourself if there are any contexts in which you don't believe it. Such caveats might facilitate you in advancing this 'schematic' further.

Going back to me not wanting to be 'preachy' about this 'mystery topic' – that's honest; I don't. But, I recognise that may seem like a contradiction, given I'm rather preachy about other topics throughout this book. A more accurate explanation is that I don't want to come across as preachy *about a belief I have*. The truth is that my beliefs about the topic, or any topic, *don't matter*, and that's primarily why I'm not getting into that discussion here. My beliefs don't matter, just as *your beliefs* don't matter, because that's all they are – beliefs. As we address throughout this book, beliefs don't carry any real weight in CT (other than the negative effect that they can have on CT), because they are not empirically supported. For example, I can believe all day long that the Earth is flat, but that's simply not going to make it so.

Concluding Thoughts

Perhaps the most solid takeaway from this chapter is that it's hard to change people's minds on something. Sure, recommendations and advice have been offered; but, there are a good few caveats – the words you use, the order in which you use them, how you use them, your rapport with the person, the person's disposition, their willingness, their open-mindedness, their 'closeness' to the topic at hand, their trust in you. The list seems to go on; and, perhaps, that's why not engaging any further is recommended in some cases (i.e. when these 'stars don't align'). To reiterate, one of the biggest problems we have in changing our minds is overcoming the notion that what we hold in our mind as true may actually not be, alongside the associated implications of this realisation (e.g. amending a worldview). We must separate fact from fiction – truth (for as long as it remains unfalsified) from belief (what we want to be true). Change is not easy – for ourselves or for others – but if we want to think critically, we must be willing, open-minded and develop an inclination for finding the truth, even if that truth is not the one we wanted.

CHAPTER 7

Eureka Moments, Problem-Solving and Creativity

Problem-solving is among the most common applications of CT, refer-ring to the generation and selection of a solution(s), among alternatives, to an identified problem in light of a likewise identified goal. Despite the strong focus of CT research on the application of *argumentation* in real-world settings (Saiz & Rivas, 2023), *problem-solving* may be the most important application of CT because it can be considered as the founda-tion for each of the other CT applications, including argumentation (Dwyer, 2017). In my first book, I discussed how problem-solving can be similarly conceptualised in two ways: (1) as a procedural map (akin to Halpern, 2014; i.e. a problem is the gap between where you are and your goal; and, in bridging the gap the problem-solver selects the best route(s) to take, through consideration of options, givens, barriers and acknow-ledgment of sub-goals) and (2) as a list of steps (see Table 7.1). Both the map and the list can be manipulated in a variety of ways to facilitate the problem-solving process (working backwards, brainstorming, recycling through steps, means–ends analysis, difference reduction, inversion, etc.).

As we can see from Table 7.1, when done right, problem-solving does not 'jump the gun'. We are methodical with it and take our time with it because we care about how problems affect us; and so we care about finding the best means of overcoming these problems (if it happens to be through verbal-reasoning or argumentation, so be it). Of course, we may not treat all problems with the same care. Some will be more important to us than others, to other people and vice versa. Indeed, problem-solving is varied across society with respect to its contextual importance and perspectives on approaches to it. Among the most common of these diverse perspectives are those based in creative thinking, which will be explored throughout the remainder of this chapter.

101

102   Eureka Moments, Problem-Solving and Creativity

Table 7.1 *Problem-solving checklist (adapted from Dwyer, 2017; Hopwood, 1974; Robbins & Judge, 2007)*

Step	Description
1. Define the problem	Identify the cause(s) of the problem and goals to be achieved, as well as ask when, where, why, how and to whom is this problem happening?
2. Gather and organise the available information	Collate the analysed information from the last step and any additionally learned information and, subsequently, structure the scenario in light of this information, according to, for example, goal(s), obstacles, options and givens.
3. Evaluate possible strategies	The strengths and weaknesses of potential strategies must be assessed in context; strategy use is dictated by both the type of problem encountered and the information that is available.
4. Generate possible solutions	Identify potential solutions that are both contextually logical and feasible, in light of the solutions' diverse implications.
5. Monitor the progress of the solution strategy	Procedural functioning must be regulated, such as through assessing whether or not results thus far are commensurate with expectations.
6. Evaluate results of the solution strategy	Assess and re-evaluate work, results and outcomes of the strategic process; such assessment might be automatic (e.g. confirming whether a solution to a mathematics problem is correct) or lengthy (e.g. assessing the success of a three-month intervention).
7. Verify the solution	Confirm that the problem has been solved and/or the goal has been achieved, following all necessary evaluations; achieved through success in light of whether or not it worked, its consequences, its feasibility and its cost-effectiveness.

Eureka Moments

Archimedes is often credited for coining the term *eureka*, from the Ancient Greek meaning 'I have found it!' Though the use of eureka isn't typically associated with literally finding an item per se, the exclamation is contextually appropriate given that the notion of 'eureka' is typically conceived of as implying that an individual has been searching for an answer, solution, invention or some other thinking-based breakthrough, and that its discovery warrants celebration. It may come to them soon after posing the question or problem scenario to themselves, or minutes, days, perhaps even years later. Regardless, when it comes, there is generally some form of excitement and/or relief that accompanies the discovery.

Arguably, the term is dated – rarely do we hear it stated aloud anymore (picture someone jumping from their seats with index finger pointed towards the sky). But, that doesn't mean that 'eureka moments' cease to occur – the celebratory feeling associated with them remains felt by anyone who has just solved a difficult problem or come up with an idea. Of course, that presents an interesting question: *should solutions that just come to us be celebrated?* If a solution doesn't work or our idea turns out not to be a good one, then obviously it shouldn't. So, when is celebration warranted? Critical thinkers are typically cautious, consistent with the nature of epistemological understanding; so, it may be the case that they may not want to 'count their chickens before they hatch' and celebrate prematurely. When we consider it from this perspective, we might ask ourselves if it's actually a bad thing that the term isn't really engaged any more. It kind of seems that the whole concept of exclaiming joy at the end of an intellectual search is a kind of gut-level response or a failure of self-regulatory processes.

Notably, the term *eureka* is the etymological root for *heuristic* – a decision-making shortcut, like a simplified experience-based protocol for problem-solving – a 'procedure that helps find the adequate, though often imperfect, answers to difficult questions' (Kahneman, 2011, p. 98). I reiterate this point about heuristics because, as we compare them, in ways, to such wonderful, celebrated 'ah ha' eureka moments – ones that just seem to come to us – it may be the case, likewise, that such 'eureka' ideas are less than optimal.

The problem with the notion of a *genuine* eureka moment is that there's no way to instantly recognise whether or not it is 'genuine' with respect to being a good idea. A solution must be evaluated before it can be confirmed as solving the problem (e.g. through simulation via trial and error). So, maybe the celebration associated with the 'eureka moment' shouldn't actually occur upon coming up with the idea or solution but, rather, once it has been evaluated and tested. Admittedly, such delay might make it a bit of an anticlimax (despite the fact that you'll still *feel* that eureka moment, given that we can't turn off intuitive judgment). But then again, if you're after a good idea or solution, sacrificing such a feeling shouldn't be an issue.

As critical thinkers, we know that we can't jump to conclusions. Instead, we engage RJ and choose not to (prematurely) engage such celebration until we know, through evaluation, whether such a solution works. Anticlimactic or not, ensuring the accuracy of an idea or solution should

104 Eureka Moments, Problem-Solving and Creativity

be the only cause for celebration; and, thus, maybe that's when the 'genuine' eureka moment occurs.

The Creative Element of Eureka Moments

Arguably, the use of 'eureka' also implies some form of novelty, given its association with invention – marrying itself, to some extent, with the novelty intrinsic to the notion of *creative thought*. Indeed, creative thinking is often associated with problem-solving (perhaps explaining the to-be-discussed common 'lumping together' of *creative* and *critical* thinking). But, before addressing what is meant by 'creative thinking', I would like for you to take a moment and consider what *you* think of when you encounter the term. Have you a conceptualisation in mind?

When we think of notions of creation and creativity, it's hard not to think of the generation of something from nothing. Of course, the truest meaning of this is borderline unfathomable. For example, cosmologists and astrophysicists have wrestled with the beginnings of the universe for as long as these sciences have existed themselves – not to mention western philosophy and, of course, the longest tradition of creation narratives in religion, theology and mythology.

But, at the same time, we recognise that creations and inventions all have a starting point or lineage. For example, consider sitting down to write a song. You might have a tune in your head inspired by a particular song from The Pogues, so you write yours with a similar chord progression. But then, you might have wanted an 'edgier vibe', so you engineer the guitars a bit to sound more like Stone Temple Pilots. Then, in terms of lyrics, for whatever reason, you're reminded of a long car ride you took with your family when you were twelve, sitting in the back with your headphones on listening to Weezer. So, you borrow from them a bit and a bit from your road trip experience and pen some lyrics. Soon enough, you have created a song. It is a new song – never heard before. Without you, this song would likely never have been brought into existence. However, it did not just appear from the ether. It was developed, little by little, influenced each step of the way by things that came before it. In terms of cognition, can something truly come from nothing? We'll return to this question a little later.

As alluded to earlier, creative and critical thinking often get 'lumped together' as buzzwords within the realm of educational outcomes, and, as a result, people often try to draw links between the two. Indeed, we see this in research as well – as a kind of a 'critico-creative thinking' (e.g. see Fisher,

The Creative Element of Eureka Moments 105

2001). This is understandable. They are both forms of goal-oriented thinking and both focus on construction – be it of a logical argument, a solution strategy or a novel creation. But, while they may share some common features, the two processes are quite distinct. For example, informational input and the products of the thinking processes can vary greatly. As creative thinking is neither the focus of this book nor even this chapter, I will not be examining it in great detail. However, the manner in which it's conceptualised and what that means in relation to applying CT are subtly important and, thus, will be discussed.

For example, in the absence of CT, creative thinking alone is not particularly practical for solving problems or drawing conclusions regarding issues we care about (Sternberg, 2002). This perspective is consistent with recent research by Long and Long (2023) who found that though CT can positively influence creative thinking, creative thinking may not positively influence CT. Though creative thinking is utilised when relatively novel tasks or situations are encountered (Sternberg, 2005), it is vital that RJ be engaged when the novel tasks or situations require careful consideration, like CT (Dwyer, 2017; see, again, Chapter 1). However, it is possible for creative thought to be complementary to CT. Indeed, it may be that the problem here isn't creative thinking per se; rather, it's the way in which creative thinking is conceptualised that is problematic.

Steve Jobs once described creative thinking in terms of 'just connecting things. When you ask creative people how they did something, they feel a little guilty because they didn't really do it, they just saw something. It seemed obvious to them after a while' (Beahm, 2011). Typically, I don't like quoting people when they have nothing to do with the research of the particular topic to which the quote pertains – especially in light of their 'celebrity'. However, I make the exception here because I think Steve Jobs knew a thing or two about creative developments in real-world scenarios and because the quote clearly demonstrates the research-based point made here, in what I think is a particularly accessible way. Simply, we connect existing things, such as ideas, to create new ones (akin to the example earlier regarding the writing of a new song). Notably, this point addresses our previous question regarding something coming from nothing. Sure, some perspectives of creativity may conceptualise it as the generation of something from nothing, but in terms of creative thinking, it seems synthesis, akin to how Jobs describes it, might be closer to the mark.

Consistent with Jobs' perspective, Sternberg (2003, 2006) describes creative thinking from a more grounded research perspective – as the convergence of intellectual abilities, knowledge, thinking strategies, personality and motivation. Subsequently, this may yield a solution or conclusion that is (1) unusual or novel and (2) appropriate or valuable (Halpern, 2014; Runco & Jaeger, 2012; Sternberg, 2010). Notably, there is an incongruence between creative thinking and CT, unless the former is conceptualised as a form of synthesis (as described by Jobs and Sternberg) or – as some in the field of CT might conceive of it – inference (i.e. CT's third core skill; see, again, Chapter 1). If conceptualised in this manner (e.g. as drawing a novel conclusion/solution through synthesising credible, evidence-based ideas), creative thinking is akin to CT. Remember, the products of CT do not have to be unusual or 'novel' (they can corroborate previously inferred perspectives), but when they are, it's through inference afforded by synthesis, consistent with Job's perspective.

Notably, the research-derived description of creative thinking is one that exhibits similarity between it and CT – and I have no problem with that in this context. Indeed, creative thinking is often conceptualised as a component of CT (e.g. again see Halpern, 2014). However, there is a difference between this conceptualisation of creative thinking and more 'popular' perspectives that reflect *thinking with creativity*. Simply, creative thinking is a process that requires evaluation and reflection – it represents good thinking. On the other hand, more 'popular' or even more traditional outlooks on creativity are problematic if our goal is to adopt cognitive processes consistent with CT (e.g. thinking outside the box).

The Problem with Thinking Outside the Box

Thinking 'outside the box' is the primary example I allude to when I refer to both 'popular' and 'traditional' outlooks on creativity. It's also the conceptualisation I imagined would most easily come to mind when I asked earlier in the chapter for you to think of what creative thinking means to you. I acknowledge the somewhat ironic nature of classifying thinking outside the box – something that should be innovative – as a 'traditional' perspective on creativity. But, given the longevity of the buzzword in the zeitgeist, perhaps it's the case that some of the novelty has indeed worn off, particularly in our current critique of it (i.e. in terms of facilitating CT).

Thinking 'outside the box' is an often-romanticised concept; and if that was indeed the conceptualisation of creative thinking you had in mind, maybe that's the reason – perhaps because it implies that the product of thought has not been restricted or bound by some governing force – there is freedom of thought and for expression of ideas. Perhaps its

The Problem with Thinking Outside the Box

attractiveness, similarly, lies in its implication that you are an individual, a rebel against the system, with autonomy to be who you are and live your own life! Yes, very romantic indeed; but it might be the case that you're just asked to apply it on Question 6 of tonight's homework. Moreover, what you actually end up generating might not be particularly practical to apply in real-world scenarios – where there are *actually* restrictions and limitations (remember, done right, creative thinking yields an *appropriate* product). Though it could be that aforementioned romanticised outlook that makes thinking outside the box so appealing, it might also be that it's just simply less burden (e.g. cognitive load) to think outside the box than having to entertain parameters and restrictions in your thinking while simultaneously trying to create something, such as a solution to a problem.

Despite how thinking might 'feel', in the context of CT, 'freedom' should not be one of those feelings. That is, with respect to being 'bound' by useful guidelines for thinking, do not confuse freedom for autonomy. For example, imagine being asked to create a piece of visual art – its topic and focus can be anything you want it to be. Now imagine being asked to do that twice a week over the course of a year. Across the hundred-plus freely creative and original pieces of art, you will likely see emerging patterns and themes. These patterns and themes might represent your interests, thoughts, biases, emotions – things very much personal to you. That's not a criticism at all – we see it in all forms of art. Hell, that's what art is supposed to be – personal expression. But, in the context of CT, this is a problem. That is, when we are liberated of the chains of a problem space's 'restrictions', it's our 'free' thinking that then shackles us, the developers of the ideas and solutions, in light of our interests, biases, emotions and the like.

It's worth considering the notion of free will here, from a behaviourist perspective. The analogy may be a bit of a stretch, but roughly the same psychological mechanics apply. For example, traditional behaviourists might posit that our choices are made not as a result of free agency but, rather, because of behavioural reinforcement over time. If we recognise that certain choices are going to yield predictable, positive outcomes consistent with lessons from the past, we're much more likely to make those choices. Consider again our coffee example from Chapter 2. We have all these options, but I'm not going to go through them all. I'm going with my usual – regular coffee, milk and two sugars. It's what I like and it's what generally works for me. So, in light of this, was choosing my usual an act of free will, or was it simply my experience doing my thinking for me?

Similar again is our argument regarding people typically not liking change. Routine is good; it's dependable. *If it ain't broke, don't fix it*, right?

Eureka Moments, Problem-Solving and Creativity

In applying this logic to concepts of creativity – and art more specifically, as in our earlier example – I'm reminded of my own art class when I was ten years old. I was good at drawing – not the best, but certainly not the worst. I'd safely say I was among the better drawers in my small class. I remember that in this particular school year, I would win praise from my teacher in the first couple of months; but then, when mid-November rolled around, the praise all but disappeared. I remember asking my teacher what was wrong with my work, and she told me that though nothing technically was wrong with it, it seemed all I drew were the same kinds of things over and over. I recall thinking that this was a fair point – I certainly had a penchant for drawing NHL goalies. But then again, they were the subjects I was best at drawing, because I drew them so much – experience, right? My freedom to draw what I wanted ended up inhibiting my ability to create something new. The irony is that, at this stage of my 'art career', I probably would have produced something more creative if some restrictions were placed on the brief.

Of course, this problem doesn't just affect creativity in terms of artistic endeavours; it also impacts problem-solving. Abraham Maslow's famous hammer aphorism springs to mind (i.e. 'when all you have is a hammer, it is tempting to treat everything as if it were a nail'). We have a tendency to approach creativity and problem-solving from an implicitly biased perspective. Simply, you use what you have – regardless of how we perceive the situation to be. It doesn't matter how free you feel you are to 'think outside the box', you are going to use whatever you have available to you to solve your problem as best you can (again, consistent with the availability heuristic), be it a hammer, a repertoire of hockey goalies or a preference for regular coffee.

Moreover, what you have available can be contextually valuable. Consider the things 'you have' from the perspective of extant literature on problem-solving: 'givens' and 'options', in practical settings, provide us parameters for working within closed conditions. On one hand, these might be perceived as restricting; on the other, they are useful tools for progress. Thinking outside the box might wrongfully ignore the one thing that can help you – the parameters. For example, if I'm provided a project brief at work, I'm likely to play by the rules and not go rogue. Using outside-the-box thinking instead of the brief provided might be cute in some educational settings;[1] but, in professional settings, it will likely be 'discouraged' when briefs have been provided.

---

[1] There is an urban myth in Ireland that on one year's national secondary school final exam (the Leaving Certificate) in English, the essay asked, 'What is courage?', with one student answering,

The Problem with Thinking Outside the Box

From a CT standpoint, the crux of the 'creativity issue' in developing solutions to problems boils down to logic and feasibility. To exemplify this in some of my previous classes, I've asked students how they would resolve the problems in Syria (as their civil war was all over the news headlines at the time). Often students return blank stares, even after a few moments of deliberation. They know that this is one of those 'million-dollar questions' and if they solved this problem, they could probably retire the very next day. Using 'creativity', some might argue that one solution would be to 'nuke' Syria. I've heard such solutions in the past – not just with respect to Syria but other countries as well. Responses to such a suggestion typically range from sarcastic giggling to utter disgust. Of course, I do not support this solution; however, for all intents and purposes associated with the problem presented (and the way it was presented), it does solve the problem. 'No more Syria (or whatever country you'd like to insert into this line), no more problem.' However, though the solution overcomes the problem, the solution also yields other, obviously, undesirable outcomes – which is not logical. Moreover, it's not feasible – morally, politically or economically. So, no matter how 'creative' a solution may be, in order to work, it must be both logical and feasible in its application; and so creativity-based problem-solving must be used with caution. Note as well the key distinction between a solution developed through 'creativity' and creative thinking. If the latter was used, the solution would not pass the 'appropriate' test, akin to how we might view feasibility from a CT perspective. Again, if we genuinely care about the outcome of our decision-making process, as we would in navigating a problem terrain such as that of a country in the midst of a civil war, *critical* thinking is necessary and *creativity* can be sacrificed.

Another interesting quirk about this particular example is the bias associated with it. Like I said, I've heard the 'nuke solution' before for a range of different countries (I mean no disrespect to Syria or any Syrian readers); however, the one common trait shared by these countries is their lack of proximity to the people making such suggestions. I wonder how many of those people who suggested nuking Syria would likewise

---

simply, 'This is courage', before submitting it as complete to the exam invigilator. Similarly, another urban myth did the rounds during my undergrad that on Professor Wörner's *Introduction to Western Philosophy* final, he picked up and placed a four-legged chair on a table and asked the class to prove that the chair did not exist. Apparently, only one student aced that particular question, the one who simply wrote 'what chair?' Both of these examples provide great representations of outside-the-box thinking, but I doubt either actually happened; and if they did, I can't imagine that they were looked upon favourably by examiners, regardless of how charming they might appear.

Eureka Moments, Problem-Solving and Creativity

recommend nuking a North American or a European country. So, despite the fact that the suggestion (arguably) 'solves' the problem on paper, that doesn't ensure that it isn't completely biased in its generation, hence highlighting the need for engaging assessment of feasibility – again, be it morally, politically or economically.

When our goal is to solve a problem, it is necessary to consider whether it is logical and feasible (appropriate). Such assessment is central to the solution evaluation process. If it fails either of these assessments, then we need to go back to the proverbial drawing board until the solution meets such criteria – again suggesting the importance of parameters for problem-solving. With that, such assessment may not always be possible. For example, in some cases, crucial, relevant knowledge might not be readily available for solving the problem (such as that necessary to examine logic and feasibility). When my class eventually did start providing potential solutions for the 'problems in Syria', they concurrently acknowledged flaws in their solutions given that they did not have enough information on Syria, the conflict or international regulations regarding either the issue at hand or their possible solutions.

On the other hand, situations where such knowledge isn't readily available might actually end up reinforcing the attractiveness of relying on thinking outside the box because that's all that can, arguably, be done on the side of the hypothetical problem-solver. Nevertheless, the critical thinker would look at the scenario and recognise that they need to gather further information before they start working on a solution, no matter how 'creative' it might be. So, if in doubt, one should not resort to proposing a creative solution before all other avenues involving CT have been considered.

Concluding Thoughts

Remember, just because an answer is 'creative' does not make it logical or feasible. I stress this point again, given the popularity of common creative thinking misconceptualisations and their staying power in the zeitgeist, as this freedom to think outside the box – differently to how others would. Of course, different doesn't always mean good.

On the other hand, when done right (i.e. consistent with the aforementioned research-based description), creative thinking is a useful process, particularly when there is a lacking evidence base from which to draw from as input (or when the desired output is not something CT yields). But,

Concluding Thoughts 111

again, this is not an evaluation of creative thinking; rather, it is a warning against popularised notions of 'creativity'.

Again, the real problem with such notions of creativity in CT scenarios is that the credibility (i.e. the source of one 'creative mind'), relevance (e.g. with respect to feasibility or appropriateness), logical strength and even bias (e.g. those who propose to bomb Syria probably don't live in Syria or have loved ones living there) are not necessarily accounted for – and these matter in situations that require CT. However, if you conceptualise creative thought as akin to some form of heightened inference ability (i.e. through the synthesis of appropriate, credible, relevant and logically sound information – connecting things) in which such issues are considered, then creativity holds value for CT. But, then, if that's the case, isn't creativity (i.e. synthesis or a form of inference in this context) already a component of CT? If so, then why all the hoopla? Indeed, what, then, is the point of the majority of this chapter?

There are two major things. First, it would be a disservice to the concept of CT to not explain its distinctions from other 'popular' forms of thought, such as those 'popular' perspectives on creative thinking (remember, the two often get 'lumped' together in terms of how they're discussed in pop culture). Likewise, again, I'm not saying that creative thinking is an inferior form of thinking – it's just a different type of thinking, to be used in different contexts. Sure, it can be used to help support CT, but only if it's done appropriately, as recommended throughout this chapter. Given that the focus of this book is on CT and not creative thinking, of course, we're going to view CT as the star of the show.

Second, even if we treat creativity as a form of inference, we are not working with this form of creativity exclusively. The other components of CT must be engaged. That is, we can think creatively by synthesising information that we have previously thought about critically (i.e. through analysis and evaluation) for the purpose of inferring a logical and feasible conclusion or solution (indeed, good creative thinkers evaluate their own process, just as critical thinkers do); thus, given this caveat, we can infuse our critical thinking with creative thinking, but we must do so, as we do with all relevant thinking, with caution (Dwyer, 2017). Hopefully, this chapter has facilitated some eureka moments for understanding!

CHAPTER 8

Critical Thinking Training

The teaching of CT is one of the most fundamental topics in CT research because of the field's typical focus: CT is important – people need it – but they must work hard to develop it. Of course, CT development doesn't occur in a vacuum. Sure, if you were interested in CT, you might read about it and, through consistent engagement over time, your ability to apply it might improve. But, that might take years. It might not happen at all.

It may be that actual CT training is the optimal way of developing CT. A large body of research indicates that CT can be taught, with such training yielding enhanced CT performance (e.g. Abrami et al., 2008; Abrami et al., 2015; Alvarez-Ortiz, 2007; Dwyer et al., 2012; Gadzella et al., 1996; Hitchcock, 2004; Niu et al., 2013; Reed & Kromrey, 2001; Rimiene, 2002; Solon, 2007; Tiruneh et al., 2014). This is not to say that *all* CT courses will enhance the CT of *every* individual who takes such a class. However, if the individual has the right disposition, at the very least, such semester-long instruction (which is the typical duration of such CT training courses) will provide the training necessary to get the ball rolling on CT development and may expedite the process. Of course, caveats to this assertion exist, particularly with respect to issues of whether what is being taught is actually CT (see, again, Chapter 1) and whether what is being taught is being taught correctly. Simply, if one of the field's primary goals is to get more people to think critically, it should not be surprising that one of the field's focuses is that of teaching CT.

Likewise, my first book on CT was written with a core focus on providing students, teachers and the general public alike an opportunity to learn what CT is and what they can do to enhance it. Indeed, the majority of the book discussed what CT is through a wide array of explanations and activities – largely, from a *teaching* standpoint. In a way, it acted as a history lesson, a CT workbook and a teaching guide.

I like to look at *this* book – the one you're currently reading – as a natural progression on that focus, dealing with ideas related to CT that transcend a detailed 'what is CT?' exposition to a more discussion-driven account of topics that are important to consider for CT more generally. Indeed, Chapter 1 covered the 'what is CT?' in a rather short and sweet manner. Though I could, likewise, rehash much of the content from those 'workbook/teaching guide' chapters in my first book here (in the context of this 'CT Training' chapter), I think discussion of observations and tips for teaching and learning CT, in more practical scenarios, might be more beneficial than simply repeating myself. Essentially, the focus of this chapter is less about what content to teach (that should be obvious from Chapter 1) than, rather, how that content *can be taught*. However, I also recognise that some of you might be saying to yourselves, 'I'm not a teacher and I'm not a student; so, this chapter doesn't matter to me.' Maybe it doesn't. However, maybe you're interested in one day taking a class in CT – maybe that's why you bought this book. Maybe you're only now thinking about such a possibility in light of reading this book – great. As earlier, it may very well be the case that to optimally enhance your ability to think critically, some form of training is necessary. If that is your goal, I'd recommend engaging such training. So, if you're not a teacher or a student, yet you're open to at some stage taking a CT course, consider the following discussion as advice on what to look for in such training.

In Preparation of Content and Materials

In the past, I've enjoyed opportunities to give talks and make presentations on developing CT courses and integrating CT into the classroom, across a diverse range of disciplines. These talks and presentations typically open up very interesting discussions with other educators around conceptualisation, instructional typology, methods of assessment and methods of delivery. As addressed previously, we've already covered conceptualisation at length in Chapter 1, so it doesn't really bear repeating here. Thus, let's start with typology.

Instructional Typology

Consistent with concerns over how CT content is taught, it's important to acknowledge that CT can be the focus of a course at varying levels. Beyond making clear the nature of CT (such as through definitions, examples and even showing people where their strengths and weaknesses, in this context, lie) is that of making explicit the nature of the instruction. For example,

114 Critical Thinking Training

according to Ennis' (1989) typology of CT courses, there are four different CT training methods:

1. *General approach* – actual CT skills and dispositions 'are learning objectives, without specific subject matter content' (Abrami et al., 2008, p. 1105).
2. *Infusion approach* – requires specific subject matter content upon which CT skills are practised, in which the objective of teaching CT within the course content is made explicit.
3. *Immersion approach* – like the infusion approach, specific course content upon which CT skills are practised is required; however, CT objectives in the immersed approach are not made explicit.
4. *Mixed approach* – CT is taught independently of the specific subject matter content of the course.

Meta-analytic research has revealed that the immersion approach – the only one that does *not* make CT objectives explicit to students – had the smallest effect on CT outcomes; that making CT objectives and requirements clear to students may be a crucial aspect of course design aimed at increasing CT ability; and that the enhancement of CT ability is greatly dependent upon how CT is taught (Abrami et al., 2008; see also Abrami et al., 2015).

Though it may seem obvious that if CT is a desired learning outcome, then it should be explicitly taught, I can't tell you how many classes I've sat through as a student where CT was identified as a core learning outcome in our first class but never mentioned again after that. This is even worse when it shows up in the class's title! Often, as well, is its appearance on graded assessment materials (e.g. a term paper); but many of those classes never bothered to detail *what* needs to be done, *when* it needs to be done or *why* it's to be done. So, how is the student supposed to know what the lecturer wants? Sometimes, it's like educators assume that students will just figure it out themselves through engaging the opportunities provided. Again, opportunities to engage CT are vital to its development; but it needs to be made clear how CT is to be applied during such opportunities – especially when CT is a core focus of the class!

Classes with dedicated CT components are more likely to succeed, as Abrami and colleagues (2008, 2015) recommend (e.g. *Critical Thinking 101*), but a class on 'CT in Psychology', 'CT in Approaches to History' or 'CT in Sociological Applications' may require a bit of extra effort, depending on how the relationship between CT and the target domain is conceptualised. For instance, in the latter example, a poor approach would be to just present classes on current events, discussed through sociological theory, and then assume that students will apply CT because you had previously presented them a set of procedural strategies. Students may fail to gain in CT ability but learn a great deal about sociological theory – the latter being nice but not necessarily the purpose of the class. On the other hand, a better approach would be to teach CT – what it is and what it involves – but to do so using examples from a domain-specific topic area (e.g. sociology, if the class is 'CT in Sociological Applications'). In this approach, the student is learning about CT and how to apply it – the primary outcome of the class – but, also learning about, say, sociological theory as a consequence of applying CT. This sounds like a win-win, but a real fear here is that students might finish the course and only be able to apply CT in domains specific to which they were learned (e.g. sociology), hence an important reason why a 'mixed approach' was found to have the strongest effect on CT outcomes (see, again, Abrami et al., 2008).

Assessment Design

With respect to the other topics that typically arise in discussion at my presentations on integrating CT into educational settings, the issue of assessment is rather simple, despite the barriers that surround it. That is, there is a wide array of CT assessments on the market (e.g. the California Critical Thinking Skills Test (CCTST; Facione, 1990b); the Cornell Critical Thinking Test (CCTT; Ennis et al., 1985); the Ennis–Weir Critical Thinking Essay Test (EWCTET; Ennis & Weir, 1985); the Halpern Critical Thinking Assessment (HCTA; Halpern, 2010); the Watson–Glaser Critical Thinking Assessment (WGCTA; Watson & Glaser, 1980)); but, unfortunately, a majority of them utilise a multiple-choice question format (MCQ). The beauty of MCQ assessment formats is that they are pretty easy for teachers and markers to grade. However, MCQs cannot appropriately measure CT, given that all it takes to answer such a question is to recognise the correct answer (e.g. see Halpern, 2003). CT educators want their students to engage, but there's no real engagement with MCQs; for example, you might be asked to answer forty MCQs in sixty minutes – that's a minute and a half per question and, I would argue, not enough time to appropriately apply RJ for purposes of arriving at a critically considered conclusion/solution. Sure, an answer might be correct, but was any real CT put into it? Moreover, one could guess the right answer when they haven't a clue – and with fairly decent odds too (e.g. 1/5, 1/4 or 1/3)!

116   Critical Thinking Training

On the other hand, open-ended questions that require longer answers have their drawbacks as well. First, such essay-style questions don't necessarily ensure that CT needs to be engaged. For example, I once took over the teaching of a CT module in which the only method of assessment was the final exam, which, for the preceding three years consecutively, asked the same question: *what is critical thinking?* The question was hilariously ludicrous, given that it perpetuated the antithesis to CT – more or less inviting students to have memorised a definition. Nowhere on the paper were students asked to critically evaluate anything. The issue here is that the open-ended question needs to elicit engagement through CT skills and RJ, not the recall of information. With that, this issue is, I suppose, easily remedied through amending the wording of the question(s). For example, you could give students two hours to answer three essay-style questions that present problem-based scenarios or arguments to evaluate. However, this leads to a second drawback of the essay-style format, which is perhaps less easy to remedy – it has been observed that such essay-length responding strategies are biased in favour of those proficient in writing (such as on the EWCTET, among other related issues, see Adams et al., 1996; Taube, 1997). That is, exam markers may be impressed with the articulate nature of certain essays and look more favourably upon them than others in terms of their evaluation of actual CT. With that, 'good communication', such as through writing, is an important aspect of CT (e.g. with respect to being clear in one's logic). However, just because someone is poor at communicating that logic doesn't mean they lack it.

Perhaps, somewhere in the 'middle' is optimal with respect to response strategy. For my assessment of domain-general CT, I use an adapted version of the HCTA as my class's final exam, where students are given sufficient time[1] to answer fifteen short, open-ended response questions (three questions each for the five common applications of CT: hypothesis testing, verbal reasoning, argumentation, problem-solving and judging likelihood and uncertainty; see Dwyer, 2017; Halpern, 2014). These short, open-ended questions allow for up to approximately five lines for a response – as opposed to a full essay.

---

[1] If in a lecture hall or exam setting, two hours are provided (if necessary), simply from a scheduling perspective. By rights, unlimited time should be allowed (i.e. to facilitate RJ), but that's sometimes not the case because of practical reasons such as the aforementioned scheduling. With that, the two hours have always been sufficient (at least to my knowledge). In some contexts (e.g. 'pre-course' assessment), students complete the assessment at home where they pretty much have as much time as they need, which does well to facilitate the RJ aspect of it all. Notably, the 'answers' are not easily found online in the event that students want to engage some 'dishonest behaviour'.

In Preparation of Content and Materials 117

Notably, this assessment isn't exactly something you can study for per se, with respect to content. Someone with an already well-developed capacity for CT could walk into the exam and do quite well without any prep. I recognise that there could be a 'fairness' issue here, particularly for those students who worked very hard and made significant progress from the course's start to finish.

To account for this, the 'final' is only worth a minor percentage of the class's overall grade. The bulk of their grade is dictated by a term paper that they are allotted a semester's worth of time to research, think about and write – a critical evaluation of some topic core to CT. So, what's the point of even measuring domain-general CT as a 'final' if it's not worth a significant proportion of the mark? Well, the other thing I do is administer a different version of the final at the outset of the class – another set of fifteen short, open-ended response questions from the original HCTA. What this facilitates is a pre-course assessment to be compared with a post-course assessment – consistent with my aforementioned research regarding mature students in CT classes (Dwyer & Walsh, 2019). This comparison facilitates a personalised perspective for students on how much their CT developed over the duration of the course. A student may only score a 'C' grade on the final, but given that they failed on the pre-class assessment (which doesn't go towards their marks), they can see that this improvement is substantial, particularly when you compare it against a 'B' grade on the final of someone who had already scored a 'B' on the pre-class assessment. Essentially, it serves as a reality check for some students and, for others, as a well-deserved boost of confidence that may have been otherwise unacknowledged.

One further methodological consideration for assessment that I wholeheartedly advocate for is assessing *often*. That is, ensure students are engaging in CT outside the classroom on a regular basis, as best you can – provide them with opportunities to develop their RJ. For example, in my dedicated CT classes, I assign short, weekly assignments (typically requiring fifteen–twenty minutes each), in addition to the term paper and pre-post assessment strategy described earlier, to ensure that my students have as many opportunities as reasonably possible to develop their CT without bombarding them with work. I say 'reasonably possible' here because I could give them more work (i.e. fifteen–twenty minutes per week isn't a lot), but in light of all the groans and pushback I get from students upon providing them their schedule of work, it appears that this is their threshold. In fairness, if they approach preparation of the term paper appropriately, they will be working on that during the week too.

118 Critical Thinking Training

Active Learning and Knowing Your Cohort

Active learning is a fundamental component of CT instruction. In fact, instruction is probably a poor word here – training is a better fit given that instruction, in the didactic sense of the word (e.g. sitting in class for an hour and listening to the educator 'teach'), should only be a portion of CT training. Specifically, CT training should utilise a mixed approach of didactic instruction *and* active learning. According to Mayer (2004), students should be cognitively engaged during learning (beyond that of constructing knowledge through listening and reading), and educators must provide them opportunities to do so, coupled with guided practice. This type of active learning provides students with a form of *scaffolding* (Wood et al., 1976), whereby they are guided didactically by their educator and also actively 'learn by doing'. Research suggests that people learn more through active learning (e.g. Hake, 1998; Laws et al., 1999; Redish et al., 1997) and, more specifically, that intensive practice of CT skills increases CT ability more so than didactic teaching of CT (Burbach et al., 2004). Moreover, active learning (such as through class exercises) provides a useful and natural break from instruction, with respect to educators simply talking to students. Such breaks are important, as research has shown that didactically teaching students for durations longer than fifteen minutes can substantially decrease attention to the source of instruction (Wankat, 2002). Essentially, students will 'turn off' if didactic instruction goes on for too long.

Worth noting, in the context of CT training, is argument mapping as a form of active learning. An argument map (which is largely distinct from a mind map or concept map; see Dwyer, 2011) is a visual representation of a logically structured network of reasoning, in which the argument is made unambiguous and explicit via a 'box and arrow' design where the boxes represent propositions (i.e. the central claim, reasons, objections and rebuttals) and the 'arrows' among propositions indicate the inferential relationships linking the propositions together (Dwyer, 2011; Van Gelder, 2002). Research indicates that training CT through argument mapping significantly enhances CT performance (Alvarez-Ortiz, 2007; Butchart et al., 2009; Dwyer et al., 2011, 2012; Van Gelder, 2001; Van Gelder et al., 2004). Learning CT with argument maps – be it evaluating previously completed maps or constructing them from scratch – can be a useful means of keeping students actively engaged and facilitating assimilation through visual representation.

With respect to knowing what educational strategies are feasible, it's important for educators to familiarise themselves with their student cohort

As the Course Unfolds 119

before even walking into the classroom (e.g. demographics). I've taught many diverse cohorts over the years, and being aware of demographics (e.g. educational level, educational history, socio-economic background, male/female split) has been very useful for how I approach my content and strategies. However, when it comes to thinking about active learning strategies in particular, perhaps the most important cohort characteristic to be aware of in advance is the number of students in the class.

Knowing your audience size is crucial for determining what level of active learning can be successfully integrated into your training sessions and/or how that active learning is conducted/represented. For example, if you have a small group of approximately ten individuals, opening the floor to collaborative discourse is a useful means of practising CT. However, if you have a lecture hall filled with 300 students, open discourse is not likely to be feasible. With a larger group, informally picking people out of the crowd and asking them what they think might work for you.[2] If you feel that you might come across like you're 'putting people on the spot' by doing this, perhaps polling your students will work better (e.g. through a 'clicker system'). The point is that, regardless of what size your audience is, you need to find a way to keep everyone actively engaged!

As the Course Unfolds

Questions

One of my favourite observations from teaching undergraduate CT is that even though students claim to, they very often don't know what educators mean by CT. Consistent with our discussion from Chapter 1, 'too many people today use the term CT in ways that are vague and at cross-purposes with how others use the term' (Couch, 2012, p. 8). Notably, a fun exercise (particularly for the educator) is to get students to define it in their own terms before presenting a definition. Assuming that there is a mistake in the definition (e.g. equating it to creative thinking, failing to acknowledge a dispositional aspect or thinking of it as a skill as opposed to a collation of

---

[2] I like this method better than the common 'raise your hand' approach (though I always encourage students to raise their hands when they have a question). As mentioned elsewhere in this book, students don't always raise their hands, and they need to do so if they're going to engage in this form of active learning. On the other hand, when students do raise their hands, it's often the same people over and over, which is less than ideal for a number of reasons. Thus, picking people out from the audience is my preferred route (I do my best to make people feel like I'm not 'putting them on the spot').

cognitive processes), such an exercise might provide you an opportunity to see where people might be getting things wrong and, perhaps, what to put additional focus on in their training. Moreover, it gives you an opportunity to 'debunk' such misconceptions from the get-go. Even though students often don't know what is meant by CT, there is a tendency for them to nod their heads in agreement with whatever educators say about it thereafter, because no one wants to look foolish.

'Does Anyone Have any Questions?'
Nothing. Not a single hand goes up. With that, maybe there genuinely are no questions, but in larger classes – say with over 100 people – it's more likely than not that there is at least one question. The lack of hands up would be of some concern had we not engaged the earlier 'definition exercise', where we can at least address a few discrepancies in conceptualising what we're talking about. For CT instruction to be effective, (1) instructors need to acknowledge the discrepancies among 'understandings' (i.e. discrepancies between educators' and students' understandings, as well as understandings among educators themselves (e.g. again see Eigenauer, 2017; Lloyd & Bahr, 2010)) and (2) students' pre-existing understandings (sometimes inaccurate) must be addressed (Bransford et al., 2000). These considerations, like CT, are metacognitive in their own right; for example, in this context, students are required to *think about their thinking* (Flavell, 1976, 1979). If the diverse perspectives that students hold prior to training are not engaged, they may fail to grasp newly taught concepts, and may fail to understand how they can coordinate their knowledge with the knowledge of others and apply it to real-world problems, which is essentially CT in practice! Besides, it's useful for everyone involved to engage discussion regarding coming to know new terms and what they mean – elaboration yields better understanding (e.g. Dansereau, 1988; Newbern et al., 1994).

The smartest man I ever met was a high school teacher of mine, Tony Nappi. He was a physicist before getting into teaching, the latter of which he did for about twenty-five years before retiring. He taught me maths during my freshman and sophomore years and, as a learned man with interests above and beyond maths and science, he taught Shakespeare as well, a class that I took in my senior year. Ours was the last class he taught prior to retirement. Nappi and I became good friends over my high school career, sharing an interest in film and film analysis. Don't get me wrong, I had no problem socialising with friends my own age; but, whenever I had the chance, I'd use one of my free periods to run up to Nappi to talk about whatever film I had seen the night before, provided he had the time.

As the Course Unfolds 121

I'll never forget my first day of classes with him as a freshman: he opened his briefcase on the desk and pulled out the syllabus, from which he read. The open briefcase, with the front facing the class, had a sheet of paper stuck to it, upon which was a single written word, large enough for the whole class to see: LIVER. Nappi finished reading the syllabus and asked if anyone had any questions. A few hands went up inquiring about liver. 'It's important to ask questions,' he responded. 'Those who ask them are typically rewarded with the information they need.' The people who raised their hand asking about liver were further rewarded through not having to do homework that night. Nappi never spoke to us about liver again, but an important lesson was learned after only five minutes of our first class.

I've since picked up this gimmick for my classes – my CT class in particular. Perhaps there's a difference between high school and university students in this regard, or maybe it's a cultural or even a generational thing, but only seldom do I get a hand up about liver. When I get no response, I'm forced to 'explain the joke'. As it turns out, that ends up being as impactful because the students get to see the disappointment on my face resulting from no one asking about it. I know this because students come back to me after the semester's completion and mention it as an important learning experience. I suppose that's why I still do it. Though silly (and sometimes embarrassing), it is worth doing even if only one person in the room gets something from it.

As Nappi was trying to get across to us, if a student has a question, they do not look foolish for asking it – it makes them look smarter. Not only does it exhibit inquisitiveness, it's also in the student's interest to do so, particularly if they don't understand what is being discussed, thus also exhibiting a desire for clarification. Nevertheless, questions often go unasked, perhaps because of shyness or because no one wants to stand out and look like they don't get it (especially if no one else is raising their hand). Thus, some might just be sitting there, still wondering, *what do you mean by critical thinking?*

Acknowledging Student Preconceptions

Further to student preconceptions regarding what CT is, it's also worth considering their preconceptions regarding their abilities. I've addressed a study I conducted with mature students a couple of times thus far, and one of my observations was that, consistent with self-serving biases such as illusory superiority (i.e. our tendency to overestimate our abilities, e.g. the tendency for most people to rate themselves as having above average intelligence, despite this being a statistical impossibility), for the most part, they thought they were already pretty good at CT, even when they weren't – well, not as good as they thought they were anyway (despite not really knowing to what CT refers). Things changed a bit after they saw the pre-module assessment (and associated scores); that's when modesty started to kick in a bit. As alluded to before, despite being written up as a study, this actually started off as more of an educational tool or class exercise – one that I think paid off and continued to pay off in future iterations of the class – consistent with the discussion of assessment strategies earlier.

Introducing students to examples of where CT can be applied, then asking them to actually do it and, subsequently, showing them how well they did has been a great motivator in that class. From the outset, students can see what they're doing right, what they're doing wrong and learn something a little more concrete about CT before they even get into the depths of the class. On the other hand, if you wait for mid-term scores or, in some cases, a final only, it's arguably too late in the game for students to amend their approach.

With that, there are indeed students who question their capability to 'keep up' in CT classes from the very get-go. The level of abstraction, even from the outset, can be intimidating to students. To simplify this abstraction, the provision of concrete examples – as discussed in the next section – will facilitate understanding and, alongside opportunities to practise and successfully apply CT, will facilitate the building of confidence in this domain, which can also be useful for approaching CT (e.g. Facione & Facione, 1992). Although, as we alluded to before, too much confidence isn't good either!

Approaches to Content Presentation and Style

CT can get really boring, especially if the focus is exclusively on abstract definitions and history. Though I love CT as a topic area (*why else would anyone write a book on it?*), I recall sitting in on some presentations/classes and having to fight off 'resting my eyes' during them. For example, when you've got the time (e.g. a full semester) to explore CT in depth, formal logic is a topic that is often covered. Symbolic logic, on the surface, is not exciting. If I start presenting phrases such as 'if p, then q' for an hour, people are going to get bored pretty quick. We need to make it fun. Arguably, that goes for *all* education.

Consider the syllogism:

All men are bastards.
Some bastards are attractive.
Therefore, some bastards are attractive.

Is this syllogism valid or invalid? Whenever I present it in class, I get laughs. I forget that it's kind of funny, because I've presented it so many times over the years; but that was a reason I initially included it as an exercise. Students don't expect 'funny' in class – especially one on formal logic; so, when there is an injection of humour, they are surprised, and this reinforces engagement.

Moreover, the example is a reflection of real-world context – not just formal logic; people can imagine someone making a statement like this. This 'concreteness' of the example allows people to better apply their learnings of formal and symbolic logic to everyday language, which is important for understanding argumentation. So, I've kept people's interest and I've increased the likelihood of understanding. That's why concrete examples are a winner.

By the way, the syllogism is logically invalid; however, many people incorrectly assume that it is valid, because they might agree with the statements. This concrete example further reinforces the notion of how emotion, beliefs and attitudes can affect how we think – another benefit! For example, I might have a student who would ace a symbolic logic exam if I presented only symbols (i.e. ps and qs) but fail to see its application in the real-world through such examples as that earlier. If I teach them both and make explicit the application, I can be more confident that the learning outcome will be achieved.

Due to the abstract nature of CT, it is easy for novices to get lost or confused and, subsequently, fail to regain focus on the lesson. By integrating humour and real-life examples, maybe even from your own life, you're giving your students something concrete on which to latch. Such examples will clarify the abstract nature of the lesson, and the humorous/personal touch may facilitate future recall of the lesson.

The content is the content, and educators out there can teach the same stuff but get very different results. It's not necessarily the content that needs to change but, rather, how it's presented. Use concrete, real-world examples. Be personable. Be funny – even if you're not funny. Try. CT gets very serious, very quickly. Take every opportunity to break that with humour.

Speaking of 'getting serious', CT often gets applied to some rather controversial topics. Don't shy away from them, unless it's appropriate to do so.[3] I make it clear to my students (particularly in CT and Social Psychology classes) that to think critically, you cannot always be 'politically correct'. It is often the case that controversial topics are those that require the most CT! Consider why such topics are controversial – obviously, people care about them; thus, they often require CT. However, that doesn't mean that you shouldn't be cautious in terms of how you present such material. For example, be cognisant of the differences between being objective and offensive – and ensure your students know too! Again, CT should be engaged when you care about a topic; and sometimes when we 'care', emotion tends to get involved – especially if said topic is controversial. Some topics cannot be avoided and need to be engaged to get to the crux of either solving a problem or deriving a conclusion for the issues that are important to us. If we truly care about the conclusions we draw, we need to question the controversial topics objectively and play *devil's advocate*, no matter how uncomfortable it may sometimes make us feel.

Another way of presenting controversial material and getting students involved is opening the floor and letting them discuss various points on a topic. It keeps students engaged, promotes active learning and helps students feel like they have a voice in not only their education but their thinking as well. My classes and I have discussed many controversial topics, such as those involving sexual violence, race, gun control and abortion. If we want our students to develop into capable individuals, able to apply CT in their daily lives, we cannot hide them from the 'big, bad world'. We need to prepare them. Of course, there are times when educators need to exercise some caution regarding what topics are appropriate and when (see again footnote 3); but, for the majority of cases, do not shy away from allowing your students to engage such issues. I suppose

---

[3] I once had a Social Psychology class on prejudice and discrimination, where the time came for an example that I usually discuss in light of a piece of research that had been conducted on a specific minority group. I looked out at my class and noticed, on that particular day, that there was one and *only* one member of said group in attendance. The student in question was on the younger side and also quite timid. Sure, who am I to make such judgments? Well, my intuitive judgment kicked in and I decided not to present the example on that particular day, instead going with another research-based example. I chose not to take the chance of potentially making this individual uncomfortable. But, again, context matters – it was the individual rather than the topic that helped me make my decision. For example, in another class, we discussed a different study regarding a different minority group, where again only one member representing said group was present. I elected to go ahead with the discussion because this student was a bit more mature and willing to engage in discussion generally. That student thanked me after class for engaging it and thought it was a very interesting and productive exercise. That could well have been the outcome in the first example, but sometimes you need to read the room. Again, intuitive judgment is often useful, and this particular scenario (i.e. deciding whether or not to run one exercise) didn't really require CT.

Underlying Themes and Concluding Thoughts 125

my statement to students, early on in my CT modules, that 'to think critically, you cannot always be politically correct' is a kind of trigger warning for them in many ways. If they're not prepared for such conversations, they're not prepared for CT – which also leads to questions regarding their preparedness for the real-world.

Underlying Themes and Concluding Thoughts

Not everyone reading this chapter teaches CT. Not everyone reading this has taken a CT course. Not everyone will ever take a CT course. That doesn't mean that they won't be able to think critically. But such people – you might be one of them – could have the positive dispositions necessary for CT, which may not be the case for many people that have or will take a CT course. Such disposition is important. It might drive them towards independent reading and learning. You don't need a fancy piece of paper to confirm that you've learned something. Sure, 'formal' education provides the proverbial 'leg-up' in many different contexts, such as in the case of formal CT training increasing the likelihood of enhanced CT, but that's not a guarantee – neither with respect to 'formal' students getting better nor 'informal'/independent learners not getting better. If you've never taken a CT course and you want to get better at CT, pursue one – be it at an institution or online. If such a pursuit is not feasible, then read; read as much as you can about the topic. I say this because a semester-long course in CT doesn't make you an expert in it. Reading a few books on it doesn't make you an expert either. What makes you a critical thinker, in this context, is a combination of background knowledge, positive disposition towards CT and a lot of experience engaging relevant opportunities. Embrace those opportunities.

This line of thinking calls to mind one of my biggest pet peeves, as alluded to in Chapter 5, when someone argumentatively tells another person to 'do their research!' What good is that going to do? As if that's going to magically grant you some expertise. Watching three hours of videos on YouTube is most certainly not research; but neither is reading a few books, from credible sources, on a specific topic area. Sure, the latter will give you a pretty good (and credible) understanding of a topic; but, it's not going to provide you the level of expertise that will put you on par with the experts. That's why we turn to experts, to see what they say. Consistent with Chapter 5, if an expert in quantum mechanics recommends something about the field – regardless of how I feel about it – I'm inclined to listen to them; because they are the credible expert, not me. I'm using their years and years of training, research, thinking and knowledge to usher me in the right direction.

The point is that you may not have the resources to devote to such pursuits, be it in terms of time, money or effort. You may not have taken a course in CT. You may not have read multiple books on CT. This book may actually be your first adventure into the field; if so, welcome – I hope you're enjoying it. Keep at it; every opportunity counts.

Likewise, I think about the blog I write on CT – I imagine there will be many of those readers who will only ever read one of my posts (as opposed to following each one). For those who only read one post, I try to provide them with something of value, something that will improve their thinking in some way, even if it's little. Again, we're not going to change a person's epistemological understanding overnight, nor over the course of a book or even the course of a semester – but each engagement helps. Sometimes, little by little will suffice, especially if that's all that's feasible. Regardless, engage and embrace each opportunity you can, no matter how small or short.

CHAPTER 9

Implications of Social Psychology on Critical Thinking and Practical Lessons Learned in Recent Years

CT is inherently a social activity. As we've discussed throughout this book, knowledge can be more simply described as information that we have gained over time – be it correct (true (for now anyway)), incorrect (misinformation or disinformation), subject to change (in light of further advances in knowledge) and/or imperfect (somewhat misinterpreted or incomplete). Humans are not born with knowledge of such information – it is acquired from somewhere. The news we hear, the books we read, the lessons we are taught in school all come from someone else; and thus, our development of knowledge is through a form of social interaction. Even when you're on your own, you are thinking in a social manner simply because you are *aware* of the existence of others (e.g. *what clothes will I wear today?*). Moreover, your environment and your interactions with it also fall under the scope of social interaction. For example, regardless of whether others are present or not, your environment is largely the result of some form of human intervention (e.g. taking a nature walk down the road on a spring evening is facilitated by the building of that road, in that location, by someone else).

Depending on where you are, you may think and act differently if people are around than you normally would in that setting alone (e.g. sitting up straight and smiling). Again, context is key too. You might have a schema for how to act in a restaurant (i.e. a cognitive script) with friends or family. Now, let's keep the presence of others and the same environment (restaurant), but instead of a friend or a family member, the person we are eating with is a romantic interest. Commonly, we call this a date. When the context changes – from dinner with your friend to a date – so too does the way in which you think and act.

It may be the case that I have never met you, the person reading this book, but right now we are interacting – I am giving you insight into my knowledge of cognition. My actions as I write this book are affecting you, as you read this. The impact of such insight will be different from reader to

128   Implications of Social Psychology on Critical Thinking

reader; but, nevertheless, there is an interaction happening. Consider another example: even in your own bedroom, though you may be alone, what you have on your wall, what you keep on your bedside table, even the style of your bed, though they might all be handpicked by you and bring you comfort, they are all outcomes of culture – the manifestations of a collective society. Simply, we cannot escape the impact of other people.

With that, the purpose of this chapter is not to explain that CT is social. The chapter's introductory paragraphs should make this point sufficiently clear. Indeed, every aspect of thought discussed throughout this book is treating cognition in terms of working in a social environment (e.g. *it depends*). The purpose of this chapter is to provide an explicit reminder that thinking is a social activity, despite what you might believe of yourself in terms of being an 'independent thinker'.

I've never really liked the term 'independent thinking' because it doesn't accurately portray the type of thinking that educators want to see. Yes, we want people to independently search for and evaluate information on their own accord, generate ideas, think about potential solutions to problems – yes, of course! However, this description is more in tune with being 'motivated to think critically' and less about the acceptability of information, because there's more to it than that – there's a metacognitive component to this as well. For example, consistent with Chapter 5, if a credible expert provides me information relevant to their topic of expertise, I'd be foolish to not listen to them and instead 'go with my gut', despite being a novice in the topic area. Am I blindly following what I'm being told? *Yes and no*. 'Yes' in the sense that I am following what I'm told (i.e. because I'm out of my depth with respect to domain knowledge). 'No' in the sense that I'm engaging metacognition, considering the nature of knowledge, evaluating the social dynamic between myself and the expert and making the decision to heed the word of the expert. I'm motivated to learn and think – so I gather as much of the most credible information that I can and apply that new knowledge in whatever way is most appropriate. 'Believing what you're told' in this context is a good thing; however, the phrasing doesn't really mesh well with the commonly held conceptualisation of independent thinking, does it?

Moreover, the problem with independent thinking is that, when you think about it, it also includes people who believe in conspiracy theories. These people will go off on their own, they'll watch a bunch of videos online, they'll 'do their research' and they'll come back with their conclusions. Sure, many of their beliefs will, likewise, be held by others in such a subculture; but their method is quite consistent with what one might propose of as 'independent thinking'. The point is, even if 'independent thinking' is an ideal (and, again, I'm not so sure it should be treated as such – rather, motivation to engage CT would be better), it's near impossible to be independent in one's thought, given that we are dependent on others and our environment with respect to targets of our thought. This example is just one that will be explored in this chapter, another purpose of which is to highlight issues and situations in the real-world that not only exemplify social impacts on our thinking (as addressed earlier), but more importantly how we can think critically about them.

'Noisy Information': Are We, as a Society, Getting Worse at CT?

Not long ago, I had an interesting conversation with someone who made the observation that, despite the growing amount of and access to knowledge in their field, individuals and companies in this field seemed to be exhibiting a shrinking knowledge base and/or ability to think critically about such an information base – seemingly getting less competent over time. This worrisome observation was made by this individual in light of countless communications where patterns of poor thinking were identified.[1]

---

[1] Though we might often hear about 'thinking ability' decreasing, we must also acknowledge that what we perceive of as modern thinking is simply a cross-section of what's out there. The rise of social media has become a driving force for globalisation, providing greater access to communication with wider ranges of people and many more opportunities to see poor thinking in action. We engage videos and stories about people saying and doing silly things. These are cathartic – often eliciting an emotional response (e.g. laughter or anger). That's why they get shared on social media and go viral. Videos of people doing what they should be doing may not be as common, because that's 'boring'; that's not going to get clicks, likes or shares. The 'fails' we watch influence and advance our echo chambers; they get shared; we grow accustomed to people doing and saying the wrong things. We grow to believe that 'the idiots are taking over'. However, what if we're just conflating all of this and are simply *more aware* of poor thinking? What if this just represents a small proportion of humanity? Again, we tend to focus more on the negatives than the positives, so such a possibility should not be surprising.

Poor thinkers online might be on their 'down time', leaving comments based on beliefs and opinions (remember, we all have them). CT may not be at the top of their list of priorities (we can't think critically all the time). So, someone says something wrong – does that mean that they don't apply CT to other things in their life? Absolutely not. Maybe they're trolling and don't actually believe what they're saying (i.e. further 'noisy' information). Others might do this as leisure or escapism. People in videos doing silly things – much of the time, all you see is less than a minute of them being 'wrong'. That's a small snapshot of their existence from which to pull about their typical behaviour/thinking ability (i.e. the mistake might be a once-off for them). Regardless, we judge them. That's human nature – over-relying on intuition and jumping to conclusions.

When we see all of this 'incorrect information', our observations facilitate schema-building regarding thinking in modern society accordingly, thus painting a negative picture. Our own cognitive biases exacerbate this. In a self-serving manner, we perceive ourselves as 'knowing better'; and we fear that others are in greater danger than they might be, because we don't often

130   Implications of Social Psychology on Critical Thinking

Of course, we both acknowledged that this perspective was a product of a sample size of one – this individual's observation. However, it made them consider such potential further; and what they concluded was that, perhaps, people are becoming less able to filter out 'noisy', peripheral information from the 'good' stuff – relevant, accurate information. For example, the rise of social media engagement begets a rise in people processing novel information in a fast, simple, thread-like manner, in which accurate and reliable data may get filtered out, thus facilitating the making of critical decisions or judgments with only a fraction of the data required for such a task.

Though I agree with some of this perspective, there are a number of caveats and exceptions that are important to make. First, consider the proposition, are we getting worse at CT? Simply, *no*. For starters, there is no such thing as 'good' CT[2] but, rather, a case-by-case basis of asking whether or not CT has been conducted. Again, just because a person *generally* thinks critically about important issues, it doesn't mean that they will use it in all situations. Some people use it more often than others, and some don't use it at all. Beyond the concept of 'care', the nature of the information itself can play a large role in whether CT will be engaged. Though CT and having a relevant knowledge base are dependent on one another to some extent, they are distinct concepts (see, again, Chapter 3).

To better understand this distinction, consider the *new knowledge economy*. Though there is nothing new about the 'new' knowledge

---

see them as having the same level of capacity as ourselves. Thus, we fear a mass dumbing down of society, when in fact it might just be a small proportion that's in danger.

That's not to say that this might all be fear-mongering. If it was, I probably wouldn't be writing this book. Just as no one can think critically all the time, everyone is susceptible to making a poor decision that can impact them in a negative way – regardless of how 'well' they generally think. CT may not be crashing as many might speculate; but that doesn't mean that generally good decision-makers cannot be misled or capable of making a poor decision in important contexts, especially in light of all the noisy information out there.

[2] I often come across reference to 'good CT', but seeing such a phrase makes me ask, *is there 'bad' CT?* Of course not. The issue of 'degrees' of CT is much like being 'kind of pregnant'. Either you are or you aren't. Likewise, you either conducted CT or you didn't. Sure, CT is never conducted perfectly (e.g. we can never eliminate all emotion from our CT) – nothing ever is – so, there's bound to be a few minor errors here and there. That said, such minor errors (e.g. missing a step in logic) do not make for *bad* CT, they just extend the amount of thinking that remains required. Worth noting in this context is that CT is as much about the process as it is the answer. Sometimes, people generate a correct answer – it doesn't mean that they used CT. If it was an important decision, that's bad (i.e. there was no CT). On the other hand, someone might engage CT and conclude that they don't have an answer. They've acknowledged uncertainty and understand that what answer they are leaning towards might well be falsified without more concrete evidence. Outcome-wise, the former example is desirable – a correct answer (albeit bereft of CT); however, from a CT standpoint, I'd be impressed with the latter's process – answer or no answer. CT was engaged; and that's 'good'.

economy, its ramifications are maintained and increasing – the exponential increase in the annual output of knowledge has been growing for over twenty years, given the constant evolution of the internet and how information is transferred. For example, it's estimated that about 500,000 times the volume of information contained in the US Library of Congress print collection was created in 2002 alone; from 1999 to 2002, the amount of new information created equalled the amount of information previously developed throughout the history of the world (Varian & Lyman, 2003); and just over twenty years ago, the development of new information was suggested to be doubling every two years (Jukes & McCain, 2002). Given how much information has actually been developed in that time, it's difficult to assess these estimations. However, it has been suggested that approximately 329 million terabytes of data are currently created each day (with roughly half of that speculated to be video data).

That said, exact figures aren't important here; rather, a staggeringly higher amount of information is available now than it was twenty years ago. If anything, our knowledge base is getting bigger and better; however, it is becoming increasingly difficult for many to distinguish accurate, quality information from 'noisy', peripheral rubbish. As a result, it is not enough to gain a knowledge base (further impacted by the need to filter it) – we *must* be able to adapt to new information, develop a capacity to engage in inquiry and constructively solve problems. These 'musts' are consistent with what we know of as CT. Another way of looking at it is that our advancing knowledge economy is presenting us more and more opportunities to engage CT; and in the case of CT development, 'practice makes perfect' (e.g. Dwyer et al., 2012, 2015).

So, in light of my aforementioned conversation, it is reasonable to suggest that no, we are not losing our knowledge base, and no, we are not getting worse at CT – on the contrary, we have greater access now to opportunities to practise and improve our CT, in light of advances in our knowledge base. However, we need to utilise CT in tandem with our knowledge base for successful information-processing outcomes. Years ago, knowledge was king. However, in light of the information explosion over the past few decades, that's no longer sufficient. That's why CT is so important in real-world scenarios.

Contextual Applications in Real-World Scenarios

The remainder of this chapter is broken down into a series of distinct sections that all share the theme of highlighting specific contexts and

132 Implications of Social Psychology on Critical Thinking

situations, in our everyday lives, where social implications play a central role in thinking. Moreover, they provide examples of the important role social psychology plays in considering CT, as well how 'noisy' information is all around us. Notably, this is not an exhaustive treatment of such examples by any means – there are many more out there for consideration; rather, it represents a selection of examples that I find both particularly interesting and commonly engaged within society, on a day-to-day basis.

Conspiracy Beliefs

Conspiracy beliefs (i.e. they are not conspiracy *theories*, given our discussion of the term in Chapter 3) have been around for hundreds of years in varying forms. Machiavelli discussed conspiracies in terms of overthrowing rulers. Indeed, conspiracies, by definition, are often real in the sense that it only takes two individuals to plot together in a malevolent manner. Famously, Brutus is said to have led the conspiracy against Julius Caesar. But, a conspiracy doesn't have to be big and elaborate. It can be small. Two classmates may work together to overthrow the leader of their social group at school by spreading rumours about them. Conspiracies happen all the time; so what makes them different to the kinds of 'conspiracy theories' we have come to know?

This is where the term 'theory' comes into play. The inaccurate use of 'theory' is used to play the role of explanation in this phrase; but, because there is no model to observe per se (see again Chapter 3) – and no credible evidence of which to speak – the 'theory' is no more than a speculation. In addition to concepts associated with falsification, theory and the like, Karl Popper also addressed conspiracy theories in his work, as an inaccurate explanation of some occurrence. Indeed, much of this book has been about shedding light on such occurrences.

Some conspiracy beliefs are easier to believe than others. Admittedly, JFK's assassination never sat right with me. Moreover, knowing that it takes only the plotting of two individuals to commit a harmful/negative act for it to count as a conspiracy, it seems a little more reasonable that the assassination was the result of a conspiracy. With that, I don't have a specific explanation ('theory') as to the who, why or any of that. Moreover, I don't claim that this assuredly happened; rather, I believe that it is plausible. Notice how I recognise that it is an unfounded belief and that I don't try to explain anything beyond that. The problem with conspiracy beliefs and their founding 'theorists' is that they often extend far beyond that, and that's what makes such beliefs so problematic (from a plausibility perspective).

Whereas some beliefs might have some plausibility (e.g. JFK's assassination), other conspiracy beliefs are ridiculously far-fetched. Consider the likelihood of not only an illuminati but one that consists of reptilian overlords that rule us all. Examples such as this one are what I find interesting about conspiracy beliefs – the threads of logic to them (or lack thereof): not only do you believe that there is an illuminati, but they also happen to be reptilian. Why not bovine or avian? Is it because we perceive 'snakes' as sneakier and more insidious than cows or sparrows? Why does it matter? Is it to make such individuals less 'human' and, thus, more susceptible to evil deeds? Such extra steps (or stretches) in logic are typically a telltale sign that I'm not going to get much actual logic from the remainder of such correspondence with this 'theorist'.

To clarify, a conspiracy belief is importantly distinct (though subtly so in some respects) from my earlier description of a conspiracy, in that a conspiracy belief refers to a falsely derived belief that the ultimate cause of an event results from the plotting of multiple omnipresent and omnipotent actors working together in pursuit of an often malevolent, unlawful and secret goal (Bale, 2007; Mandick, 2007; Swami et al., 2014; Swami & Furnham, 2014). Research suggests that belief in conspiracy 'theories' is correlated with lower levels of education (Douglas et al., 2016), lower crystallised intelligence, lower analytic thinking and lower open-mindedness (despite 'theorists' often calling for others to open their minds and 'do their research'), as well as higher scores on intuitive thinking (Swami et al., 2011; Swami et al., 2014). Research further suggests that not only does roughly half of the American public surveyed believe in at least one conspiracy 'theory' (Oliver & Wood, 2014), those who believe in one are likely to believe in other conspiracy 'theories' as well (e.g. Goertzel, 1994; Van Prooijen, 2012).

We often see conspiracy beliefs come to the spotlight following catastrophes and events that challenge social order (Van Prooijen & Jostmann, 2013). For example, think of all the new beliefs resulting from the COVID-19 pandemic. Consistent with our discussion regarding humans' desire to 'fill in the gaps' where uncertainty may exist, conspiracy beliefs develop in a similar manner – as a means of explaining complex scenarios that many of us may never fully understand. Of course, though what 'fills in the gaps' may fail to provide accurate information, it does provide an explanation simple enough to comprehend, helping to make 'sense' of the world – and, at the same time, provide a form of closure. Indeed, research

134   Implications of Social Psychology on Critical Thinking

indicates that belief in conspiracy theories is significantly correlated with a desire for closure (Swami & Furnham, 2014).

Consistent with previous discussion regarding people's relationships with certainty and confusion, the notion that random events with negative outcomes can occur can be existentially problematic. Consider the well-established representativeness heuristic (Tversky & Kahneman, 1974), which refers to our often poorly developed mental shortcut for engaging information of a probabilistic nature (e.g. some people believe that their six 'random' lotto numbers, which they always play, have better odds of being drawn than the numbers 1–6; of course, this is incorrect – both are equally likely given the true nature of randomness and because neither the lotto machine nor the balls it draws have a memory). Simply, people are poor at conceptualising the nature of randomness. When random, catastrophic events occur (e.g. natural disasters), people are often poorly equipped to 'deal' with them in terms of cognitive processing. So, we develop causal explanations as a means of facilitating this desired closure and alleviating the negative feelings associated with uncertainty. Thus, the development of conspiracy beliefs acts as such explanations, which may also serve as a coping mechanism that provides reassurance (Newheiser et al., 2011; Van Prooijen, 2012) to those who might feel powerless – be it in the aftermath of a tragedy or in more general economic, social or political ways (Swami & Furnham, 2014).

Furthermore, this concept of *powerlessness* is also important to consider; for example, ever notice how there are seldom 'nice' conspiracy beliefs doing the rounds on the internet – like, how a network of teens are secretly getting together to help the sick and suffering? Perhaps a reason for this is that conspiracy beliefs are not only about 'explaining' an event but also about power struggles and the notion of returning 'control' to those who might be perceived of as powerless. Tragic events are often blamed on some institution of power (typically one already disliked by the 'theorist'), thus creating a scapegoat (e.g. consistent with *scapegoat theory*). In this sense, no matter how powerful the conspirators might be, the individual takes back control, to some extent, by 'figuring out the conspiracy', 'calling out the conspirators' and 'spreading their message'. For the most part, however, such 'revolutionary' thinking consists of watching a few hours' worth of videos online, typically cherry-picked by individuals with the same perspective. Such thinking might be revolutionary, but it doesn't seem particularly effortful. If only 'doing one's research' was this easy.

Despite generally being more agreeable (Swami et al., 2011), conspiracy theorists often claim to be 'sceptics' and to 'think critically'. It seems likely that they fail to see the difference between what we know of as CT and efforts to critique structures of power – albeit without offering real alternatives (Swami & Furnham, 2014). Consistent with our discussion of CT dispositions, though scepticism is an important CT disposition, it must be applied to all sides of an argument and not just in a manner that rationalises a confirmation bias. Just as important as scepticism is open-mindedness – on which, as addressed earlier, 'theorists' typically score low (NB: open-mindedness is subtly, but importantly, distinct from personality measures of agreeableness). Specifically, open-mindedness is not just blindly accepting the information that's provided; it's about being open to changing your mind in light of new evidence, detaching from your beliefs and focusing on unbiased thinking void of self-interest, as well as being open to constructive criticism and new ideas. Pennycook et al. (2015) distinguish types of open-mindedness in a manner that alludes to the agreeable issue described earlier: *reflective* open-mindedness searches for information as a means to facilitate critical thought, whereas *reflexive* open-mindedness is accepting of information without much processing – making the latter more 'open' to misinformation. Perhaps the latter description is what people mistakenly confuse for the open-mindedness we talk about in terms of CT; and it may explain why scepticism (which can also be misinterpreted as the opposite of open-mindedness) might be perceived, by some, as more important for CT.

If you ever argued with a conspiracy theorist, 'open-minded' – in the reflective sense – may not be your first description of their thinking. Consistent with research by Swami and colleagues, more recent research by Quinn et al. (2020) found that higher CT disposition towards open-mindedness predicted lower scores on 'control of information' conspiracy beliefs (i.e. beliefs regarding unethical control and suppression of information by institutions such as the government, the media, scientists and corporations). Moreover, higher scores on disposition towards perseverance predicted lower scores on both 'government malfeasance' beliefs and 'malevolent global conspiracy' beliefs, and higher scores on disposition towards attentiveness predicted lower scores on 'extra-terrestrial cover-up' beliefs. Furthermore, these results suggest that those with specific inclinations towards conducting CT may be less likely to believe in specific types of conspiracy beliefs.

With that, as we discussed in Chapter 6, changing anyone's mind is not an easy task; so, a focus on conspiracy believers here isn't exactly fair in the context of discussing open-mindedness. But, the same issues we previously discussed remain at play here – issues further enhanced when the

136   Implications of Social Psychology on Critical Thinking

conspiracy in question blames an institution or person to which the 'theorist' is already opposed. Individuals are more likely to believe conspiracy theories if they are biased in favour of the individual's pre-existing views, such as distrust of science or the government (Swami & Furnham, 2014).

The reasons why people fall into believing in conspiracy theories are numerous and complex. Though, in the grand scheme of things, conspiracy 'theories' represent a belief structure that reflects people's attitudes and values, which is hard to change once developed. We will continue to observe this trend throughout the remainder of this chapter, as we discuss value-signalling, politics and the similarly inclined 'fake news'.

Value-Signalling

In Chapter 2, we introduced the practice of virtue- or value-signalling, referring to a behaviour that publicly expresses commitment to a belief system that often demonstrates one's perceived good character or moral correctness with the (implicit or explicit) intent of enhancing social standing. The point was made that to truly understand the concept, a distinction should be made between virtue and value. That is, value is, perhaps, a better description because the stance in question does not require others to hold it in similar regard – let alone agree with it – for it to be of some value. That is, to be valuable, it only requires one person to value it (e.g. the signaller). On the other hand, being virtuous may have the connotation of being globally accepted or, at least, by the many. Arguably, this is potentially dangerous because such connotations may facilitate emotion-based, anti-CT behaviours, such as those that bully, shame and ridicule those who disagree with such 'virtuous' perspectives.

I recall a comment left as feedback on one of my blog posts, which stated: 'In the U.S. at least, a student offering [CT] that may go against the Stalinist PC [i.e. political correctness]/SJW [social justice warrior] propaganda model on university campuses is academic suicide. Why put a grade at risk for something that you believe in? Intellectual integrity is passé.' I do not know how true this perspective is, nor do I know (if it is true) how widespread such models are on university campuses (relative to the hoopla one might see on social media, where topics such as 'social justice' are value-signalled in many circles). With that, this is not the first time I have heard such an assertion as a cause for concern. Indeed, 'social justice' is 'valued' and has become both a primary focus of many university mission statements and infused into many curricula. Regardless of such scope,

I think it's a genuine shame that any individual, even if it's just one, should feel that they cannot practise intellectual honesty and integrity – especially in an educational setting – without fear of being chastised by students or even by educators.

Similarly, why would someone on a social media site risk being ridiculed (e.g. being unfairly referred to as a GMO 'shill', a pro-Illuminati 'troll', a whatever-phobic or something-ist) in a public forum for supporting an 'unpopular' perspective, even though they have critically thought about it? Inaction can be viewed as a conscientious move. Again, who cares about social media?[3]

Now, consider what happens when unpopular, though logically considered, perspectives are similarly silenced or ignored. Often, the emotion-driven and misinformed positions take centre stage (i.e. 'whoever screams loudest' or 'the squeaky wheel gets the grease'). Due to a less presented opposition, the abundance of popular perspectives available on social media generates further buy-in, reinforces echo chambers and a belief that the observable position is the only (e.g. valued/virtuous) position, and develops into a form of status quo.

In recent years, rather concrete examples have popped up in the news, including the protesting and banning of academics from radio stations and public-speaking events, in light of statements (despite being well-considered positions based on extensive research) that 'offended' certain individuals and their associated social groups. It seems illogical that efforts to promote people's rights should come at the cost of restricting other people's rights; but individuals are entitled to their opinions, and they are certainly entitled to be offended. With that, being offended – an emotionally charged stance I might add – does not entitle the offended party to being accommodated, as if they were morally superior or even empirically supported.

Furthermore, being offended is not being oppressed. Likewise, you are not oppressed if someone has a differing opinion to you. Neither scenario

---

[3] Further to our previous discussion of the 'who cares' perspective, in this context, I say this as someone in their late thirties, who didn't grow up with social media, who would have no qualms with deleting his profiles off all platforms. But, what about a teenager who has always known social media, who uses it as a genuine means of socialising? I recognise that experiences/perspectives of individuals like me, in this context, will be much different than a teenager's. Furthermore, keeping this hypothetical teenager in mind, this rationale ties in quite consistently with many of the psychological mechanisms we associate with cyber-bullying (e.g. consider the aforementioned chastisement earlier). The point is, in modern society, such 'opposition' is difficult to avoid, and many people – particularly younger people – may feel forced to care about such issues because of social implications.

makes you a victim. Just because you value something that someone else does not doesn't make you virtuous (again, the importance of distinguishing value and virtue with respect to its signalling); moreover, it is far from virtuous to force emotion-based opinions of virtue/value on to others who do not subscribe to the same ideology as you. If anything, it's consistent with a form of bullying, like that discussed in footnote 3.

Returning to the point regarding inaction or non-response, consider also that it can be argued that a strategised form of social thinking is being utilised here – one that enhances our social standing and one that ultimately benefits us. For example, it's socially prudent to either ignore or simply accept the fact that people believe something that has poor supporting evidence. You don't need to be the person who gets into arguments with everyone who showcases beliefs inconsistent with yours or even evidence.

According to Saiz & Rivas (2023), an ultimate goal of CT is personal well-being. We use CT to solve problems so as to make our lives better. If the beliefs and perspectives that we present on social media don't really matter in the grand scheme of things, who cares? We focus our attention and CT on the things that do matter – the things that affect our well-being. If you let social media and topics on such platforms affect your well-being, then perhaps it's time to re-evaluate how you engage social media.

Some of you may say that's all well and good until the topic under investigation is something that's important. Well, what's important? Many people will think politics is important; some will not (see shortly for further discussion). Some will see healthcare and education as important – and they are, depending on the context (recall Chapter 2). For example, alternative medicines, such as homeopathy, are nonsense (i.e. there is no empirical research to support their use, as opposed to, say, a wealth of evidence-based research on actual medicine). I know that and, hopefully, you do too. For a long time, I would post about the dangers of these on social media, as well as educational pieces on the topic. I still do and still will (because that's an important topic to me – though I recognise that it might not be important to you); but I'll never get as worked up about it as I once did. Why?

Just because there are misinformed people in the world doesn't mean that everyone is misinformed. Large populations of people do not depend on me for information. Consistent with our discussion about others being more intellectually capable than we often give them credit for, I realise that most people can make the right decisions for themselves. If I post something and it gets engagement, it's typically from others who already agree

Contextual Applications in Real-World Scenarios 139

with my perspective. Preaching to the choir doesn't help anyone. We must not overestimate the value of our own personal input. Moreover, my post is not likely going to change the minds of alternative medicine users – the actual target of such posts; so, again, what's the point? Look after your own health and education, as well as the health and education of your family. That's what you need to focus on. Other people will do their thing, just as you'd be expected to be let to do your thing.

Such freedom, of course, is one of the beauties of living in a modern, western society. I understand that those of us who do are very lucky – not everyone lives this way. I will not get further into such conversation here, not only because such an existence is outside the remit of my 'knowledge' but also because I don't like discussing politics. Speaking of which . . .

Politics

When I first came of age when I could legally enjoy a beer, my father gave me one piece of advice for conducting myself in bars and pubs: 'don't talk about religion or politics'. I always considered this a good piece of advice and still do. In fact, I try to avoid talking about politics altogether.

Nevertheless, too often do I see people disregard this guideline, much to their detriment. Of course, most occurrences of such disregard that I observe happen online. Consistent with cognitive mechanisms of social psychology, there is perhaps a veil of anonymity (despite usernames typically being displayed), a sense of courage or even the notion of physical distance one might feel when engaging with a screen, as opposed to another human being, that facilitates our ability or even sense of freedom to discuss such ideas. Either way, consistent with the growth of the internet and information, so too have we seen growth in political conversation among non-politicians.

Politics is a funny thing. It's like religion in that both reflect a standpoint or perspective regarding the world around us that is based on some ideology – how it works (or how it should work). However, where it's not (largely) acceptable to criticise someone for their religious beliefs, it is a pastime for many to do so with regard to politics.

Seldom do I scroll the home pages of any social media platform without seeing numerous politically based sentiments: 'this guy's an idiot' or 'that woman is evil'. It's no longer taboo to discuss politics in public – never mind force-feeding one's 'take' to anyone among the masses who will listen (whether they agree or not). Sometimes, I'll read threads on leisure pages and someone will find a way, despite the lack of relevance, to spout hate

140   Implications of Social Psychology on Critical Thinking

towards the leader of their political rivals. Even our modes of relaxation, leisure and escapism are no longer safe from political debate.

I don't want to sound as if I'm falling prey to the decline bias, but in my younger adult years, I recall there being much more centrist or compromising views on politics; now it appears that you *have to be* a conservative or a liberal. However, I'm also cognisant that, consistent with the earlier rationale regarding how it seems that CT is lessening, perhaps these 'one or the other' perspectives are simply those that are being screamed the loudest from the rooftops. Maybe centrist perspectives are still alive and well – it's just that the people who hold them don't want to share them, consistent with my father's advice. Be that as it may, regardless of what the majority perspectives might be, it remains that politics has been in existence for a long time and will continue to be a point of controversy.

That said, it's worth recognising that politics is useful in facilitating the change we want to see in the world; and as much as some would like to avoid political discussion (myself included), it needs to be engaged from time to time. Indeed, I enjoy observing political debate among open-minded thinkers, where everyone's goal is to work through a means of achieving the best outcome for the governed people, regardless of 'sides'.

As addressed earlier, it seems in many ways that the political divide has increased over the years. Years ago, when political conversations were held, people seemed to care less about what party the debaters were from. If a good idea was presented, it was supported. That was the main thing – supporting an idea, not an ideology. If a candidate, regardless of party, promoted multiple ideas that you supported, then chances were that you would, in turn, support them. But now, it seems what really matters is the party that's represented – the individual candidate matters less (depending on how much 'dirt' you can drag up on them). To reiterate, I know that sounds like a 'back in my day' form of argument; and I'm sure that the dichotomous outlook on politics is not as extreme as it may 'seem' – like I said, in reality, I wouldn't be surprised if centrist perspectives make up the majority. However, what is real is that extreme perspectives are very often front and centre, they are antagonistic, they create substantial noisy information for 'non-affiliated' voters to sift through and they have the potential to sway people to believe in or vote for a person based on non-critically considered information.

In terms of my personal application of CT in the political landscape, I don't support any particular party. I am neither conservative nor liberal. Sure, I personally support ideas from both camps, but such support doesn't make me one or the other. With that, isn't it rational to consider both sides?

Contextual Applications in Real-World Scenarios 141

As discussed, when many people think of the word *argument*, they might think of phrases such as 'heated exchange', or words such as 'fight' (verbal that is). Of course, this is not an accurate interpretation of the word. A friend of mine once told me about an argument he had with his wife about some topic at a small gathering of immediate family. When his mother-in-law cut in to demand that no fighting should take place under her roof, both he and his wife turned to her and responded that they were not fighting at all. They simply disagreed with each other's perspectives and were, thus, arguing to convey their individual rationales.

Upon initial reading of this, such a scenario might be interpreted as a rather cringy experience – 'arguing' at a family gathering. But such a perspective only further exemplifies the generally biased view of 'arguing'. If anything, I think the ability for spouses to engage each other in debate is really healthy. Argumentation – as this couple were conducting – is vital for the decision-making process, particularly if the subject is one about which both participants care. It's not about conflict; it's about presenting ideas followed by a network of supports and rebuttals that help facilitate either acceptance or rejection. Of course, if you start yelling at one another and engage name calling (*ad hominem*), then that's another story.

As we addressed in Chapter 1, any transfer of knowledge that includes words such as *but, because, however* and *therefore* is an argument. Pardon the pun, but I would *argue* that you would be hard-pressed to find any page-long piece of text (excluding obvious things like instructions) that doesn't contain some form of argument. Despite arguments being all around us, unfortunately political debates often become heated arguments because of emotional investment in our beliefs and ideologies. Consistent with CT, for argumentation to be successful, both sides of the argument require appropriate consideration.

If you were to think critically about *all* politically oriented topics, it is unlikely that you would wholeheartedly side with conservatives or liberals all of the time. In politics, you should be able to 'pick and mix' policies you support, regardless of the party. Politics should not be about *us versus them*; rather, it should be about identifying a candidate(s) that you believe will best represent you and what you value.

Political stances are ill-structured problems – there is no absolutely correct answer. We must realise that politics would not exist if one side was always 'correct'. Over time, the 'wrong' side would have been weeded out and the 'correct' escalated in standing. But this has not happened. If there was a definitively correct way to govern, it's reasonable to suggest that we would have adopted it by now. There is a constant back and forth in favour of the disparate parties. So, what does that tell us about CT in politics?

142   Implications of Social Psychology on Critical Thinking

Again, politics is a lot like religion – they both represent a standpoint or perspective on the world around us that is based on some belief system. As critical thinkers, we know that beliefs are not facts. If and when we engage in political discussion, we must acknowledge this in the stance we take. Furthermore, if we find that one of our stances is consistent with that of a particular party, we must not take for granted that said party is consistent with our perspectives on other topics.

Politics is not black and white. Like most other things in life, there are many shades of grey. Arguably, that's why wholeheartedly following a side, be it left or right, should be selected against. Neither side has all the answers.

In order to enhance CT around politics, avoid thinking in terms of sides, parties and agendas. Consider a political topic that's important to you. Apply CT to that topic. Pick a new topic and repeat. Amend your conclusions in light of new learnings, be open to changing your mind about your beliefs and remember, these perspectives are your beliefs and you're just as entitled to yours as someone else is to theirs. This point is further reinforced by the notion that such beliefs are developed in light of what people believe to be 'right and just' – and the notion of what is morally 'right' or 'just' is by no means universal (again, see value-signalling). Morality is a social construct. It's relative – what's unjust to some might be no problem for others, and, likewise, what one believes to be acceptable might be perceived as completely unjust to another.[4] Again, this is why political debate lives on.

---

[4] Consider the 'trolley problem': imagine a runaway trolley speeding down railway tracks. Up ahead, there are five people tied to the tracks and the trolley is headed straight for them. You are in the train yard, safe and secure, standing next to a lever. If you pull this lever, the trolley will switch to a different set of tracks; but, this different set of tracks has one person tied to them. You have only two options: (1) do nothing, allowing the trolley to kill the five people on the first track or (2) pull the lever, actively diverting the trolley on to the second track where it will kill the one person. This ethical dilemma is interesting because it forces a decision in light of differing moral standpoints; for example, *five dead people is worse than one, so pulling the lever is the optimal option* versus *five people dying is preferred to my active involvement in the killing of one individual*. Hopefully, you can see the different ethics at play. This example can be fleshed out further, with amendments to the situational context. For example, had you said that you would pull the lever, you might be again presented the same scenario, but this time, the one person on the second track is a loved family member. Personally, I've yet to meet anyone who would pull the lever in this altered scenario (and I appreciate their honesty). Let's say you did choose to pull the lever in the original example; you might then be asked to consider the same scenario, but instead of there being a second track or a lever that you have the option of pulling, you are now placed on a bridge standing next to an obese man who is large enough to stop the runaway trolley. Given the option, would you choose to do nothing or push the man off the bridge and into the way of the trolley? Though the outcomes of the options don't change, the ethics of the situation might: *pulling a lever (albeit knowing it will kill someone)* versus *physically pushing a man to his death (regardless of the fact that it saves five others)*. Again, there is no 'right' answer to these. Morality is subjective.

Indeed, politics is a funny thing. Seriously, it can be *literally* funny. Consider the mass introduction of the term 'fake news' to the world. I genuinely laughed when I first heard it in the political context it was used. Though fake news has evolved to connote the notion of dispelling information that contradicts one's stance (i.e. it's easy to declare 'fake news' if the information in question goes against your beliefs), its intended use – that of calling out misinformation – is an important aspect of applying CT in real-world scenarios.

Fake News and Misinformation

Though the term is relatively new, the concept of fake news is not – be it with respect to spotlighting misinformation or dispelling contradictory perspectives. We have seen people in action simply saying those two words to dismiss, without rationale, information inconsistent with their own views. In this context, it is a tool for the antithesis of CT. On the other hand, the term can be a useful tool for making the concepts regarding misinformation and disinformation more accessible to larger populations (though that's assuming we can 'shake off' the aforementioned negative connotation). Nevertheless, it remains that misinformation still exists and people still fall for it. Indeed, research indicates that students struggle to evaluate the credibility of information online (Wineburg & McGrew, 2016) and that approximately only 2 per cent of children (i.e. 9–16-year-olds) have the critical literacy skills necessary to identify whether a news story is fake (Commission on Fake News and the Teaching of Critical Literacy in Schools (UK), 2018).

One consideration that requires greater detail here (though alluded to earlier in this chapter with respect to how things might seem on social media) is whether or not the acknowledged trend of 'fake news' and the spread of misinformation is actually as big of a societal problem as we might be led to believe (e.g. as in footnote 2 in Chapter 10). According to some, there is no substantial evidence to suggest that the spreading of misinformation is actually having as large a negative effect as reported. For example, research suggests that we might exaggerate the negative effects of misinformation because of a form of 'third-person effect' in which we perceive others as more vulnerable (or gullible) to misinformation than we might be ourselves (e.g. see Altay & Acerbi, 2024). According to Mercier (2017), communication, such as through means that misinformation/fake news is often disseminated, isn't particularly useful for changing minds. Sure, if you already believe the misinformation or information related to it,

144   Implications of Social Psychology on Critical Thinking

it may reinforce your stance; but, if you were initially sceptical of the misinformation, it may not have the negative impact such 'alarmist' reports might suggest.

Be that as it may, one thing that is easily observed is the *reach* of fake news. For example, research by Basch et al. (2021) revealed that thirty-five million people viewed an identified set of 100 TikTok videos regarding COVID-19 vaccines. Approximately 50 per cent of views were of videos encouraging vaccine uptake, and 40 per cent were of videos discouraging vaccine uptake. That's a lot of views one way or another. With that, I understand how such reports of such 'potential impact' may be on the alarmist side of things, given that seeing isn't necessarily believing, in the sense that just because I engaged misinformation doesn't mean I buy into it. For example, in research by Guo et al. (2023) on the efficacy of social media warnings of misinformation, the watching of a video doesn't mean that the warning failed. Hell, I watch videos that spread misinformation for fun – sometimes to have a laugh and also to see what kind of nonsense is out there (e.g. things I should be aware of in terms of my research on CT). To my knowledge, I have not yet been corrupted by such misinformation (but, as is the nature of this book, I could be wrong).

So, it's perhaps the case that, in terms of research like that of Basch and colleagues, the number of views isn't particularly telling (even though 'likes' were similarly spread in that study – perhaps that's more telling). Nevertheless, it is tough to dispute that, given these numbers, misinformation isn't being spread or celebrated (e.g. through likes) in some way. Moreover, just because alarm might be exacerbated by the notion that people often believe that others are more vulnerable to misinformation than they are doesn't mean that such spread (and potential for influence) isn't problematic.

Indeed, one problem with a large portion of this research is that it's based on self-reported data. Again, people are very kind to themselves as a result of various self-serving and my-side biases; so, when it comes down to it, an individual may not be likely to report falling prey to misinformation, and, more importantly, they might not be aware that they did! For example, according to Lyons et al. (2021), though it may be the case that not that many people report seeing or sharing misinformation (e.g. Barthel et al., 2016), if that is the case, then it may also be that people have a difficult time identifying it. Thus, it may not be that there's an exaggeration of misinformation out there; rather, it may be that many are poor at identifying it – which, of course, brings us back to square one in terms of suggesting caution and emphasising the need for CT in such contexts.

Fake News and Misinformation   145

Moreover, Lyons and colleagues continue, in the event that there is a worrisome amount of misinformation out there and people don't acknowledge seeing or sharing it, statistically speaking, it is reasonable to suggest that people may also fail to recognise their inability in context. Consistent with much discussion throughout this book, it may be the case that people often misjudge their capacity to think critically – they believe they do it even when they don't. Moreover, many people who share misinformation don't know that it's inaccurate (if they did, that would render it deliberate, thus making it disinformation as opposed to misinformation). Thus, in cases where misinformation is not deliberate, it represents evidence of a failure to identify the 'fake news' and indicates that, at some level, it is a problem. With that, perhaps the 'level' of the problem need not be a concern in the context of CT, in that you could fall for 'fake news' or misinformation often; but if it's in reference to things that aren't important, then the negative effect might be negligible. On the other hand, of course, if you have a tendency to fall for misinformation often (despite how little it matters), that trend may well translate to important decisions too. However, when it comes to the level of the problem – on a case-by-case basis – contextually speaking, *it depends*.

So, why do we fall for erroneous information? Arguably, this question is one of the fundamental inquiries made throughout this book – we've been answering it as we go along. However, perhaps a nuanced look – in light of real-world social contexts, such as value-signalling, social media and politics – is warranted and places a nice cap on this chapter.

Consistent with the confirmation bias, we favour information that *confirms* our existing beliefs. If we don't appropriately account for this and these types of bias blind spots (see, for example, Pronin & Hazel, 2023), we're more likely to fall for fake news if we agree with what is being said or if we believe its plausibility. It works the other way around as well – such bias will yield unwarrantedly enhanced scepticism (arguably, we can label this *cynicism*) for information we *dislike* or refutes our beliefs.

Of course, we can't be present to witness everything that happens in the world; and thus, for hundreds of years, we have put our faith in news outlets to succinctly report to us what has happened. Traditionally, we trusted our sources of news in that the information they provided us was true; and, in doing so, we put trust in the source's credibility. But, we can no longer blindly do this. Over the years, an increase in outlets has flooded the news market, thus furthering competition. This has also altered the manner in which the news is reported. Indeed, people often don't even get their news from 'traditional' news outlets anymore, but rather from digital

146   Implications of Social Psychology on Critical Thinking

and social media companies, in which credibility may be even more of a concern.

Nevertheless, we want our information fast because we have been primed to get it fast. I remember a time when if you wanted information on a current event, you'd have to hope it was covered in the newspaper, on the radio or on the evening TV news. Nowadays, we can just type a few words into our phone and the information we want, from a wide array of sources, pops up on screen. A series of questions arise: *are we really attending to and cognitively engaging what is being said, or are we just looking for a quick answer? How deep are we evaluating? Are we patient enough to engage this properly? Are we even evaluating, or are we just skimming through before moving on to the next article?*

Consider again the headline 'flip-flops cause cancer' from Chapter 6. Fake news. Using the same logic, one could sensationally report that *baldness causes cancer*, given that a lack of hair on one's head would enhance exposure of their skin to the sun much like flip-flops do. In reality, a more truthful report would have read: 'protecting yourself from the sun is important'; but, that wouldn't get clicks or sell papers. Remember, we are cognitively lazy; so, even if you don't care about flip-flops, don't wear them and won't be going on holidays anytime soon, then you may well skip this article or simply not attend to it enough to recognise that it's nonsense. However, a residual effect of the reporting may be that the bogus headline sticks with you. You may even relay the misinformation in conversation at a later time. Even though you don't care about the headline – the fake news – you can still indirectly be a vehicle for transferring it to others. Moreover, it's also worth noting that you don't even have to believe the headline for this strategy to work. Sure, I read the bogus article on flip-flops, to see how one could jump to such a conclusion; but the news outlet still wins here because they got my 'click'.

Fake news is often sensationalised as a marketing tool. Like propaganda, it can evoke and breed emotions such as fear, confusion and/or anger in its audiences. If you're emotional, you're less likely to be thinking rationally and are more susceptible to falling for fake news and other forms of misinformation and disinformation.

Familiarity with the information in question also plays a role. As alluded to in the discussion on changing people's minds, the *illusory truth effect* refers to the phenomenon in which the more we have been exposed to certain information, the more likely we are to believe it. This, of course, applies to misinformation as well. So, imagine seeing headlines such as those linking flip-flops and cancer on a frequent basis. Regardless of the information's status as fake news or otherwise, implicitly we're more likely to believe the news that's frequently presented to us. The same applies to examples of value-signalling, as discussed earlier.

Another similarity with value-signalling that influences whether or not we 'fall' for fake news is social pressure. Consider one of the bestselling 'how to' books of all time: *How to Win Friends and Influence People* (Carnegie, 1936). The success of this book can, in many ways, be attributed to people's recognition of social influence's importance in real-world situations and, likewise, the influence of social pressure. Since the dawn of social media, social pressure mechanisms have, arguably, become easier to observe. For example, if you say something that someone doesn't like, they might unfriend or block you; if it's something they *really* don't like, they might report you; the more you have in terms of friends, followers, likes, views or clicks, the more influence you and your signalled values have. Such 'pull' may also lend you a form of illusory credibility; that is, the more people 'like' someone and 'follow' them, the more inclined people will be to trust the information they present, regardless of their expertise or credibility. Social influence plays an important role in how we consume information; but, just because this individual is likeable doesn't ensure that the information they are sharing is legitimate.

Consistent with nudge theory (Thaler & Sunstein, 2008), our environments and society at play within them can influence the manner in which we think and make decisions. Social pressure can be one such manipulation. You might say, 'I think for myself; I don't let other people affect my decisions'; but, social pressure doesn't have to be as obvious as in the example earlier regarding unfriending and promotion. Influence can be much more subtle.

Consider the longitudinal effects of your echo chambers. How many people, groups or organisations on your subscribed feed present information with which you disagree? It may be that you've blocked, hidden, unfriended or unfollowed other parties with different views, thus curating your own network of influence. You may well be aware of what you observe; but are you aware of what you're not observing? This notion is akin to our earlier discussion of how experts are more likely than novices to be aware of what they don't know.

Let's step outside the world of social media and into something a little more 'real'. Friendships and romantic relationships are built around similarity. Indeed, we are more likely to socialise with people who are similar to us, for example, with respect to political and religious beliefs. We are moulded by the people around us. This applies to education as well. Recall

148 Implications of Social Psychology on Critical Thinking

my perspective on the importance of a centrist approach to political parties and political belief systems – research indicates that over the past few decades, the ratio of American psychology professors/lecturers voting for a liberal presidential candidate has grown from 4:1 to 17:1, with further research suggesting that this gap is increasing (Duarte et al., 2015; Langbert, 2018). The political leanings of educators are likely to, at least, be implicitly transferred, in some way, to their students through their explanations, examples and conversations in class. Of course, I'm not saying educators are inappropriately trying to recruit or convert students to join their political ideologies; rather, I'm exemplifying that this is the same type of influence your friends and family might have on you – frequent engagement over time with an individual, such as an educator, facilitates an implicit influence. Nevertheless, I do find these numbers concerning in light of the exposition on politics earlier.

Again, what makes this important to consider with respect to misinformation, however, is that just because the majority of whatever particular group (i.e. family, neighbourhood, school, faith group, political party) *believes* something does not make it true. When we are tasked with separating fact from fake news, only objectivity can yield an appropriate response. Being aware of your social groups' thinking, attitudes and beliefs is important in this context, as is being aware of the implicit effects they may have had on you in terms of believing what you do and your potential bias.

Now that we understand some of the reasons for why we fall for fake news, a good question is, *how do we spot it?* The simplest answer I can provide here is *caring*. If the topic you're engaging is important to you, dedicate the appropriate time and effort to evaluate it. That's not to say that you have to engage all aspects of CT, but at the very least, you should be applying the skill of evaluation.

If we care about the news we consume, we must evaluate it through a critical lens – digging deeper into the article, assessing the sources of the claims, looking for strong evidence, searching for replication across other news outlets and considering the credentials of the author, publisher and/ or website. That's a lot of work just to get the news. In this sense, our digital world presents us quite a contradiction: information is supposedly now at our fingertips – much easier and faster to acquire than it has ever been before; yet, it takes more effort (and time) now to get information that you can reasonably trust to be true. In many ways, the news outlets/ digital media have passed the research aspect of their job on to the consumer. Now, I'm not saying this is the case for all outlets; but knowing that fake news is out there and not knowing which outlets to trust and when creates a need for evaluation of all reports – especially if you care about the particular report in question.

Of course, there is an intellectual responsibility here as well – and though it doesn't quite fit the bill of 'spotting' fake news, another important consideration here is how to avoid spreading it. If you are going to share information with others, you should evaluate it as described earlier and in Chapter 1. Don't be part of the problem. I'm not saying that you might purposefully spread it, but I know how easy it can be to see a headline and then instantly click whatever type of 'share' button there is. If the information regards a serious topic, do your part and critically evaluate before sharing. If it's misinformation, not only are you potentially misleading some people, other people may very well catch you out for it and you'll look foolish. Besides, people love calling out others on social media. Don't give them the ammunition; don't look foolish. Evaluate the information. If you're still unsure of the information's truth or credibility following said evaluation, don't share it. Recognise uncertainty and exercise caution.

Concluding Thoughts

Misinformation can be dangerous. Arsonists in the UK set fire to over seventy-five cellular phone towers, spurred by belief in the conspiracy that 5G was in some way associated with or responsible for COVID-19. Social media users exploit their platforms to preach of their values and upstanding, regardless of the evidential accuracy of such messages. A cohort of Americans dangerously and unlawfully stormed the Capitol Building as a protest consistent with their political beliefs. Parents who don't trust/ understand medical treatment/healthcare (be it for distrust of science, religious beliefs or faith in alternative medicine) potentially put their children in harm's way. People get hurt and people die either directly or indirectly from misinformation.

Throughout this chapter, I kept reiterating the question *who cares?* Some of you may see it as just part of a writing technique, which it is in part. But it is also earnest. Much like society as a whole, we can look at the application of thinking in terms of being concerned solely for yourself and your loved ones, concerned for humanity and society as a whole, or somewhere in between. You care about your thinking, likely the thinking of your near and dear and, perhaps, if you're an educator, the thinking of your students. But do you really care about the thinking of people you don't know and will never meet? Your position on this is up to you. I'm surely not going to judge you.

150   Implications of Social Psychology on Critical Thinking

When I first got into this research topic area, I approached such scenarios with the point of view that I could potentially make a difference to society through my work. As the years have gone by, it's not that I've become jaded, it's that I no longer engage that youthful idealism that many of us had. It's not likely that I will ever have the reach of which I once dreamed. Accounting for a few caveats, it's been estimated that it takes approximately seventeen years on average for research evidence to make it to clinical practice (Morris et al., 2011) – we're talking about healthcare research here. That's important, not the 'dropping' of some rapper's fifth studio album. But, researchers are not rock stars, celebrities or influencers. I get that. Sure, I can strive to make a difference in my research fields; but I am not a household name. The point is, I am realistic about the fact that not everyone will hear my message; not everyone will care about the message I send. Some people will never care to engage CT, and some will believe they already do. This is a shame; but it's also an example of why you shouldn't necessarily care about what other people think (especially those you don't know) – because you don't know if they know how to think critically.

So, it may well be the case that you don't care about other people's thinking. It's not important to you. However, it is important to acknowledge that others' thinking can influence you – either in small ways (e.g. implicit influence of people in your social groups or community) or in larger ways (e.g. new bills and laws created to appease a majority perspective that contradicts empirical evidence). Thus, though what others think may not be important to you now, their thinking may be of importance to you later down the line. Be cognisant of these outcomes, but don't sweat the small stuff either. People are people; and people are different – with different beliefs, attitudes and experiences. Accept that. Just because you value the appropriate application of thinking through CT for important issues doesn't mean others will value the same appropriate approach. Accept that as well. Just be sure to apply that appropriate approach in contexts that are important.

CHAPTER 10

How Can We Really *Think Critically?*
Engaging and Expressing Critical Thinking in Our Everyday Lives

In Chapter 1, we answered one of the big questions: *what is CT?* Not only did we discuss what it is, but also what it consists of and things you'll need to do it. Of course, the theoretical nature of these explanations provides only an abstract understanding of it. Given human nature, however, I'm sure most people read that chapter and nodded along, thinking to themselves that they already do that or are already inclined towards those ways of processing information – and maybe that's the case; I mean, you are reading this book! But, despite numerous examples of these processes working in the real-world, perhaps what's missing from that description is a more practical means of exemplifying how that's done in our day-to-day lives. This concluding chapter aims to fill in such potential gaps, through various concrete examples and discussion of how we can better apply CT in our everyday lives (e.g. Table 10.1; see also Dwyer, 2017; Halpern, 2010, 2014). This chapter will also serve as a collated summary of many of the concepts we've discussed throughout the book.

CT as Expression

Clarify the Definitions of Important Terms

Think of a time you have observed two sides arguing and the argument's end eventually occurs because someone finally recognises that they're talking about two different things. 'Well, yeah – if that's what you mean by X, then sure, I see your point.' Up until then, the two sides thought they were arguing over, for example, 'fruit'; but, they were really comparing apples and oranges. Language plays a large role in argumentation; and we often overestimate the commonality of our points of view and perspectives (akin to *false consensus*). So, when we introduce a term in conversation – regardless of how common it might be – we assume, because of this perceived commonality, that others are on board with our interpretation of

151

How Can We *Really* Think Critically?

Table 10.1 *Real-world applications of CT (adapted from Dwyer, 2017; Halpern, 2014)*

Application	Description
1. Argumentation	Recognising the structure of arguments and how to judge their strength or weakness.
2. Verbal reasoning	Recognising what follows what through the use of induction, deduction and falsification.
3. Hypothesis testing	Understanding the limits of correlational reasoning and how to know when causal claims cannot be made.
4. Judging likelihood and uncertainty	Applying relevant principles of probability and avoiding overconfidence in certain situations.
5. Problem-solving	Identifying the problem goal, and generating and selecting solutions among alternatives.

its meaning. Of course, this is not always the case – I cannot say how many arguments I have encountered because of this confusion and, sometimes, the two sides leave the argument never knowing that they were talking about two completely different things.

In one of my classes, I have an exercise on structuring argumentation, in which the word *efficiency* is presented in one of the propositions. After letting the class discuss the proposition, I eventually ask them to define 'efficiency'. In a class of twenty students, I might see some thematic overlap (e.g. productivity, speed, meeting deadlines, qualities and standards or some combination of two or more of these), but for the most part, different descriptions are presented across the class. Imagine arguing with someone over how best to enhance 'efficiency' in your workplace and then finding out later that you define it in different ways. It'd be frustrating to learn that you've wasted your time unnecessarily arguing over different things. Regardless of whether you're expressing your thinking in written or spoken format, it's a good idea to define key terminology from the outset to ensure clarity over what is actually meant within your argument.

Address the Importance of the Topic

It's not uncommon to hear of people being referred to as 'someone who argues just for the sake of it'. Indeed, I've been referred to that way and that's because I often *play devil's advocate* and use the *Socratic method*, of course, for the purpose of optimising outcomes – even though it is sometimes to my detriment.[1] However, these tools of argumentation are typically used by someone questioning an argument, as opposed to the individual making it (though such tools are useful for evaluating one's own argument). In terms of the person making the argument, it would certainly seem like a waste of time and energy making the argument simply for the sake of it. It's only logical that there should be a purpose. The argument one makes must be important, in some way, to warrant discussion. Such importance and, indeed, the purpose of this argument should be made clear and transparent as early in the argument as possible.

Obviously, you care about the topic regarding which you're expressing your CT. But, that doesn't mean other people necessarily care about it. If you want to create 'care' and, hopefully, engage others in this CT, then they need to understand the importance that you're trying to convey.

It's the importance that grabs the audience's attention, while clarity and transparency[2] maintain it. Unfortunately, the logic and the research referenced may not be as attention-grabbing, but without it your stance will be quickly debunked. A simple way of addressing these issues is to ask yourself how clearly you might answer the following: *what is this argument's purpose? Why is it important? Why should others believe it?*

Do Your Research – Properly

As I've mentioned elsewhere in this book, by 'do your research', I don't mean the clichéd response from conspiracy believers. I mean read actual peer-reviewed research (sure, that's not necessarily primary research that you conducted yourself, but it's better than being in the dark about a topic you care about). If the language used in such research lacks accessibility or

---

[1] Sometimes, when my wife makes a statement or indicates that we should act in a certain way, I might question her or request a rationale. Often, I know I've gone wrong before the last word of my sentence leaves my mouth; and I apologise, explaining it as an *occupational hazard*. She lets it go most times, but from time to time it does genuinely annoy her. It is patronising. Of course, that's not my intent; but, that's how it comes across. I know this because that's how it feels when people do it to me. My wife doesn't need second-guessing – if the decision she made was important, I should be confident that she applied CT, because like me, she highly values evidence-based decision-making. Socrates was notorious for questioning people like this, and look where that got him! The point is, though it's important to engage scepticism, playing devil's advocate, caution and all of these wonderful things related to CT, intellectual humility is also vital. We must remember that (1) other people can think critically as well – such decisions don't always have to fall down to us and (2) there's a time and a place – for example, even if you're right, playing devil's advocate should be selected against or at least amended in many interpersonal settings.

[2] In our ever-evolving world of fast news, 'fake news' and incomplete news, transparency cannot be viewed as a potential for weakness, but rather strength in credibility.

is difficult to understand (there's a lot of language in certain research I find very difficult to navigate), find a credible source that explains the relevant studies. Yes, this takes time and work. Yes, it is easier to simply watch a bunch of videos and call yourself 'educated'. But, if you really care about the topic, you will sacrifice the time and effort to gain a genuine evidence-based perspective.

Google Scholar (not just 'regular old googling') is a place for sourcing the original peer-reviewed journal articles. Moreover, everyone is biased; so you will already have a point of a view on a topic before you even start your search – this is natural. However, don't feed into confirmation bias and corrupt the search. Avoid seeking out information that simply supports your existing point of view – consider both sides (or the multiple sides) and be honest with yourself about the information you choose to use. Analyse, evaluate and, then, infer.

Just as you need to be diligent in evaluating others' findings and conclusions, you need to apply the same type of assessment to your own. Make sure you do in your thinking what you would like to see from others. As a critical thinker, practise what you preach. Remember, consistent with the nature of this book's very title, whatever you conclude is subject to later evidence-based falsification; and because you cannot *prove* your conclusions, you need to be cautious in the manner you present them. That's why it's important to present conclusions such as 'A *may* enhance B', or 'research *suggests/indicates* that X increases/decreases Y'. Even if all the research points in one direction, be sure to exercise caution.

CT and Writing

You may see this heading and ask yourself, *who sits down and writes?* We're not in school anymore! Sure, academic and/or professional writers fit the bill; but, you may also naturally intuit that, apart from these, writing is an activity that the majority of the population doesn't engage very often. But, after reflecting for a moment, hopefully, by this stage in your journey through this book, you recognise that CT isn't just something we apply to other people's expressions of thoughts; it's something we must apply to our own – and we all write from time to time, often in situations where CT is quite applicable. You don't have to be a professional writer or an academic. Your job may require you to write reports. An application for a new position may require some lengthy open-ended response. You may often go through threads on social media posts and leave a comment. These all represent opportunities to express your CT through writing.

If it's the case that you don't see the relevance of writing even after this reflection, then I ask you to substitute the word 'composition' for writing. If you're someone who genuinely doesn't write often, fine; but you are definitely someone who thinks. As you think, you piece ideas and propositions together. You are composing and creating a narrative of logic through this composition. Thus, you can treat the CT you conduct 'in your head' (e.g. for purposes of application in conversation) as you would if you were writing. So, regardless of how frequently you do write, there will be some relevant advice and points to consider for you in this section on writing.

Writing is a rather unique form of expression because the nature of the process grants you a very useful resource: time. As previously discussed, when you are engaged in a 'live' conversation that would benefit from CT, you are often put on the spot – you won't necessarily have access to research or the time to pull out your phone and laptop to have a look. But, in many cases when you are writing, you're sat down with a reasonable amount of time to compile the resources you need. Make the most of that opportunity: reference research and draw from a credible evidence base.

With that, I recognise that there is often stress and tedium associated with the writing process, especially for those who do not often do it. Even some academics joke about how they procrastinate so as to avoid writing. I think it's fair to suggest that many people do not find writing to be an easy or enjoyable task; and ensuring the successful integration of CT into one's writing often increases the perceived workload associated with it. However, just because something is sometimes challenging doesn't mean that it's not worth pursuing. Thus, it's useful to discuss a few strategies for integrating CT into one's writing to better express such thinking.

Know the Nature of an Argument

As we discussed in Chapter 9, an argument isn't just a heated debate; it's an activity of reason aimed at increasing (or decreasing) the acceptability of some claim or point of view. The simplest description of an argument might be that regarding any piece of text that contains words such as *because, but, however, therefore, thus, on the other hand, yet* and the like. These words and phrases act as signallers to the reader about the inferential relationships between and among sentences. Arguments typically consist of a central claim, supports for that claim, objections to that claim and rebuttals that object to the objection – the 'signallers' help the reader identify the nature of each proposition in this context. For example, if the word *but* is used at the beginning of a sentence, I know that the

156   How Can We *Really* Think Critically?

information to follow in that sentence in some way refutes what had previously been stated. Thus, it has been signalled to me that an 'objection' to the claim is being presented. Use of the word *because* signals to me that a reason is being provided to support the previously stated claim. A critically thought out argument will address both, if not multiple, sides of the story – think of it as playing devil's advocate in written form – and so understanding the appropriate use of such 'signalling' words and phrases is important.

Develop an Organised Structure

It's a writing rule of mine that not a single word should be written in earnest before I've developed an organised outline for the argument in question (argument-mapping, as described in Chapter 8, is highly recommended in this context). Organisation is an important disposition towards CT, and being this way inclined implies a level of preparedness that will allow you to adapt and cope with the potential 'surprises' that may be encountered during the writing process. Simply, you do your thinking before your writing, and then you know exactly what will be committed to your pages before a single word is typed or written. Over the years, I've developed a template[3] for how I approach written argumentation (see Figure 10.1) – one that I use regularly and share with students (who have fed back to me how useful it has been to them throughout their collegiate careers). At the macro level, we start with an *introduction, body* and *conclusion* – the old stalwarts of any well-organised manuscript are obvious fixtures. But, when we move down a level, we see that 'reasons' and 'objections' also require appropriate organisation, so as to ensure a coherent, logical flow not unlike a narrative (e.g. through either *formal* or *informal logic*).

How to Start Writing an Argument

One flaw I see time and time again is that of starting with a central claim. Of course, you're writing an argument about a topic. Why would you be

---

[3] The argument template recommends starting with 'something quotable'. Note that it does not recommend starting with a quote. Too often, as an educator, I see students submitting psychology papers starting with quotes by individuals such as Gandhi who, despite being in a way 'inspirational', never conducted any relevant research to the topics discussed. Thus, such quotes essentially act as a space filler and fail to add anything useful to the CT attempt at hand. The 'something quotable' recommended should either be a direct quote from a relevant expert in the field or an attention-grabbing proposition that is directly relevant to the topic under investigation.

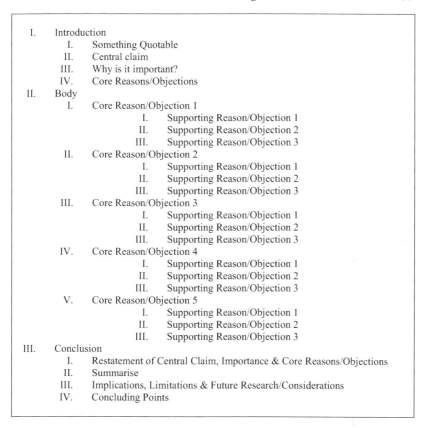

Figure 10.1 Example template for an argument

arguing if you didn't already have a perspective? This is where most people get it wrong. The nature of human bias will always make it so that you, at least, lean towards one side or the other before engaging the evidence base, but it's the CT process that allows you to evaluate that bias and amend it as appropriate. Consider, again, argument maps. The conclusion (i.e. the central claim) is presented at the top of the map, front and centre. The same goes for traditional outlines that you might remember from school (as in Figure 10.1). I implore you to leave these blank or insert a placeholder when developing your argument. Do not bias yourself, any more than you already are, before even starting the argument development process. Draw the conclusion 'organically' from reasonably derived inferential relationships that form in light of the evidence base that you collate.

158 How Can We *Really* Think Critically?

As mentioned earlier, I always develop an outline prior to writing a single word of my argument, knowing that structure is key to a coherent, logical argument. However, I'm stretching the truth there a bit. Where I actually start, akin to another earlier recommendation, is by defining key terms that I know will be relevant to the argument I make. In addition to the previously described rationale as to why defining terms is so important, sometimes, clarifying these terms will highlight certain ideas and concepts that I might otherwise have missed in the development of my outline (it also ensures that you'll never be stared in the face by a blank screen, wondering what to write).

Once I've defined key terms, I explain why they're important and/or relevant, and how they're related to the topic I'm discussing. It is generally at this stage that their pertinence to my argument's goal becomes clearer, and this is generally a big help to my writing process. The process of defining and drawing links among terms and concepts may seem like an obvious starting point to many; but, it's important that this is done from the start, because they also accustom you to other important opportunities to integrate CT into your writing (e.g. self-regulating against emotion, engaging organised logic and objective, open-minded approaches to the propositions considered).

'Quality, Not Quantity'

Don't get me wrong, quantity is important. If you don't present enough information, it may affect the impact of your argument, which may make it not as convincing as it could be – and if you're a student, it might affect your grade as well. With that, you want to be thorough with the evidence base you present, including all the relevant reasons and objections that are appropriate to discuss. Of course, there is a way of doing this while also being succinct and concise. For example, consider in advance what an appropriate word count might be. If you're in an educational setting, this may already be prescribed for you. If for a work report, you might be suggested a number of pages. For other purposes, you might consider what is proportionally appropriate in light of what is representative of the evidence base.

Depending on the context, I typically adhere to the advice that good arguments generally contain three to five core propositions to support or refute a claim. Each of those three to five core propositions requires justification (or refutation) as well; and so each needs another three to five reasons/objections. That is, three to five reasons/objections for those three to five core propositions. Obviously, not all arguments are the same, and so the 'three–five for three–five' guideline might only provide you an anchor for length (though it is a reasonably wide-ranging anchor – I'd recommend somewhere between twelve and twenty credible propositions). You may also wish to elaborate on some of these propositions (if relevant to the argument), thus adding further content. In cases where there are only nine propositions to discuss (following a genuinely thorough search of the literature), make a greater effort to critically evaluate the points that are available. With that, I'd personally rather see ten points discussed and evaluated well than twenty-five points merely slapped on to a document.

One of my high school English teachers told us about the time she got an 'F' on her first college English assignment, despite it being her best subject. Next to the stain of the big red 'F' was some memorable feedback: *avoid glorious bullshit*. The line is of particular relevance here as it reflects the need to omit waffle from one's writing. If length is a concern (as it should be – either because of prescribed limitations or to be concise and succinct), then unnecessary verbiage should not appear in your argument. Every paragraph, every sentence, every word has a purpose. If what you write doesn't have a purpose (other than adding words to your piece), remove it. For example, unless you're writing a literary piece, adverbs are often a good place to start cutting.

Write as if Your Granny Was Reading

Consistent with the notions of 'quality, not quantity' and 'avoiding glorious bullshit', just because the argument is wordy or reads complex doesn't make it good writing, a good argument or evidential of CT. Again, the coherence and logic are what matter. If you're writing about a specialist topic, it's likely that the language you use will be somewhat complex, particularly to someone not experienced in that topic area. Being able to simplify a complex concept so that others can understand it is a much better example of good writing – and another way to ensure that coherence. This is of particular relevance to people submitting graded writing, such as students. Teachers examine their students' writing for the purpose of understanding. The ability to paraphrase complex information into something accessible to novices is a primary indicator of learning and a facilitator of teaching – not the repeating of complex information, word for word, from a few different texts. 'Write as if your granny was reading' because if she can understand it, so will others – and that exemplifies that you understand it too!

Recognising That Some People Don't Want Your Expression

Back to the notion of *who cares?* – if you don't care, then there's no real need to apply CT in that scenario. Save your time and energy for a topic you do care about. However, it's also important to realise that people may not care about what you think is important. Consider again our discussion of value-signalling.

Expressing your ideas, no matter how well thought out they might be, requires a purpose. If your purpose is to inform or educate, think about your audience. Is your audience open to education, debate or receiving information? If yes, great – you've got yourself a dialogue for CT! If not, well, consider again footnote 1 from earlier in this chapter about playing devil's advocate in inappropriate personal or professional settings – there's a time and a place. If your audience doesn't care (or doesn't seem likely to change their mind), your efforts will likely be futile; and, if you are acquainted with the audience, you might even run the risk of decreasing your social standing as a result of your 'preaching' or what they might view as a value-signalling.

Sometimes, you might be 'preaching to the choir'. In such cases, you might be helping these people reinforce their perspectives, by providing new useful information to help them further understand an idea. That's great! Other times, however, the choir might not be as 'devout' as you might think, and what you might actually be doing is 'poisoning the well' in a manner consistent with the backfire effect, as discussed in Chapter 6. Consider the following example:

> Imagine a societal issue has arisen in which a minority group feels that they're being viewed unfavourably. Let's say 15 per cent of the population are culprit for this negative sentiment – either being prejudiced or discriminatory towards said minority group. Now, let's say a separate 10 per cent of the population start a campaign to fight this injustice to the extent that people hear this message at least once a day, either through posters, through personal stories, by both traditional and social media, and even integrated into contexts that seem to lack relevance. Consistent with the earlier postulation, I wonder how many of that initial 15 per cent are going to change their minds because of such campaigns. Unfortunately, it's not likely to be very many – I'm not saying no one, but I imagine numbers would be much lower than for what's hoped (in light of understanding the cognitive mechanics behind 'changing minds'). On the other hand, what I'd be concerned about is the remaining 75 per cent of the population who neither discriminate nor are prejudiced against the minority group (but are not actively engaged with the campaign against injustice) and see how they react to such consistent 'education'.

To give this example greater context, I recall speaking with a friend of mine, who is a member of a minority group, about this very topic. Of course, he wasn't happy with the prejudice or discrimination he has faced in the past. But now, as society has become more 'inclusive', he worries that over-saturation of the equality message may do more damage than good. He suggested that while those prejudiced against his community are unlikely to change (regardless of how much 'education' they receive through societal campaigns), those previously accepting and embracing of inclusivity may grow fed up with such campaigning, which may lead to negative perspectives in the future (where there were none before). That's not to say that people shouldn't be challenged if they act in a discriminatory manner; however, we must also recognise the possibility that attempts to combat such antisocial behaviour – through presentation of such argumentation – may not always yield the desired outcomes we hope to achieve.

A Tale of Two 'CT's

Throughout this book, I've presented arguments about what CT is and what it is not. It is a complex process of knowledge, skills, dispositions and self-regulation – and that's a simplified description! I've argued that without the interaction of all of these, though an individual might be doing 'good' thinking that yields a reasonable resolution, it is not CT per se.[4] On the other hand, CT – in the 'true' sense – is not always feasible. Indeed, I also acknowledged countless times when we should only apply CT to topics we care about. But, what if there were two types of CT? For example, one might be the 'true' form of CT that we've discussed throughout this book, and the other form might be one that's less tedious, less time- and resource-consuming and, perhaps, easier to engage. In the case of the latter, consider the notion of *mindware*.

---

[4] For example, though a large body of good research has examined CT ability in children and how it can be enhanced in this cohort, I remain sceptical of whether what these children are doing is actually 'CT' as we conceptualise it here. For example, such research might observe enhancement in a battery of outcomes, such as problem-solving and verbal reasoning (i.e. outcomes associated with CT); but that's not CT *per se*. I make this point because, consistent with a Piagetian developmental perspective (and, indeed, many post-Piagetian perspectives), I have my doubts that many children, let alone many teenagers, will have reached the developmental level of abstract reasoning necessary to appropriately conduct CT (e.g. engage in epistemological considerations associated with reflective judgment, adequately self-regulate thinking, understand the nature of developing a positive disposition towards thinking, etc.). Thus, while children can improve their cognitive performance on applications associated with CT, I would argue that it's, perhaps, not necessarily CT as we conceptualise it.

162 How Can We *Really* Think Critically?

Mindware: 'Fighting Fire with Fire'

In Chapter 1, I mentioned that I once had a very thought-provoking conversation with a colleague about some people who get so 'good' at CT that it's no longer effortful – it becomes automatic. Of course, the problem here is that when thinking becomes automatic, it's relying on skills- or knowledge-based heuristics and no longer on RJ. Acknowledging this, the following recommendation might, at first, seem contradictory to what has been suggested throughout this book. But, as we are now at a crossroads in CT (see shortly for further elaboration), it is perhaps now necessary to 'fight fire with fire' through using this 'other' potential form of CT.

Despite my faith in CT training as a means of developing in people the ability to conduct CT, I must admit the following seems, in many ways, like a pretty lazy answer with respect to its simplicity: 'if they don't know how to do it, teach 'em!' Yes, research indicates that CT can be successfully taught – provided of course certain conditions are met and boxes ticked in terms of instructional design (e.g. where CT is appropriately conceptualised and delivered; see again Chapter 8). However, one of the most obvious issues is that people may very well not have the opportunity to engage such education (e.g. not being able to attend college or other similar courses – or even not wanting to engage 'term-long' CT training).

The concept of 'fighting fire with fire' is one potential solution here. Consider the approach akin to Hitchens' razor (i.e. *what can be asserted without evidence can be dismissed without evidence*): if people naturally engage cognitively lazy thinking practices, then deal with it through 'cognitively lazy thinking practices'. More precisely, if people want to deal in nice, neat little packages, then let's give them nice, neat little packages. Though I acknowledged before that there might be some level of hypocrisy, for someone who values CT and its thorough nature – with respect to strategies such as Hitchens' razor – consider also, again, the notion of reasoning by analogy (Halpern & Dunn, 2021). Strategies such as this are simple; and though incomplete in terms of providing a full and thorough explanation, they succeed in making their point succinctly and concisely, in a 'currency' of information processing that we, for the most part, can all 'deal in'. *See what I did there?*

The higher-order cognition literature, such as that discussed in this book, often ignores that successfully overcoming the influence of biases and intuitive judgment in cognitive tasks is largely dependent on stored knowledge of various types (e.g. epistemological understanding) – not just self-regulation (Stanovich, 2018). Stanovich refers to this kind of knowledge as 'mindware' and cites Perkins (1995) and Clark (2001) in his conceptualisation of the term as knowledge bases, rules, procedures and strategies that can be retrieved from memory for combatting cognitive laziness and miserliness (e.g. on heuristics and biases tasks) in efforts to facilitate decision-making and problem-solving (Stanovich, 2009, 2018). Here's where the contradiction/hypocrisy comes in: mindware kind of sounds like a heuristic or a network of schemas, right? Well, isn't it heuristic and schema-based thinking we're supposed to be combatting? Like I said, 'fighting fire with fire'. Moreover, Stanovich addresses this notion through identifying a common conceptual flaw in the interpretation of dual-processing literature (i.e. reflective versus intuitive judgment): that all errors must be fast and that all correct responses must be slow. Obviously, this is not the case when we consider concepts such as naturalistic decision-making and recognition-primed decision-making (RPD).

Naturalistic decision-making refers to how people make practical decisions in real-world settings, wherein domain-specific intuitions can be explained according to the RPD model (Klein, 1989, 2008). RPD describes how people apply their domain-specific knowledge according to a repertoire of 'patterns' that organise the primary variables (e.g. potential causal factors) operating in the situation that is to be judged (Klein et al., 1986). These patterns allow individuals to quickly identify relevant environmental cues, anticipated outcomes, possible goals for a given situation and, subsequently, to select an appropriate reaction(s). The RPD model was developed based on qualitative data from interviews conducted with fireground commanders regarding occupation-related emergency events/problem situations (Klein, 1989, 2008). Fireground commanders reported not 'making choices', 'considering alternatives' or 'assessing probabilities', but, instead, acting and reacting on the basis of prior experiences – 'generating, monitoring and modifying plans to meet the needs of the situations' (Klein, 1989, p. 139). Simply, when faced with a situation that requires quick decision-making (within or relevant to domain-specific knowledge – e.g. fireground commanders reacting to a blazing inferno), that individual can quickly apply the patterns they have learned to their current situation (Klein, 2008). Interestingly, this research suggests another link between expertise (see again Chapters 4 and 5) and CT: when experts need to make a quick decision, provided it is within the confines of their domain-specific knowledge, expertise-based 'heuristics' may suffice as a substitute for CT when it is not practical to conduct CT.

This perspective supports the argument that the term 'heuristic' can really mean two different things, despite both referring to 'mental shortcuts'. One way of looking at it is how we have done so throughout this book – flawed, biased and prone to silly mistakes (in those times that it is 'wrong'). The other way of looking at it arises from domain-specific, integrated knowledge garnered through effortful practice. For example, 'conducting science' is no easy task, but through a heuristic – or mindware – such as the 'scientific method', the complex task is, arguably, streamlined (e.g. for understanding or for following steps), to some extent.

From a mindware perspective, for example, when confronted with novel information that requires consideration, we *recognise* situations in which CT may be necessary and we *remember* to not jump to a conclusion and, instead, take our time with it. According to Stanovich, the mindware necessary to succeed in context is diverse, encompassing knowledge in the domains of probabilistic reasoning, causal reasoning, scientific reasoning and numeracy. Notably, the goal of such requirements is core to CT.

Admittedly, things like probabilistic reasoning and causal reasoning may sound rather intimidating to those who don't know anything about them. The beauty of a mindware approach is that it provides 'mini-modules' of context-relevant knowledge. That is, one doesn't need a comprehensive understanding of causal reasoning to be able to apply core principles in context. Consider previously used examples throughout this book in terms of the aforementioned usefulness of reasoning by analogy: measuring women's shampoo preferences (probabilistic reasoning), and Nicholas Cage and swimming pool drownings (causal reasoning), both in Chapter 5.

Specifically, consider again the 'Nicholas Cage and drownings' as well as the 'sex offenders and consumption of water' examples. In fairness, the concept of 'correlation does not mean causation' may not be the easiest to understand if you've never taken classes in statistics, research methodology or CT. 'Teaching' a full elaborate explanation to a complete novice might be a step too far, especially if they don't fully understand how this ties in with their goal. Arguably, more bang for their buck is attained from these simple examples – along with the tagline that 'correlation does not mean causation'. Altogether, these might be said to represent a piece of mindware – and, perhaps, an effective piece too, given what they do. For example, to some, the Nicholas Cage example has an element of humour; people like humour and they remember humour.

On the other hand, the 'sex offender and water consumption' example is not only emotion-evoking because of the topic, but, in a way, it also trolls the hypothetical 'type of people' who often make these mistakes. Arguably, no one wants to be one of 'these people' (i.e. making 'silly mistakes'; e.g. consider risk aversion and social desirability, in context); thus, the example might implicitly reinforce caution in engaging similar situations so as to not look foolish.

Another example might be to ask people to picture themselves googling a controversial topic that they're passionate about (I can't imagine many people under a certain age not having done this, so the scenario is certainly relatable) and then asking them to identify what information they hope pops up in the results. If their hopes and reality overlap, then recommend searching the topic in alternative ways, perhaps even with a negative slant, so as to ensure engagement of differing perspectives. Of course, this is a means of ensuring balanced information is yielded; but it is also a practical and simple lesson for how we can work to overcome confirmation bias.

More recently, this line of thinking has been advanced with particular relevance to the CT training literature, in terms of encouraging CT mindware development as a sort of surrogate for more formal CT training (e.g. for those without opportunities, resources or time to engage such education). That is, if people could learn and use these mini-modules or pieces of mindware, they would likely make better decisions than they would otherwise (Eigenauer, 2024). According to Eigenauer, this might imply that barriers previously perceived as insurmountable (e.g. regarding social conformity, tribalism, biases and 'unthinking' emotional replies) are 'merely default techniques for navigating a complex world without the proper thinking tools and . . . with the proper thinking tools, they could be overcome more consistently' (p. 2). Consistent with the work of Stanovich and Klein, Eigenauer reminds us that heuristic-based decision-making is an evolutionarily advantageous way of dealing with complex issues, and not merely as a flaw in the nature of decision-making, especially in the absence of more effective strategies (e.g. not having the time to apply RJ and, more broadly, CT per se).[5] 'Easily-learned modules' (relatively speaking) of cognitive and metacognitive strategies would provide an accessible

---

[5] In conversation with Eigenauer about this topic, he told me about a student who came into class and thanked him for his lesson on 'amygdala hijacking', which 'kept the student out of jail'. As many of you might well know, the amygdala is the part of the brain most associated with emotional processing – 'amygdala hijacking' works here as a piece of mindware representing the idea that some environmental stimulus is influencing one's emotional reactivity, which could negatively impact decision-making. The student was out with his girlfriend when a guy started hitting on her. The student walked around his car with the intention of fighting; but, halfway around, he said to himself, 'my amygdala is being hijacked' and stopped. He calmly said, 'c'mon, babe, let's go'. This invaluable piece of mindware (certainly from the student's perspective anyway) is purely 'heuristic' (see the earlier discussion regarding Klein's research and two notions of 'heuristic'). However, just as timely as this mindware was, so too might be other examples provided throughout this discussion, in which case, Eigenauer advises, they are potentially more employable, learnable and valuable than the kind of CT that requires prolonged and effortful intervention.

166 How Can We *Really* Think Critically?

introduction to CT and its underlying principles to individuals who otherwise would not receive such training; and, indeed, such modularisation disguises the education as a series of tips or advice, for the benefit of those who might resent the notion of 'benefiting' from education, as if what they're currently doing is 'wrong' (Eigenauer, 2024). Again, fighting fire with fire.

Consider some of my simplified descriptions of CT from Chapter 1 and reword them as such tips or advice: 'play devil's advocate'; 'take your time and use caution with thinking'; 'leave emotion at the door'. Arguably, these tips suffice, to some extent, as useful pieces of mindware. Perhaps the addition of a one-liner to explain, along with a concrete, cathartic example for good measure, ensures a nice, neat package. I'm excited to see this mindware proposition fleshed out and explored in future research.

CT in Reality

I must admit, I probably have an optimistic perspective on how people might engage CT, despite occasionally displaying what might be perceived of as cynical stances – addressed here and there throughout the book. Such stances may not necessarily be cynical though. I'd say 'sceptical' is a fairer label. Hell, scepticism is an integral part of the CT process. Be that as it may, regardless of my scepticism, I acknowledge that my outlook probably is over-optimistic (e.g. *how often are you really going home and dedicating time to research and to think about something you engaged in social conversation?*). To counter this optimism, I find myself, on countless occasions, recommending saving one's CT for important decisions and situations, and that if you don't apply every facet of CT (i.e. the requisite skills, dispositions and RJ), then it's largely debatable as to whether or not what you're doing is, indeed, CT. But, the preceding discussion regarding the development of CT-related mindware is more than just a practical suggestion as to how one might enhance their CT (e.g. in lieu of more formal CT training). It also yields potential implications about the nature of how people think, in real time, about topics that may be important to them and further makes me question the nature of my aforementioned optimism/scepticism.

For example, let's say you're in conversation with someone and a topic is brought up – one that you care about – but, you're at a restaurant or in a work meeting or some other setting that doesn't facilitate you in going online and looking up relevant, credible research to corroborate the new information for further engagement. CT takes time to 'do right'.

Moreover, consistent with what I've said throughout this book, RJ is necessary for you to appropriately apply CT. So, not only would I typically recommend finding time to engage a credible resource in relation to the new information you encountered, I'd also recommend you take your time in considering it. Certainly, the notion of 'sleeping on it' is sound advice in the context of CT. Indeed, avoidance of being hasty with our decision-making is key for CT. Have you ever read an email or received a text message that has infuriated you? You probably started a reply that exhibited your anger, but you ultimately thought better of sending it. You might have put off replying until the next day, once you had cooled down. This cooled-down response was likely more considered, coherent and logical than the more emotionally driven response you had drafted the day before. This is RJ in action. Of course, taking your time to reflect is ideal.

However, I recognise that having such time is often a luxury. So, when we think about being put on the spot in a restaurant or in a work meeting, we may not be given the time to appropriately apply CT. Your boss might deliver you a complex question that they want the answer to now. What can you do? Without an evidence base in front of you from which to extrapolate an answer, your response may rely on various cognitive and metacognitive mechanics. You may pull from memory of past research you have read, you may recall and apply specific fundamentals of RJ, you may engage open-mindedness and scepticism through something like playing devil's advocate or you may apply specific skills that allow you to quickly eliminate certain propositions from the argument. The possible ways you could approach this scenario are endless.

What makes this 'everyday' type of encounter so interesting is that each of the examples regarding what you could do is a part of CT. Sure, CT in the formal sense (i.e. as presented throughout this book) isn't necessarily being applied in this example, but if the conclusion you draw yields an outcome to a satisfactory standard for the purpose of your thinking – consistent with that you would have drawn had you access to credible resources in real time – then how much of a difference does it really make? In the short term, it makes none. In the short term, all that matters is that a reasonable response is provided – consistent with that of a critically thought out answer.

In the long term, it might matter; and perhaps that's why I'm so pedantic about engaging all aspects of CT (i.e. in its true form). It's human nature for us to find the simplest means of accomplishing a task (i.e. consistent with satisficing, using heuristics, relying on intuition and the very nature of humans being cognitively lazy). If we become so 'good' at applying processes associated with CT, like in the example earlier, I'd worry that one might engage 'true' CT less and less over time. Such a routine of not applying true CT might have adverse effects on disposition and self-regulation, thus further decreasing the likelihood of subsequent application of true CT. Thus, while I see great promise in the prospect of promoting CT mindware as a kind of educational strategy (and am indeed looking forward to future research on it) – particularly for those who might otherwise never have an opportunity to engage formal CT training – or even as a means of an introduction to CT (e.g. consider again my 'tips for CT'), I am sceptical of its promotion as a replacement for CT education and am wary of it becoming a potential replacement for the conceptualisation of CT that the field has worked so hard to build over the years. All in all, however, when CT is not feasible, the use of certain aspects of it, such as through mindware, is an optimal way of approaching the situation.

Final Thoughts

We are at a crossroads in the world of CT. Arguably, the debate as to what CT is and of what it consists is over. A majority of experts are in agreement regarding the nature of skills, dispositions and the goals of their application. Perhaps the more practical issue is not what the CT experts think but rather how individuals who teach CT – be it to themselves or others – engage what the experts think. If the sources of CT training misconstrue its conceptualisation, then what is being trained may not be CT – perhaps just specific aspects of it (that may or may not be conducive to CT, in isolation (e.g. creative problem-solving)).

A large body of research indicates that CT can be enhanced through CT education, but the success and quality of such training really boils down to what is being taught and how it is being taught. Of course, I recommend that CT teachers and those who wish to learn about CT on their own familiarise themselves with CT research before commencing such education; but if you're reading this concluding chapter now, it's not likely that you're one of those for whom I'm fearful.

My fear is for the educators not reading this book or any research on CT. It's likely they don't know what they don't know, and this will continue until the time comes when they do appropriately engage the research. Just as I would not recommend a novice in physics to teach a class in physics, I wouldn't recommend a novice in CT to teach that either. I'd like to think most individual novices in physics would recognise their

Final Thoughts

lack of domain-specific knowledge enough to decline the opportunity to teach it; but, on the other hand, given the nature of CT (i.e. its domain generality and broad scope, alongside our human nature to make assumptions about our own cognitive abilities), unfortunately I wouldn't be surprised if there was greater confidence in one's novice thinking to just 'give it a go'. Obviously, this should not be the case.

So, the simple recommendation here is that if we want to enhance CT across populations, people should seek a credible education in it – from an educator who knows how to teach it. But, as we've addressed, not everyone is in a position to do this. The question becomes, what about the people who can't afford or don't have the time for such education/reading? Sure, picking up a book or two on the subject might suffice in some cases. Indeed, a goal of this book has been to shed light on what CT is and how it can be applied in real-world settings. I do hope these 'thoughts on critical thinking' have been usefully educational.

The previous recommendation regarding mindware might fit the bill in some ways as well. A series of short, freely available videos on some social media platform might do well in this respect. Will this give people a comprehensive perspective on CT? Probably not. There would probably need to be a lot of these videos, and people might need to see all of them to get the complete picture; but, at least they'd be getting useful 'mini-lessons' even if they just watched one or two such videos. Of course, that also requires a desire to engage.

When I was little, my mother used to say 'where there's a will, there's a way', and I think this adage might be at the heart of the CT problem we face at this crossroads. Interestingly, it is inextricably linked with the concept of disposition towards CT. That is, for CT to be enhanced, people must want to enhance it – and that requires engagement. This is the crossroads of which we speak. We know what CT is; we know it can be improved; so, who will make the effort to engage opportunities to enhance it? The crossroads faced is one that asks the population at large to 'put up or shut up' in the sense that people may fancy themselves critical thinkers, but if they have never engaged research or training in it, how able can they be? Again, a key goal here for individuals must be to seek opportunities to engage CT.

Given the wide range of topics discussed throughout the course of this book, it seems a bit reductive to attempt to summarise and tie *everything* together into a nice thematic thread, despite our love for wrapping things up into nice, neat little packages. CT is just not that straightforward. Maybe if it was, more people would be doing it. Then again, that latter speculation might just be my biased perspective on things, based on my experiences and observations regarding how people act in light of their cognitive processes. Nevertheless, I'd like to close with something useful; and so, despite the difficulty I engaged in Chapter 1, regarding how to simplify CT's conceptualisation, I offer simplified recommendations for how we might enhance our CT in day-to-day settings, assuming that more formal training in CT is not feasible:

> Save your CT efforts for topics and decisions that you care about or may impact you in important ways. Don't sweat the small stuff – that's bad for your mental well-being. Conduct CT when you're rested and able. If you're tired or lack the energy, you're going to stop caring (which counteracts your initial care of the topic from the outset) or, worse, make mistakes that might impact an important decision. Don't jump to conclusions. Take your time – reflect. Play devil's advocate with yourself and ask yourself questions about the topic and the nature of your knowledge and the information you have available. Acknowledge your emotions, biases and experiences and evaluate both the role and the impact they're having on your thinking process. Address these concerns and maintain as much objectivity as possible. Self-regulate your thinking and filter out as much noisy information as you can. Motivate yourself and engage opportunities to practise your CT.

References

Abel, T., & McQueen, D. (2020). Critical health literacy and the COVID-19 crisis. *Health Promotion International, 35,* 6, 1612–1613.

Abrami, P. C., Bernard, R. M., Borokhovski, E., Waddington, D. I., Wade, C. A., & Persson, T. (2015). Strategies for teaching students to think critically: A meta-analysis. *Review of Educational Research, 85,* 2, 275–314.

Abrami, P. C., Bernard, R. M., Borokhovski, E., Wade, A., Surkes, M. A., Tamim, R., & Zhang, D. (2008). Instructional interventions affecting critical thinking skills and dispositions: A stage 1 meta-analysis. *Review of Educational Research, 78,* 4, 1102–1134.

Adams, M. H., Whitlow, J. F., Stover, L. M., & Johnson, K. W. (1996). Critical thinking as an educational outcome: An evaluation of current tools of measurement. *Nurse Educator, 21,* 23–32.

Altay, S., & Acerbi, A. (2024). People believe misinformation is a threat because they assume others are gullible. *New Media & Society, 26,* 11, 6440–6461.

Alvarez-Ortiz, C. (2007). Does philosophy improve critical thinking skills? Unpublished Master's thesis, University of Melbourne, Australia.

Anderson, J. R. (ed.) (1981). *Cognitive skills and their acquisition.* Hillsdale, NJ: Erlbaum.

Anderson, L. W., & Krathwohl, D. R. (2001). *A taxonomy for learning, teaching, and assessing: A revision of Bloom's taxonomy of educational objectives.* New York: Addison-Wesley.

Andolina, M. W., Jenkins, K., Zukin, C., & Keeter, S. (2003). Habits from home, lessons from school: Influences on youth civic engagement. *Political Science and Politics, 36,* 2, 275–280.

Anticevic, A., Repovs, G., Corlett, P. R., & Barch, D. M. (2011). Negative and nonemotional interference with visual working memory in schizophrenia. *Biological Psychiatry, 70,* 1159–1168.

Bale, J. M. (2007). Political paranoia v. political realism: On distinguishing between bogus conspiracy theories and genuine conspiratorial politics. *Patterns of Prejudice, 41,* 1, 45–60.

Bargh, J. A. (1997). The automaticity of everyday life. In R. S. Wyer (ed.), *The automaticity of everyday life: Advances in social cognition,* Vol. 10, 1–61. Hove, UK: Psychology Press.

Barthel, M., Mitchell, A., & Holcomb, J. (2016). Many Americans believe fake news is sowing confusion. *Pew Research Center, 15*, 12.

Bartlett, F. (1932). *Remembering: A study in experimental and social psychology.* New York: Cambridge University Press.

Barton, K., & McCully, A. (2007). Teaching controversial issues: Where controversial issues really matter. *Teaching History, 127*, 13.

Basch, C. H., Meleo-Erwin, Z., Fera, J., Jaime, C., & Basch, C. E. (2021). A global pandemic in the time of viral memes: COVID-19 vaccine misinformation and disinformation on TikTok. *Human Vaccines & Immunotherapeutics, 17*, 8, 2373–2377.

Baumeister, R. (2003). The psychology of irrationality: Why people make foolish, self-defeating choices. *The Psychology of Economic Decisions, 1*, 3–16.

Beahm, G. (ed.) (2011). *I, Steve: Steve Jobs in his own words.* London: Harper Collins.

Bensley, D. A. (1998). *Critical thinking in psychology: A unified skills approach.* Pacific Grove, CA: Brooks & Cole.

Bezanilla, M. J., Fernández-Nogueira, D., Poblete, M., & Galindo-Domínguez, H. (2019). Methodologies for teaching-learning critical thinking in higher education: The teacher's view. *Thinking Skills and Creativity, 33*, 100584.

Bloom, B. S., Engelhart, M. D., Furst, E. J., Hill, W. H., & Krathwohl, D. R. (1956). *Taxonomy of educational objectives: The classification of educational goals. Handbook 1: Cognitive domain.* New York: McKay.

Boekaerts, M., & Simons, P. R. J. (1993). *Learning and instruction: Psychology of the pupil and the learning process.* Assen: Dekker & van de Vegt.

Brabeck, M. M. (1981). The relationship between critical thinking skills and development of reflective judgment among adolescent and adult women. Paper presented at the 89th Annual Convention of the American Psychological Association, Los Angeles, 24–26 August.

Bransford, J. D., Brown, A. L., & Cocking, R. R. (2000). *How people learn.* Washington, DC: National Academy Press.

Brown, A. (1987). Metacognition, executive control, self-regulation, and other more mysterious mechanisms. In F. Reiner & R. Kluwe (eds.), *Metacognition, motivation, and understanding*, 65–116. Hillsdale, NJ: Erlbaum.

Burbach, M., Matkin, G., & Fritz S. (2004). Teaching critical thinking in an introductory leadership course utilizing active learning strategies: A confirmatory study. *College Student Journal, 38*, 3, 482–493.

Butchart, S., Bigelow, J., Oppy, G., Korb, K., & Gold, I. (2009). Improving critical thinking using web-based argument mapping exercises with automated feedback. *Australasian Journal of Educational Technology, 25*, 2, 268–291.

Butler, H., Dwyer, C., Hogan, M., Franco, A., & Almeida, L. (2012). Extending the validity of Halpern critical thinking assessments: Cross-national applications. *Thinking Skills and Creativity, 7*, 112–121.

Cader, R., Campbell, S., & Watson, D. (2005). Cognitive continuum theory in nursing decision-making. *Journal of Advanced Nursing, 49*, 4, 397–405.

References 173

Carnegie, D. (1936). *How to win friends and influence people*. New York: Simon & Schuster.

Casey, H. (2018). *Transformative learning: An exploration of the BA in community and family studies graduates' experiences*. Doctoral dissertation, National University of Ireland, Galway, Ireland.

Chuah, L. Y. M., Dolcos, F., Chen, A. K., Zheng, H., Parimal, S., Chee, M. W. L. (2010). Sleep deprivation and interference by emotional distracters. *SLEEP, 33*, 1305–1313.

Clark, A. (2001). *Mindware: An introduction to the philosophy of cognitive science*. New York: Oxford University Press.

Commission on Fake News and the Teaching of Critical Literacy in Schools (2018). *Fake news and critical literacy: Final report*. London: National Literacy Trust.

Cook, J., & Lewandowsky, S. (2011). *The debunking handbook*. St Lucia, Australia: University of Queensland.

Couch, M. (2012). Approaching critical thinking. In Center for Catholic Studies, *Critical thinking: Summer seminars, 10*, 8–9. South Orange, NJ: Seton Hall University.

Dansereau, D. F. (1988). Cooperative learning strategies. In C. E. Weinstein, E. T. Goetz & P. A. Alexander (eds.), *Learning and study strategies: Issues in assessment, instruction and evaluation*, 103–120. Orlando, FL: Academic Press.

Dawson, T. L. (2008). *Metacognition and learning in adulthood*. Northhampton, MA: Developmental Testing Service, LLC.

de Hoog, N., & Verboon, P. (2020). Is the news making us unhappy? The influence of daily news exposure on emotional states. *British Journal of Psychology, 111*, 2, 157–173.

Denkova, E., Wong, G., Dolcos, S., Sung, K., Wang, L., Coupland, N., & Dolcos, F. (2010). The impact of anxiety-inducing distraction on cognitive performance: A combined brain imaging and personality investigation. *PLoS ONE, 5*, e14150.

Dewey, J. (1933). *How we think: A restatement of the relation of reflective thinking to the educative process*. Lexington, MA: Heath & Co.

Dolcos, F., & McCarthy, G. (2006). Brain systems mediating cognitive interference by emotional distraction. *Journal of Neuroscience, 26*, 2072–2079.

Douglas, K. M., Sutton R. M., Callan, M. J., Dawtry, R. J., & Harvey, A. J. (2016). Someone is pulling the strings: Hypersensitive agency detection and belief in conspiracy theories. *Thinking & Reasoning, 22*, 57–77.

Duarte, J. L., Crawford, J. T., Stern, C., Haidt, J., Jussim, L., & Tetlock, P. E. (2015). Political diversity will improve social psychological science. *Behavioral and Brain Sciences, 38*, e130.

Dunwoody, P. T., Haarbauer, E., Mahan, R. P., Marino, C., & Tang, C. C. (2000). Cognitive adaptation and its consequences. *Journal of Behavioral Decision Making, 13*, 1, 35–54.

Dwyer, C. P. (2011). *The evaluation of argument mapping as a learning tool*. Doctoral thesis, National University of Ireland, Galway.

(2017). *Critical thinking: Conceptual perspectives and practical guidelines.* Cambridge: Cambridge University Press.

(2023). An evaluative review of barriers to critical thinking in educational and real-world settings. *Journal of Intelligence, 11,* 6, 105.

Dwyer, C. P., Campbell, D., & Seery, N. (2025). An Evaluation of the Relationship Between Critical Thinking and Creative Thinking: Complementary Metacognitive Processes or Strange Bedfellows?. Journal of Intelligence, 13(2), 23, doi.org/10.3390/jintelligence13020023.

Dwyer, C. P., Harney, O., Hogan, M. J., & Kavanagh, C. (2016). Facilitating a student-educator conceptual model of dispositions towards critical thinking through interactive management. *Educational Technology Research and Development, 65,* 1, 47–73.

Dwyer, C. P., Hogan, M. J., & Stewart, I. (2011). The promotion of critical thinking skills through argument mapping. In C. P. Horvart & J. M. Forte (eds.), *Critical thinking,* 97–122. New York: Nova Science Publishers.

(2012). An evaluation of argument mapping as a method of enhancing critical thinking performance in e-learning environments. *Metacognition and Learning, 7,* 219–244.

(2014). An integrated critical thinking framework for the 21st century. *Thinking Skills and Creativity, 12,* 43–52.

(2015). The evaluation of argument mapping-infused critical thinking instruction as a method of enhancing reflective judgment performance. *Thinking Skills and Creativity, 16,* 11–26.

Dwyer, C. P., & Walsh, A. (2019). A case study of the effects of critical thinking instruction through adult distance learning on critical thinking performance: Implications for critical thinking development. *Educational Technology and Research, 68,* 17–35.

Eigenauer, J. D. (2017). Don't reinvent the critical thinking wheel: What scholarly literature says about critical thinking instruction. *NISOD Innovation Abstracts, 39,* 2.

(2024). Mindware: Critical thinking in everyday life. *Journal of Intelligence, 12,* 2, 17.

Ennis, R. H. (1987). A taxonomy of critical thinking dispositions and abilities. In J. B. Baron and R. J. Sternberg (eds.), *Teaching thinking skills: Theory and practice,* 9–26. New York: W. H. Freeman.

(1989). Critical thinking and subject specificity: Clarification and needed research. *Educational Researcher, 18,* 4–10.

(1996). *Critical thinking.* Upper Saddle River, NJ: Prentice-Hall.

(1998). Is critical thinking culturally biased? *Teaching Philosophy, 21,* 1, 15–33.

(2018). Critical thinking across the curriculum: A vision. *Topoi, 37,* 165–184.

Ennis, R. H., Millman, J., & Tomko, T. N. (1985). *Cornell critical thinking tests.* Northbend, OR: Critical Thinking Co.

Ennis, R. H., & Weir, E. (1985). *The Ennis–Weir critical thinking essay test.* Pacific Grove, CA: Midwest Publications.

Facione, P. A. (1990a). *The Delphi report: Committee on pre-college philosophy.* Millbrae, CA: California Academic Press.

References

(1990b). *The California critical thinking skills test (CCTST): Forms A and B: The CCTST test manual.* Millbrae, CA: California Academic Press.

Facione, P. A., & Facione, N. C. (1992). *CCTDI: A disposition inventory.* Millbrae, CA: California Academic Press.

(2001). Analyzing explanations for seemingly irrational choices. *International Journal of Applied Philosophy, 15*, 2, 267–268.

Facione, P. A., Facione, N. C., & Giancarlo, C. A. (1997). *Setting expectations for student learning: New directions for higher education.* Millbrae, CA: California Academic Press.

Fischer, K. W., & Bidell, T. R. (2006). Dynamic development of action, thought, and emotion. In W. Damon & R. M. Lerner (eds.), *Handbook of child psychology: Theoretical models of human development (6th edition)*, Vol. 1, 313–399. New York: Wiley.

Fisher, A. (2001). *Critical thinking.* Cambridge: Cambridge University Press.

Flavell, J. (1976). Metacognitive aspects of problem solving. In L. Resnick (ed.), *The nature of intelligence*, 231–236. Hillsdale, NJ: Lawrence Erlbaum Associates.

(1979). Metacognition and cognitive monitoring: A new area of psychological inquiry. *American Psychologist, 34*, 906–911.

Gadzella, B. M., Ginther, D. W., & Bryant, G. W. (1996). Teaching and learning critical thinking skills. Paper presented at the 26th International Congress of Psychology, Montreal, 19 August.

Gambrill, E. (2006). Evidence-based practice and policy: Choices ahead. *Research on Social Work Practice, 16*, 3, 338–357.

Gestsdottir, S., & Lerner, R. M. (2008). Positive development in adolescence: The development and role of intentional self-regulation. *Human Development, 51*, 3, 202–224.

Glaser, E. M. (1941). *An experiment in the development of critical thinking.* New York: Teachers College of Columbia University, Bureau of Publications.

Goertzel, T. (1994). Belief in conspiracy theories. *Political Psychology, 15*, 731–742.

Goldberg, M. (1990). A quasi-experiment assessing the effectiveness of TV advertising directed to children. *Journal of Marketing Research, 27*, 445–454.

Goleman, D. (1995). *Emotional intelligence.* New York: Bantam.

Guo, C., Zheng, N., & Guo, C. (2023). Seeing is not believing: A nuanced view of misinformation warning efficacy on video-sharing social media platforms. *Proceedings of the ACM on Human–Computer Interaction, 7*, CSCW2, 1–35.

Hake, R. (1998). Interactive-engagement vs. traditional methods: A six-thousand student survey of mechanics test data for introductory physics courses. *American Journal of Physics, 66*, 1, 64–74.

Halpern, D. F. (2003). The 'how' and 'why' of critical thinking assessment. In D. Fasko (ed.), *Critical thinking and reasoning: Current research, theory and practice.* Cresskill, NJ: Hampton Press.

(2010). *The Halpern critical thinking assessment: Manual.* Vienna: Schuhfried.

(2014). *Thought and knowledge: An introduction to critical thinking (5th edition).* Hove, UK: Psychology Press.

References

Halpern, D. F., & Dunn, D. S. (2021). Critical thinking: A model of intelligence for solving real-world problems. *Journal of Intelligence*, *9*, 2, 22.

Hamm, R. M. (1988). Clinical intuition and clinical analysis: Expertise and the cognitive continuum. In J. Dowie & A. S. Elstein (eds.), *Professional judgment: A reader in clinical decision making*, 78–105. Cambridge: Cambridge University Press.

Hammond, K. R. (1981). Principles of organization in intuitive and analytical cognition. Report No. 231, Center for Research on Judgment and Policy, University of Colorado, Boulder, CO.

　(1996). Upon reflection. *Thinking & Reasoning*, *2*, 2–3, 239–248.

Hitchcock, D. (2004). The effectiveness of computer-assisted instruction in critical thinking. *Informal Logic*, *24*, 3, 183–218.

Holmes, J., & Clizbe, E. (1997). Facing the 21st century. *Business Education Forum*, *52*, 1, 33–35.

Hopwood, A. (1974). *Accounting and human behaviour*. London: Accountancy Age Books.

Iordan, A. D., Dolcos, S., & Dolcos, F. (2013). Neural signatures of the response to emotional distraction: A review of evidence from brain imaging investigations. *Frontiers in Human Neuroscience*, *7*, 200.

Johnson, M. K., Raye, C. L., Mitchell, K. J., Greene, E. J., Cunningham, W. A., & Sanislow, C. A. (2005). Using fMRI to investigate a component process of reflection: Prefrontal correlates of refreshing a just-activated representation. *Cognitive, Affective, & Behavioral Neuroscience*, *5*, 339–361.

Jukes, I., & McCain, T. (2002). *Minds in play: Computer game design as a context of children's learning*. Mahwah, NJ: Erlbaum.

Kahneman, D. (2011). *Thinking fast and slow*. London: Penguin.

Kahneman, D., & Frederick, S. (2002). Representativeness revisited: Attribute substitution in 240 intuitive judgment. In T. Gilovich, D. Griffin & D. Kahneman (eds.), *Heuristics and biases: The psychology of intuitive judgment*, 49–81. New York: Cambridge University Press.

King, P. M., & Kitchener, K. S. (1994). *Developing reflective judgment: Understanding and promoting intellectual growth and critical thinking in adolescents and adults*. San Francisco, CA: Jossey Bass.

　(2004). Reflective judgment: Theory and research on the development of epistemic assumptions through adulthood. *Educational Psychologist*, *39*, 1, 5–15.

King, P. M., Wood, P. K., & Mines, R. A. (1990). Critical thinking among college and graduate students. *The Review of Higher Education*, *13*, 2, 167–186.

Klein, G. A. (1989). Recognition-primed decisions. In W. Rouse (ed.), *Advances in man–machine systems research*, *5*, 47–92. Greenwich, CT: JAI Press, Inc.

　(2008). Naturalistic decision making. *Human Factors: The Journal of the Human Factors and Ergonomics Society*, *50*, 3, 456–460.

Klein, G. A., Calderwood, R., & Clinton-Cirocco, A. (1986). Rapid decision making on the fireground. In *Proceedings of the Human Factors and Ergonomics Society 30th Annual Meeting*, Vol. 1, 576–580. Norwood, NJ: Ablex.

References

Kruger, J., & Dunning, D. (1999). Unskilled and unaware of it: How difficulties in recognizing one's own incompetence lead to inflated self-assessments. *Journal of Personality and Social Psychology, 77*, 6, 1121–1134.

Ku, K. Y. L. (2009). Assessing students' critical thinking performance: Urging for measurements using multi-response format. *Thinking Skills and Creativity, 4*, 1, 70–76.

Ku, K. Y. L., & Ho, I. T. (2010a). Dispositional factors predicting Chinese students' critical thinking performance. *Personality and Individual Differences, 48*, 54–58.

(2010b). Metacognitive strategies that enhance critical thinking. *Metacognition and Learning, 5*, 251–267.

Langbert, M. (2018). Homogenous: The political affiliations of elite liberal arts college faculty. *Academic Questions, 31*, 2, 186–197.

Langley, A. (1995). Between 'paralysis by analysis' and 'extinction by instinct'. *Sloan Management Review, 36*, 63.

Laws, P., Sokoloff, D., & Thornton, R. (1999). Promoting active learning using the results of physics education research. *UniServe Science News, 13*, 14–19.

Lewandowsky, S., Cook, J., Ecker, U. K., Lewandowsky, S., Cook, J., Ecker, U. K. H., & Newman, E. J. (2020). Under the hood of the debunking handbook 2020: A consensus-based handbook of recommendations for correcting or preventing misinformation. Center for Climate Change Communication. www.climatechangecommunication.org/wp-content/uploads/2020/10/DB2020paper.pdf.

Lewandowsky, S., Ecker, U. K., Seifert, C. M., Schwarz, N., & Cook, J. (2012). Misinformation and its correction: Continued influence and successful debiasing. *Psychological Science in the Public Interest, 13*, 3, 106–131.

Lieberman, M. D. (2003). Reflexive and reflective judgment processes: A social cognitive neuroscience approach. *Social Judgments: Implicit and Explicit Processes, 5*, 44–67.

Lloyd, M., & Bahr, N. (2010). Thinking critically about critical thinking in higher education. *International Journal for the Scholarship of Teaching and Learning, 4*, 2, 1–16.

Loftus, E. F. (1974). Reconstructing memory: The incredible eyewitness. *Psychology Today, 8*, 7, 116–119.

(2005). Planting misinformation in the human mind: A 30-year investigation of the malleability of memory. *Learning & Memory, 12*, 4, 361–366.

Loftus, E. F., & Palmer, J. C. (1974). Reconstruction of automobile destruction: An example of the interaction between language and memory. *Journal of Verbal Learning and Verbal Behavior, 13*, 5, 585–589.

Long, R., & Long, Y. (2023). The influence of critical thinking on creativity: A moderated mediation analysis. *Social Behavior and Personality: An International Journal, 51*, 12, 12844E–12852E.

Lowenstein, G. (1996). Out of control: Visceral influences on behavior. *Organizational Behavior and Human Decision Processes, 65*, 272–292.

Lyons, B. A., Montgomery, J. M., Guess, A. M., Nyhan, B., & Reifler, J. (2021). Overconfidence in news judgments is associated with false news susceptibility. *Proceedings of the National Academy of Sciences*, *118*, 23, e2019527118.

Mahmood, K. (2016). Do people overestimate their information literacy skills? A systematic review of empirical evidence on the Dunning–Kruger effect. *Communications in Information Literacy*, *10*, 2, 199–213.

Mandick, P. (2007). Shit happens. *Episteme*, *4*, 205–218.

Maybery, M. T., Bain, J. D., & Halford, G. S. (1986). Information-processing demands of transitive inference. *Journal of Experimental Psychology: Learning, Memory, and Cognition*, *12*, 4, 600–613.

Mayer, R. E. (2004). Should there be a three-strikes rule against pure discovery learning? The case for guided methods of instruction. *American Psychologist*, *59*, 1, 14–19.

McGuinness, C. (2013). Teaching thinking: Learning how to think. Presented at the Psychological Society of Ireland and British Psychological Association's Public Lecture series, Galway, Ireland, 6 March.

Mercier, H. (2017). How gullible are we? A review of the evidence from psychology and social science. *Review of General Psychology*, *21*, 2, 103–122.

Miyake, A., Friedman, N. P., Emerson, M. J., Witzki, A. H., Howerter, A., & Wager, T. D. (2000). The unity and diversity of executive functions and their contributions to complex 'frontal lobe' tasks: A latent variable analysis. *Cognitive Psychology*, *41*, 1, 49–100.

Morris, Z. S., Wooding, S., & Grant, J. (2011). The answer is 17 years, what is the question: Understanding time lags in translational research. *Journal of the Royal Society of Medicine*, *104*, 12, 510–520.

Most, S. B., Chun, M. M., Widders, D. M., & Zald, D. H. (2005). Attentional rubbernecking: Cognitive control and personality in emotion-induced blindness. *Psychonomic Bulletin and Review*, *12*, 654–661.

National Academy of Sciences, National Academy of Engineering, Institute of Medicine (2005). *Rising above the gathering storm: Energising and employing America for a brighter economic future*. Committee on Prospering in the Global Economy for the 21st Century, Washington, DC.

Newbern, D., Dansereau, D. F., Patterson, M. E., & Wallace, D. S. (1994). Toward a science of cooperation. Paper presented at the annual meeting of the American Educational Research Association, New Orleans, April.

Newheiser, A.-K., Farias, M., and Tausch, N. (2011). The functioning nature of conspiracy beliefs: Examining the underpinnings of beliefs in the Da Vinci Code conspiracy. *Personality and Individual Differences*, *51*, 1007–1011.

Niu, L., Behar-Horenstein, L. S., & Garvan, C. W. (2013). Do instructional interventions influence college students' critical thinking skills? A meta-analysis. *Educational Research Review*, *9*, 114–128.

Norris, S. P. (ed.) (1992). *The generalizability of critical thinking: Multiple perspectives on an educational ideal*. New York: Teachers College Press.

References

Oliver, E. O., & Wood, T. J. (2014). Conspiracy theories and the paranoid style (s) of mass opinion. *American Journal of Political Science*, *58*, 952–966.

Pennycook, G., Cheyne, J. A., Barr, N., Koehler, D. J., & Fugelsang, J. A. (2015). On the reception and detection of pseudo-profound bullshit. *Judgment and Decision Making*, *10*, 6, 549–563.

Perkins, D. N. (1995). *Outsmarting IQ: The emerging science of learnable intelligence*. New York: Free Press.

Perkins, D. N., & Ritchhart, R. (2004). When is good thinking? In D. Y. Dai & R. J. Sternberg (eds.), *Motivation, emotion, and cognition: Integrative perspectives on intellectual functioning and development*, 351–384. Mawah, NJ: Erlbaum.

Popper, K. R. (1934/1959). *The logic of scientific discovery*. London: Routledge.

Pronin, E., & Hazel, L. (2023). Humans' bias blind spot and its societal significance. *Current Directions in Psychological Science*, *32*, 5, 402–409.

Quinn, S., Hogan, M. J., Dwyer, C. P., Finn, P., & Fogarty, E. (2020). Development and validation of the student-educator negotiated critical thinking dispositions scale (SENCTDS). *Thinking Skills and Creativity*, *38*, 100710.

Redish, E., Saul, J., & Steinberg, R. (1997). On the effectiveness of active-engagement microcomputer-based laboratories. *American Journal of Physics*, *65*, 1, 45.

Reed, J. H., & Kromrey, J. D. (2001). Teaching critical thinking in a community college history course: Empirical evidence from infusing Paul's model. *College Student Journal*, *35*, 2, 201–215.

Rimiene, V. (2002). Assessing and developing students' critical thinking. *Psychology Learning & Teaching*, *2*, 1, 17–22.

Robbins, S., & Judge, T. A. (2007). *Organizational behavior (12th edition)*. Upper Saddle River, NJ: Pearson Prentice Hall.

Rubinelli, S., Ort, A., Zanini, C., Fiordelli, M., & Diviani, N. (2021). Strengthening critical health literacy for health information appraisal: An approach from argumentation theory. *International Journal of Environmental Research and Public Health*, *18*, 13, 6764.

Runco, M. A., & Jaeger, G. J. (2012). The standard definition of creativity. *Creativity Research Journal*, *24*, 1, 92–96.

Saiz, C., & Rivas, S. F. (2023). Critical thinking, formation, and change. *Journal of Intelligence*, *11*, 12, 219.

Salovey, P., & Mayer, J. D. (1990). Emotional intelligence. *Imagination, Cognition, and Personality*, *9*, 185–211.

Shackman, A. J., Sarinopoulos, I., Maxwell, J. S., Pizzagalli, D. A., Lavric, A., & Davidson, R. J. (2006). Anxiety selectively disrupts visuospatial working memory. *Emotion*, *6*, 40–61.

Siegel, H. (1999). What (good) are thinking dispositions? *Educational Theory*, *49*, 2, 207–221.

Simon, H. A. (1957). *Models of man*. New York: Wiley.

Slovic, P., Finucane, M., Peters, E., & MacGregor, D. G. (2002). Rational actors or rational fools: Implications of the affect heuristic for behavioral economics. *The Journal of Socio-Economics, 31*, 4, 329–342.

Solon, T. (2007). Generic critical thinking infusion and course content learning in Introductory Psychology. *Journal of Instructional Psychology, 34*, 2, 95–109.

Soroka, S., Fournier, P., & Nir, L. (2019). Cross-national evidence of a negativity bias in psychophysiological reactions to news. *Proceedings of the National Academy of Sciences, 116*, 38, 18888–18892.

Stanovich, K. E. (1999). *Who is rational? Studies of individual differences in reasoning.* Mahwah, NJ: Erlbaum.

  (2009). *What intelligence tests miss: The psychology of rational thought.* New Haven, CT: Yale University Press.

  (2018). Miserliness in human cognition: The interaction of detection, override and mindware. *Thinking & Reasoning, 24*, 4, 423–444.

Staw, B. M. (1976). Knee-deep in the big muddy: A study of escalating commitment to a chosen course of action. *Organizational Behavior and Human Performance, 16*, 1, 27–44.

Sternberg, R. J. (2002). Raising the achievement of all students: Teaching for successful intelligence. *Educational Psychology Review, 14*, 4, 383–393.

  (2003). The development of creativity as a decision-making process. In R. K. Sawyer (ed.), *Creativity and development*, 91–138. New York: Oxford University Press.

  (2005). The theory of successful intelligence. *Revista Interamericana de Psicología/Interamerican Journal of Psychology, 39*, 2, 189–202.

  (2006). The nature of creativity. *Creativity Research Journal, 18*, 1, 87–98.

  (2010). The dark side of creativity and how to combat it. In D. H. Cropley, A. J. Cropley, J. C. Kaufman & M. A. Runco (eds.), *The dark side of creativity*, 316–328. Cambridge: Cambridge University Press.

Stewart, T. R., Heideman, K. F., Moninger, W. R., & Reagan-Cirincione, P. (1992). Effects of improved information on the components of skill in weather forecasting. *Organizational Behavior and Human Decision Processes, 53*, 2, 107–134.

Strack, F., & Deutsch, R. (2004). Reflective and impulsive determinants of social behavior. *Personality and Social Psychology Review, 8*, 3, 220–247.

Strack, F., Martin, L. L., & Schwarz, N. (1988). Priming and communication: Social determinants of information use in judgments of life satisfaction. *European Journal of Social Psychology, 18*, 5, 429–442.

Swami, V., Coles, R., Stieger, S., Pietschnig, J., Furnham, A., Rehim, S., & Voracek, M. (2011). Conspiracist ideation in Britain and Austria: Evidence of a monological belief system and associations between individual psychological differences and real-world and fictitious conspiracy theories. *British Journal of Psychology, 102*, 443–463.

Swami, V., & Furnham, A. (2014). Political paranoia and conspiracy theories. In J. W. van Prooijen & P. A. M. van Lange (eds.), *Power, politics, and*

References

paranoia: Why people are suspicious of their leaders, 218–236. Cambridge: Cambridge University Press.

Swami, V., Voracek, M., Stieger, S., Tran, U. S., & Furnham, A. (2014). Analytic thinking reduces belief in conspiracy theories. *Cognition, 133*, 3, 572–585.

Sweller, J. (2010). Cognitive load theory: Recent theoretical advances. In J. L. Plass, R. Moreno & R. Brünken (eds.), *Cognitive load theory*, 29–47. New York: Cambridge University Press.

Tan, C., Niculae, V., Danescu-Niculescu-Mizil, C., & Lee, L. (2016, April). Winning arguments: Interaction dynamics and persuasion strategies in good-faith online discussions. Proceedings of the 25th International Conference on World Wide Web, 613–624. International World Wide Web Conferences Steering Committee.

Taube, K. T. (1997). Critical thinking ability and disposition as factors of performance on a written critical thinking test. *Journal of General Education, 46*, 129–164.

Teichert, T., Ferrera, V. P., & Grinband, J. (2014). Humans optimize decision-making by delaying decision onset. *Plos One, 9*, 3, e89638.

Thaler, R. H., & Sunstein, C. R. (2008). *Nudge*. London: Penguin.

Tiruneh, D. T., Verburgh, A., & Elen, J. (2014). Effectiveness of critical thinking instruction in higher education: A systematic review of intervention studies. *Higher Education Studies, 4*, 1, 1–17.

Trussler, M., & Soroka, S. (2014). Consumer demand for cynical and negative news frames. *The International Journal of Press/Politics, 19*, 3, 360–379.

Tversky, A., & Kahneman, D. (1974). Judgment under uncertainty: Heuristics and biases. *Science, 185*, 4157, 1124–1131.

University of Western Australia (2007). ACE and NSSE. www.catl.uwa.edu.au/CATLyst/archive/2007/1/ace_and_nsse

Valenzuela, J., Nieto, A.M., & Saiz, C. (2011). Critical thinking motivational scale: A contribution to the study of relationship between critical thinking and motivation. *Journal of Research in Educational Psychology, 9*, 2, 823–848.

Van Gelder, T. J. (2001). How to improve critical thinking using educational technology. In G. Kennedy, M. Keppell, C. McNaught & T. Petrovic (eds.), *Meeting at the crossroads: Proceedings of the 18th Annual Conference of the Australian Society for Computers in Learning in Tertiary Education*, 539–548. Melbourne: Biomedical Multimedia Unit, University of Melbourne.

(2002). Argument mapping with Reason!Able. *APA Newsletter: Philosophy & Computers, 2*, 1, 85–90.

Van Gelder, T. J., Bissett, M., & Cumming, G. (2004). Enhancing expertise in informal reasoning. *Canadian Journal of Experimental Psychology, 58*, 142–152.

Van Prooijen, J. W. (2012). *Suspicions of injustice: The sense-making function of belief in conspiracy theories*, 121–132. Berlin Heidelberg: Springer.

Van Prooijen, J. W., & Jostmann, N. B. (2013). Belief in conspiracy theories: The influence of uncertainty and perceived morality. *European Journal of Social Psychology, 43*, 1, 109–115.

References

Varian, H., & Lyman, P. (2003). *How much information?* Berkeley, CA: School of Information Management & Systems, UC Berkeley.

Wankat, P. (2002). *The effective, efficient professor: Teaching, scholarship and service.* Boston, MA: Allyn and Bacon.

Watson, G., & Glaser, E. M. (1980). *Watson–Glaser critical thinking appraisal.* New York: Psychological Corporation.

Wineburg, S., & McGrew, S. (2016). Why students can't google their way to the truth. *Education Week, 36*, 11, 22–28.

Wood, D. J., Bruner, J. S., & Ross, G. (1976). The role of tutoring in problem solving. *Journal of Child Psychology and Psychiatry, 17*, 89–100.

Wood, P. K. (1993). Context and development of reflective thinking: A secondary analysis of the structure of individual differences. Unpublished manuscript, University of Missouri, Columbia.

Zimmerman, B. J. (1989). Models of self-regulated learning and academic achievement. In B. J. Zimmerman & D. H. Schunk (eds.), *Self-regulated learning and academic achievement: Theory research and practice*, 1–25. New York: Springer-Verlag.

Index

active learning, 118–119, 124
analyse, 12, 40, 73, 154
analysis, 7, 10–12, 18, 20, 28, 72, 101, 111, 120
anecdotal evidence, 11, 42, 50, 66–68, 95
applications, 101, 114–116
argument, 5, 9–13, 16–18, 21, 26, 28, 38,
    66–68, 83, 90, 92, 94, 105, 107, 118, 135,
    141, 152–153, 155–159, 163
  argumentation, 91, 94, 101, 116, 123, 141,
    151, 153, 156, 161
  slippery slope argument, 85
argument mapping, 118, 156
  argument map, 118, 157
assessment, 10–11, 15, 66, 110, 113–117, 122, 154
attentiveness, 14, 135
automaticity, 17
  automatic thinking, 17

backfire effect, 86, 88, 90, 160
balance, 6, 10, 21, 165
bias, 6, 10–12, 14, 16–18, 21, 26–29, 33, 37,
    44–45, 48, 50–55, 60–61, 71, 84, 86,
    89–90, 94, 98–99, 107–111, 116, 121,
    134–136, 140–141, 144–145, 148, 154,
    157, 162, 164–165, 170
  cognitive bias, 9, 31, 47, 51, 129

care (about your thinking), xii, 4, 18, 23–31, 54,
    61, 73, 79, 92, 101, 105, 109, 124, 130,
    137–138, 140–141, 146, 148–150,
    153–154, 160–161, 166, 170
certainty, 17, 20, 33, 35, 37, 43, 45, 76, 134
  uncertainty, 7, 12, 14, 17, 37, 42, 48, 57, 71,
    89, 116, 133–134, 149, 152
Cognitive Continuum Theory, 20, 29
cognitive load, 23, 30, 37, 107
common belief, 69–71, 79
common sense, 11, 66, 68–71, 77
comprehension, 10, 32
conspiracy beliefs, 41, 69, 132–135
conspiracy theories, 128, 132, 134, 136

COVID-19, 4, 65, 133, 144, 149
creative thinking, 101, 104–107, 109–111, 119
  creativity, 104–106, 108–109, 111
credibility, 3, 6, 10, 12, 35, 37, 43, 48, 50, 54,
    61, 63, 66–67, 69, 71, 73, 75–77, 81, 84,
    90, 93, 111, 143, 145–147, 149

debunking, 47, 90
decision fatigue, 23, 37
decision-making, 9, 14, 21, 23, 25, 28, 30–31,
    47, 51, 54, 60–61, 73, 77–79, 85–86,
    97–98, 103, 105, 109, 141, 163, 165, 167
disinformation, 65–66, 127, 143, 145–146
disposition (critical thinking), 6–7, 9, 13, 19, 21,
    28–29, 91, 93, 99–100, 112, 114, 119, 125,
    135, 156, 161, 166, 168–169
Dual-process theory, 20
Dunning–Kruger effect, 49

emotion, 6, 21, 26, 28–29, 54, 61, 72, 92–93,
    95, 97–98, 107, 123–124, 136–138, 146,
    158, 164, 166
  emotional, 28–29, 57, 67, 92–97, 100, 137,
    141, 146, 165, 167
epistemology, 42, 44–45, 80
eureka, 102–103, 111
evaluation, 2, 7, 10–12, 14, 18, 28, 63, 66,
    102–103, 110–111, 116–117, 148–149
  evaluate, 3, 12, 18, 61, 72–74, 76, 88–89,
    102–103, 116, 128, 138, 143, 148–149,
    154, 157, 159, 170
executive function, 16, 32
experience, 3, 20–21, 24, 46–48, 50–56, 61–62,
    67–68, 79, 86–87, 95, 97, 104, 107, 125
expertise, 8, 21, 35, 44, 48–49, 54, 59, 61,
    70–71, 73–77, 125, 128, 147, 163
  expert opinion, 11, 66, 73–74, 76, 79

fake news, 4, 33, 136, 143–149
falsification, 6, 38–42, 132, 152, 154
flip-flops, 80–81, 146

183

Index

gravity, 34–36, 41, 43, 57

heuristic, 9, 24, 31, 48, 52, 89, 103, 162–165, 167
  availability heuristic, 90, 108
  representativeness heuristic, 134
Hitchens' razor, 92, 95, 162
hot–cold empathy gap, 85
hypothesis, 34, 38–39, 41–42, 69, 116, 152

inference, 7, 10–12, 18, 28, 72, 106, 111
inquisitiveness, 14–15, 45, 121
instructional typology, 113
intrinsic goal orientation, 14
intuition, 21, 54, 77, 163, 167
  intuitive, 17, 20–21, 70, 133
  intuitive judgment, 20, 24, 47, 54, 70, 96–97,
    103, 124, 162–163

judgment, 10, 14, 16, 21, 23, 31, 52, 80

knowledge, 3–4, 10, 14, 17, 19, 21, 32–36,
    38–43, 45, 51–52, 55, 57–58, 61, 63, 71,
    73, 76, 88–90, 106, 110, 118, 120,
    125–131, 139, 141, 144, 161–164, 169–170

long-term memory, 32, 88

magical thinking, 43
Mandela 'effect', 58–61
metacognition, 10, 16, 128
  metacognitive, 5, 7, 9, 16, 21, 120, 128, 165,
    167
mindware, 161–166, 168–169
misinformation, 4, 41, 64–66, 75, 87–88, 90
  misinformation effect, 57, 59–61
Momo hoax, 65
motivation, 11, 14, 25, 106, 129

naturalistic decision-making, 163
news, 26–27, 40, 53, 56, 64–65, 72, 76, 80–81,
    94, 109, 127, 137, 145–148, 153
Nicholas Cage, 77, 164
noisy information, 130, 140, 170
Nudge Theory, 147

Occam's Razor, 60–61, 78
open-mindedness, 14–16, 95, 99–100, 133–136, 167
  open-minded, 15, 88, 93, 100, 135, 140, 158
organisation, 14, 18, 156
outside-the-box thinking, 108

perseverance, 14–15, 99, 135
personal experience, 11, 42, 49–50, 55, 66–68, 79
personality, 13, 106, 135
persuasion, 83, 92

playing devil's advocate, 6, 8, 18, 156, 160, 167
Pluto, 34, 40
politics, 26–27, 99, 136, 138–140, 145, 148
probability, 152
problem-solving, 3, 9, 18, 24, 31, 60, 101,
    103–105, 108–110, 116, 161, 163, 168
proof, 36–39, 41–42, 92

quasi-rationality, 21, 25, 70

rationalisation, 96–98, 100
recognition-primed decision (RPD), 163
reflection, 14
reflective judgment, 5–6, 9, 12–13, 16, 21, 70,
    116, 166
relevance, 6, 10, 12, 88, 99, 111, 139, 155,
    159–160, 165
remembering, 46
  misremembering, 47, 58–60
research (as an information source), 2–4, 6–8,
    13, 15, 18–19, 28, 30, 36, 38–40, 42–45,
    47, 51, 58, 64, 66–67, 69, 71–77, 79, 83,
    86, 90–93, 95, 101, 104–105, 112, 114,
    117–118, 125–126, 128, 133–135,
    137–138, 143–144, 148, 150, 153–155,
    162–164, 166–169
response tendency, 13

satisficing, 25, 50, 80, 167
Scapegoat Theory, 134
scepticism, 14–16, 45, 81, 135, 145, 153, 166–167
schema, 17, 26, 30, 37, 49, 58, 75, 88–89, 96,
    127, 163
self-regulation, 16, 19, 83, 161–162, 168
shampoo, 78, 164
skills (critical thinking), 5–7, 9, 11–13, 15–16,
    19, 21, 26, 28, 48, 114–116, 118, 143,
    161–162, 166–168
social media, 136–139, 143–147, 149, 154, 169
statistics (as information source), 66, 77–79, 164

theory, 13, 15, 34–36, 38–39, 41–43, 51, 76, 83,
    115, 120, 132–133
toothpaste, 36–38
training (critical thinking), 3, 8–9, 47–48,
    112–114, 118–120, 125–126, 162,
    165–166, 168–170
truth-seeking, 14–15

value-/virtue-signalling, 27
verbal reasoning, 116, 152

working memory, 32
writing, 1–3, 36, 45, 74, 84, 105, 116, 149,
    154–159

Printed in the United States
by Baker & Taylor Publisher Services